Richard B. Finnegan is professor and chairman of the Political Science Department at Stonehill College. The Stonehill programs in Irish studies and in international studies are also under his direction. Dr. Finnegan is the co-author of *Law and Politics in the International System* (1979) and the author of many journal articles.

IRELAND

WESTVIEW PROFILES
NATIONS OF
CONTEMPORARY WESTERN EUROPE

IRELAND

The Challenge of
Conflict and Change

Richard B. Finnegan

Westview Press / Boulder, Colorado

For Joanne, Richard, and Scott

Westview Profiles/Nations of Contemporary Western Europe

Published in 1983 in the United States of America by
Westview Press, Inc.
5500 Central Avenue
Boulder, Colorado 80301
Frederick A. Praeger, President and Publisher

Library of Congress Cataloging in Publication Data
Finnegan, Richard B.
  Ireland: the challenge of conflict and change.
  (Westview profiles. Nations of contemporary western Europe)
  Bibliography: p.
  Includes index.
  1. Ireland—History—1922–   . 2. Northern Ireland—History—1969–   . 3. Ireland—History.   I. Title.   II. Series.
DA963.F56   1983   941.5   83-6974
ISBN 0-89158-924-4

Printed and bound in the United States of America

Contents

Illustrations

Preface

This book is designed to serve two purposes. The first is to introduce the reader to Ireland—its history, society, economy, government, politics, and the hard tangle of Northern Ireland. The second purpose is to chart the process of modernization and change that has swept across Ireland in the past twenty years. That change, initiated in the sphere of economic development, has had an effect on virtually all aspects of Irish life. Therefore, this introduction to the central elements of Ireland has a contemporary focus and displays a nation undergoing substantial transformation. For the past decade or more, Northern Ireland also has been wracked by intense change, to say nothing of intense conflict.

An obligation thrust upon all who write about Ireland is clarification of terminology. The term *Northern Ireland* refers to the six counties of Ireland that are incorporated into the United Kingdom and ruled from London. That region of Ireland, with the addition of three counties now in the Republic of Ireland governed from Dublin, was the traditional province of Ulster. In this book the name Ulster will be used to refer to Northern Ireland. Although this usage is not absolutely precise, it can be justified on the grounds that to refer continuously to the "six counties of Ulster" would be pedantic. A similar difference exists with the city of Londonderry, which was originally called Derry—and still is by the Catholics of Ulster—but was renamed Londonderry in the seventeenth century by Protestant planters. The Republic of Ireland still lists the city as Derry on maps.

The terms *Catholic* and *Protestant* are used to refer to the two communities in Northern Ireland. Although overtly religious terms, they are used in this book as ethnic labels, expressive of the key difference between the two communities, rather than as a theological distinction. As explained in Chapter 9, these terms tend to make what is actually a political and cultural division into a religious one.

Thanks are due to people, too numerous to list, from whom I have learned something about Ireland over the years. I especially want to thank John Stack and Martin McGovern. Paul D'Espinosa helped with my editing of the manuscript, and Dimity Wilcox and Peggy Karp patiently typed it. I must also thank my wife, Joanne, for her patience with such a project.

Errors in the book are, of course, my responsibility, as is whatever is useful or informative to the reader. I hope the latter outweighs the former.

Richard Finnegan

ix

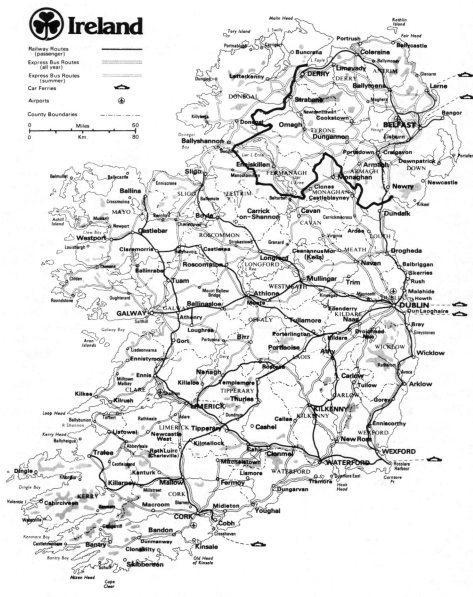

Map of Ireland. (Courtesy, Irish Tourist Board)

Introduction

A student of Ireland can find three different Irelands. First, on this small island can be found some of the most attractive tourist areas in Europe. The jutting Cliffs of Moher rival those of the Algarve in Portugal. The mountains and lakes of County Kerry glisten with beauty and charm. The ancient stone forts, monasteries, churches, castles, and stately homes provide a rich fare of beauty, history, and architecture. Visiting the western part of Ireland includes enjoying vistas of thatched-roof cottages, quaint villages, friendly pubs, and traditional Irish music; to the north lies the barren granite beauty of Donegal. Nearly 2,000 miles of seacoast (approximately 3,200 km) incorporate seashore villages and beautiful bays. Medieval banquets are held at fifteenth-century Bunratty Castle. In Dublin, there are the Curragh races, the Dublin Horse Show, shopping on Grafton Street, the National Museum, the productions at the Abbey Theatre, the Joyce Museum, and Trinity College Library, and all attractions are enhanced by the warm hospitality of the Irish people. This Ireland draws thousands of visitors each year from the United States, Britain, and the Continent.

Another Ireland is that of the Irish people, and it is different from the whirlwind Ireland of the tourist. The beauty in the west of Ireland is host to an area in decline as rural poverty dots the landscape, urbanization drains the area of people, and those Irish speakers remaining dwindle in number. Beautiful barren areas of County Mayo contain giant chemical plants; lovely bays are host to oil depots. County Clare is a duty-free zone bustling with light industry. The cities, especially Dublin, are skirted by new sprawling suburbs, and in the city centers Bauhaus buildings house international business offices. Slums, unemployment, and poverty coexist with new factories producing pharmaceuticals, chemicals, computers, and electronic components. In Dublin, the hub of Ireland, politicians and bureaucrats struggle with inflation, economic growth rates, currency fluctuations in the European Monetary System, tax policy, agricultural output, foreign debt, crime, and social welfare programs, in addition to flying back and forth to Brussels to attend meetings of the European Commission.

In the schools, churches, and homes, the people confront new ideas and values spilling into Ireland as a result of tourists, television, and travel. The settled ways and firm beliefs of the old Ireland are battered by changing attitudes toward sex, religion, work, consumerism, and education. The Irish

1

Farmland in County Clare. (Richard Finnegan)

people are becoming more numerous, better educated, younger, more urban and suburban, and more aware of the possibilities for Ireland; they have higher expectations than did previous generations. The politicians run to keep up as the political parties and political leaders attempt to adapt to a new agenda of issues and to a new electorate. The clamor of interest groups presses on Dublin, not only the old interest groups of labor, farmers, and industry, but also new groups such as women, students, and environmentalists. The Catholic Church, still a powerful pillar of Irish society, is caught in a wave of change and struggles to reconcile paternal encouragement of piety and devotion with secular challenges to traditional practice and doctrine.

The third Ireland is geographically integrated with the first two but politically separated by an international boundary. Northern Ireland (or Ulster), part of the United Kingdom along with Great Britain, is not only divided from the rest of Ireland but divided within itself. The two ethnic communities of Northern Ireland, Catholics and Protestants, live in a state of persistent tension and conflict, which occasionally flares into ruthless bloodshed. Two urban areas, Belfast and Londonderry, contain the bulk of the population. Each city is marked by rows of burnt-out houses and empty, bricked-up buildings. Streets are closed off at night with giant gates. Shoppers are searched at a fence that closes off the Belfast city center to potential bombers. The streets are busy not only with ordinary traffic but also with British armored vehicles on patrol. At night a bombing or a shooting calls forth retaliation by armed groups, and the two communities are again driven apart by the wedges of fear, sadness, and hostility. Economic decay, high unemployment, an unpopular military presence, skilled terrorists, and prisoners on hunger strikes are the everyday experience of this Ireland. The economic decisions are made in London. The politicians in Ulster are without a government in the province, are wedded to their respective communities, and are committed to virtually irreconcilable positions.

Of the three Irelands the latter two are the concern of this book. The tourist's Ireland should not be missed, but knowing that Ireland alone is to fail to understand the two central dilemmas of contemporary Ireland: the process of rapid economic and social change in the Republic of Ireland and the bitter fruit of the political relations between the two communities in Ulster.

The modernization process began some twenty years ago and was initiated by a period of relatively rapid economic growth in the Republic of Ireland. The new crisis in Northern Ireland began in 1968 as the result of a civil rights movement in Ulster. The people on the island have been caught up in the rapid currents of these two changes—some positive, some negative, but all touching virtually everyone in some way.

Michel Peillon notes, "In any event to catalogue social change in Ireland under the single label of *modernization* does not get us very far."[1] Peillon is correct in that the term *modernization* has been used predominantly to refer to nations striving to break the bonds of colonization, politically and socially mobilize their populations, develop an industrial economic base, and foster a sense of nationhood.

Ireland accomplished these goals to a greater or lesser degree in the 101 years from 1848 to the declaration of a republic in 1949.[2] However, the status of the Republic of Ireland in the 1950s, and even up to the present, was hardly that of a modern industrial nation. Not only did Ireland economically lag behind U.S. and European standards, but social and cultural patterns and values retained a traditional quality as well.

The process of change that has taken place in Ireland has thrust the values, processes, and structures of modern European industrial nations onto the Irish political, economic, social, and cultural scenes. The effect has been to generate an unprecedented degree of prosperity coupled with problems of unemployment, international debt, and inflation; a transformation of the educational system; the decline of rural Ireland and problems of mass urbanization such as crime, drugs, and inadequate housing; a blunt challenge to the values and role of the church; and a new political agenda as the result of a new suburban, young electorate and the economic transition. It is difficult to resist labeling this process "modernization," as these social dynamics are certainly close to those of the most developed nations of North America and Western Europe. Thus, although Ireland has not accumulated the capital base and wealth of the industrial nations, the economic, political, and social issues in this small country are essentially the same as those in the more developed nations.

Ireland is a small country located on the northwest perimeter of Europe, and Great Britain is traditionally both a hovering presence and a barrier to the Continent.[3] A visitor can travel from one end of Ireland to the other in a matter of hours as the distance from north to south is only 302 miles (480 km) and from east to west, a shorter 171 miles (266 km). The total size of the island is 32,595 square miles (84,421 sq km): The Republic of Ireland comprises 27,136 square miles (70,282 sq km) and Northern Ireland, 5,459 square miles (14,139 sq km). The total geographical area is approximately the same as the size of Austria and slightly smaller than that of Portugal or Hungary. Compared to the United States, the whole island is the size of the

Location of Ireland. (Courtesy, Irish Tourist Board)

state of Maine; Northern Ireland is about the same size as Connecticut.

Ireland was traditionally divided into four provinces—Leinster, Munster, Connacht, and Ulster—and is currently divided into thirty-two counties—twenty-six make up the Republic of Ireland, and six compose Northern Ireland. Leinster comprises twelve counties in the east and southeast of the Republic, bounded by the counties of Louth, Longford, Offaly, Kilkenny, and Wexford. Six counties make up the province of Munster, in the south and southwest; the counties of Clare, Tipperary, and Waterford form its boundaries. Connacht, in the west and northwest of the Republic, is composed of Galway, Roscommon, Leith, Sligo, and Mayo counties; Cavan, Monaghan, Donegal, and the six counties of Northern Ireland make up the province of Ulster.

The population of the island is 4.9 million, slightly smaller than that of the Commonwealth of Massachusetts. The population density of Ireland is quite low compared to other European states. Belgium has only one-third the area and almost twice the number of people. In 1975 Ireland's population density per square kilometer was 44, the lowest in the European Community, while that of the Netherlands was almost eight times higher at 332. The population distribution in both the Republic of Ireland and Northern Ireland is heavily urban. Dublin, the largest city on the island, has a population, including suburbs, of over 1 million people, approximately one-third the whole population of the Republic of Ireland. Cork, Limerick, and other towns and cities are also substantial population centers, and in the Republic over 60 percent of the population can be considered urban. In Northern Ireland the two cities of Belfast (with a population of close to 400,000) and Londonderry (approximately 60,000) account for nearly one-third of the population.

Both regions are characterized by an east-west split, which is as culturally distinct as the north-south split is politically distinct. The province of Ulster is bisected by the River Bann. To the east of the river the Protestants are more heavily concentrated, and the Catholics tend to live in the west and, in fact, are a majority in the city of Londonderry. Industry is concentrated in the eastern sector of Ulster, especially in Belfast, which was the first industrial area of Ireland. The rural areas of west Ulster have suffered deterioration. Population has declined, and little industrial development has taken place. In the Republic the province of Connaught in the west has also suffered a decline in population and, despite the efforts of the government to encourage industrial development there, remains less affluent than the more urbanized east. The last remaining Irish-speaking areas are sprinkled in a fringe along the western coast, but the decline of the use of that language has been accelerating in recent years. In the western areas the decline has resulted in a population that is more female than male, more old than young, more poor than affluent, and the people tend relatively inefficient small farms.

The religious affiliation of the people in the Republic is 94 percent Catholic and 3.5 percent Church of Ireland; the remainder are mostly Methodists or Baptists, and there is a tiny percentage of Jews. Northern Ireland is composed of 34 percent Catholics, 26 percent Presbyterians, 21 percent Church of Ireland, and 19 percent Methodists, Baptists, or members of other denominations. On the island as a whole the Catholics make up nearly four-fifths of the population, and Protestants constitute the remaining one-fifth.

The first three chapters of this book indicate how the relationship between Ireland and Great Britain engendered the development of Irish nationalism, which in turn produced Irish independence. That independence, however, revealed the divisions among the Irish people and, in fact, produced the political separation of Ulster and the unsolved puzzle of Irish nationhood. In the sixty years after independence the two sections of Ireland took separate paths: the south seeking to realize full independence; the north, to consolidate Protestant rule within the United Kingdom. In Chapters 4 and 5 social, economic, and cultural changes in the Republic are traced, and Chapters 6 and 7 discuss the transformations in government and politics. The impact of economic development on virtually every sphere of society has generated stress and tension as old values conflict with the new forces of urbanization, materialism, and secularism. The government has had the responsibility of managing this modernization, and the changes have generated new political pressures, a new electorate, a new agenda of issues, and changes in party leadership, structure, and style.

Chapters 8 and 9 cover Northern Ireland and trace the development of that province and the renewal of communal violence that has plagued Ulster for more than a decade. The explosion of violence in Ulster has made the people of Ireland once again face the question of Irish nationhood and has revealed the reciprocal impact of the politics of the two regions upon one another. Thus the dual pressures of modernization and communal violence are currently raising again the questions that were raised in the last century when Irish nationalism emerged: What are to be the central social and cultural values of the Irish people? and What is the structure of the political order to be?

NOTES

1. Michel Peillon, *Contemporary Irish Society* (Dublin: Gill and Macmillan, 1982), p. 1.

2. See Joseph Lee, *The Modernization of Irish Society 1848-1918* (Dublin: Gill and Macmillan, 1973).

3. The constitution of the Republic of Ireland calls the country Éire, or Ireland in English, and claims sovereignty over the whole of the island. Within the United Kingdom the province of Ulster is called Northern Ireland. To further confuse matters, the whole island was called Ireland prior to 1920. Thus the name Ireland can refer to the whole geographical unit or to the Republic of Ireland alone.

1

From the Celts to O'Connell

Henry Ford once said, "History is bunk."[1] This dismissal of history is akin to calling a magnificent tapestry just a collection of threads, which, of course, it is not. A tapestry is a reflection of the lives and ideas portrayed in its composition, and like art, history is subject to interpretation and reinterpretation as successive generations refocus their collective memories in the light of their current experiences. This process is no less true for Irish history than it is for the history of any other nation, but it is particularly true for the Irish as their experience has been intertwined with the destiny of their largest neighbor to the east.

At least two major historical traditions have coexisted since the Norman invasion of Ireland. One is the Irish tradition; the other, the British tradition. Even today the children in Ulster are taught two different histories. The Protestants are taught the history of England and the British history of Ireland, and what they learn forms the backdrop against which those children interpret their experience. The Catholic children are taught the Irish tradition, with its stress on the Celtic, Catholic, and nationalist dimensions, and it is this image that shapes their comprehension of the world. This chapter places greater stress on the latter tradition as it provided the foundations for modern Irish nationalism and the creation of the Irish state. Clearly the other tradition cannot be ignored, and it will be dealt with in discussing Northern Ireland.

THE CELTIC AND NORMAN CONQUESTS

The Celts, originating in the center of Europe, had developed an empire that, by the fourth century B.C., was caught in the vise of the Germans and the Romans. Moving westward the Celts, or Gauls as they called themselves, conquered Britain and Ireland about 350 B.C.

Socially the Celts lived in loosely knit communities, and politically the Celtic tradition of fragmentation prevailed. Ireland was broken down into over 100 little states, called *tuatha*, each with a chief or king. The *tuatha* were grouped into five kingdoms, which are partially reflected in the four provinces of contemporary Ireland. In the first century A.D. there emerged a high kingship, which, in theory, was superior to the heads of the other kingdoms.

The religion of the Celts, Druidism, was filled with pagan mysticism, taboos, and privileges. Druid priests were ascribed magical powers for casting spells and defeating enemies. To people steeped in this lore the partially

7

legendary St. Patrick brought the Roman culture and civilization, the Latin language, and Christianity. During the ensuing centuries the blending of Celtic culture and Christian faith took a unique form. The combination of the powerful monastic tradition and the customs and traditions of the Irish church came to be called "Celtic particularism."

This fortuitous blend of Celtic culture, politics, and social structure and the learning and language of Christianity produced the golden age of Ireland in the seventh and eighth centuries. The writing of Irish history began with the adoption of the Latin alphabet to write Gaelic. Thus the ability to record the law of the Gaels, or Brehon law; the songs, poetry, and scholarship of the bards and monks; and the events of the political and social order was developed about the year 600. The imprint of this culture upon the Irish gave them a distinctive religious, cultural, and political identity to which they could refer during the long struggle with the British from the twelfth to the nineteenth centuries. British imperialism confronted an integrated, highly developed culture and began the slow, uneven process of Anglicizing it. The Celtic and Catholic components of Irish nationalism are rooted in that golden age of over two and one half centuries of Celtic achievement. In the nineteenth century, despite the dominance of the English language in Ireland, it was this cultural heritage, however romanticized, that contributed to the rising nationalist movement.

The decline of the golden age began with the invasions from Scandinavia. The Danes and Norwegians began to strike out, attacking and controlling the islands in the North Atlantic. In the century from 830 to 1014 the Norse invaders founded Dublin and conquered Wexford, Waterford, Cork, and Limerick. With the Irish kings defeated, the Scandinavians were in control of Ireland by the end of the tenth century. The Irish challenge to this rule produced one of the more notable figures in the history of the Irish monarchy—Brian Boru.

Brian Boru began his ascent by defeating the Norse rulers in Munster and becoming king of that province from 976 to 1014. In the north another king, Malachy, rose to defeat the Norse at Tara and then went on to drive the Scandinavians from Dublin. The two Irish kings divided up Ireland, and Brian had the Norse settlements under his vassalage. In 1002 Malachy conceded the high kingship to Brian, and Brian had but one task left—to defeat an incipient challenge to his rule. At the Battle of Clontarf the Norse and Irish were defeated by Brian, and the sway of the Scandinavians was at an end. Brian was slain at the battle, but his rule had brought significant achievements beyond the defeat of the Scandinavians. He had claimed the high kingship of the Gaelic people and thus had accomplished what few high kings before had achieved—a semblance of unified monarchical authority. He was deeply committed to Christianity and had undertaken a program of restoration of the monasteries, churches, libraries, and cultural levels, which had declined under the rule of the Scandinavians. His death, however, revived the pattern of political conflict among the provincial kingdoms of Ireland, which now included Celticized Norse settlers who had intermarried with the Irish and had integrated into the loose Irish political and social structure.

The period of Scandinavian dominance weakened the Irish church as "Celtic particularism" deteriorated into landlord abbots, simony, nepotism, and the protection of parochial, secular, and family interests. The practices that had inspired the church to engage in reform movements on the Continent were prevalent in Ireland, and thus they drew the attention of Rome.

Dermot McMorraugh, a king of Leinster, bears a special burden in the nationalist history of Ireland as it was at his invitation that Richard Fitz Gilbert de Clare, the earl of Pembroke known as Strongbow, went to Ireland in 1170. Strongbow's agreement with McMorraugh was to gain him a wife, Mc-Morraugh's daughter, and a kingdom. Since the Irish resistance was disorganized and Norman military skills and weaponry were superior, Strongbow extended his conquests beyond Leinster. At this point Henry II began to fear a rival Norman kingdom in Ireland and, under the authority of a much disputed papal bull, went to claim his title as lord of Ireland.[2] He distributed the land in Ireland to his loyal Norman barons and some Irish provincial kings who agreed to pay him tribute. Thus the initial invasion of Ireland by the Normans was more like a sporadic consolidation of conquered land in the eastern part of the island. Intermittent conflict with the native Celtic Irish was accompanied by a slow integration of the Normans into the Irish cultural milieu. Intermarriage, adoption of the Irish language, and general acceptance by the Irish created several layers of Norman influence over the next two centuries. In the Leinster area around Dublin, called "the Pale," the English influence was greatest, and it was characterized by English law, customs, and administration. The second layer of influence was in the east and south where the Norman feudal system took hold, but the Norman rulers increasingly adopted the Irish culture. Least influenced were Ulster in the north and areas in the west of Ireland in which the rule remained essentially Gaelic.

Political authority was vested in an Irish Parliament convened in 1297. It was exclusively ecclesiastical and Norman, and no native Irish were invited. This first Parliament condemned the cultural integration of the Normans and labeled as "degenerate English" any people who adopted Celtic language and mores. The often-cited example of the attempt to preserve the Englishness of the Normans are the Statutes of Kilkenny enacted in 1366. These laws forbade intermarriage, wearing Irish dress, recognizing the Brehon law, speaking the Gaelic language, adopting Irish children, and maintaining Irish poets. Not only a reflection of cultural superiority, the statutes also signaled the somewhat insecure status of the Normans in Ireland. By the fourteenth century the Normans were in a defensive position, but the traditional political divisions of Ireland prevented the accumulation of power necessary to drive the Normans out of the country. By the fifteenth century, the political arrangement gave the Anglo-Irish descendants of the original Norman conquerors substantial home rule (with some areas still under Gaelic rule) and left them resentful of royal authority and inclined to ignore it.

The Tudor monarchs observed that the expanding imperial role of Britain was threatened by the vulnerability of Ireland. The lack of English authority beyond the Pale, coupled with the less than total devotion of the Hibernicized Norman aristocracy, was a potential opportunity for England's enemies. The task of asserting the authority of the crown was formidable. The Anglo-Irish independence would have to be curbed, and English law would have to be extended to all of Gaelic Ireland. Compounding the difficulty was the task, in fact never accomplished, of extending the Protestant Reformation into Ireland after Henry VIII's break with Rome. Henry VIII tried to garner the adherence of the Gaelic chieftains by having them turn over their lands to him, whereupon he would return the lands, grant titles to the chieftains, and they would administer the land as vassals of the king. Moreover, in 1541 Henry had himself designated king of Ireland by the Irish Parliament.

Of greater consequence in fueling Irish antagonism and deepening the political and cultural gap between the Irish and the English were the attempts by Edward VI and Elizabeth I to impose the reformed Anglican church doctrine and liturgy on Ireland. Such edicts as Edward VI's outlawing of the Mass drew the wrath of the Gaelic Catholic Irish and shattered the process of cultural integration that had served as a buffer against complete conquest by the English. The difference between ruler and ruled (except in Gaelic areas) was now defined not only by property and by culture but also by religion. The Catholicism of Ireland became the hub of Irish identity and later one of the pillars of Irish nationalism. The English responded to this insistence on Catholicism with a condescending crusade to eliminate the alien, irrational, and disloyal disease of "popery." In the latter part of the sixteenth century the Gaelic (and Anglo-Irish) lords came to the realization that the extension of English law and Protestantism could only lead ultimately to their own downfall.

In the 1590s the Irish came as close as they were going to come to defeating English rule. The earl of Tyrone, Hugh O'Neill, and the earl of Tyrconnell, Hugh O'Donnell, marshaled support from the lesser Gaelic nobles throughout Ireland. For nine years they withstood the English assault but, despite success at the outset, were finally defeated by the superior forces of the Royal Army. The struggle ended in 1603 when O'Neill surrendered. O'Donnell fled to Spain, and a few years later O'Neill and about 100 Irish chieftains from the north feared a conspiracy against their lives and went to the Continent.

This "flight of the earls" left the way open for the completion of the English conquest and the elimination of a Gaelic Ireland with its own traditions, law, and society. The flight of the earls also led to the plantation of Ulster, a strategy adopted by James I to firmly establish English control of the land. Plantation consisted of granting land confiscated by the crown to "planters," or landlords, who would farm the land. James I siezed the O'Neill and O'Donnell lands, nearly one-fourth of the island. Beginning in 1607 English planters and especially Scottish settlers went to Ulster so that by 1641 only one-seventh of the acreage was in Catholic hands. Thus Ulster eventually became a Protestant colony, and the distinct ethnic majority of that province was established.

The pattern of rebellion, defeat, and then plantation was to continue. In 1641 the Anglo-Irish and Catholics mounted another effort to throw off English domination and were quite successful in controlling a substantial portion of Ireland. They formed a government, the Confederation of Kilkenny, which then proceeded to splinter into factions, thus preventing any coherent organization of resistance. Oliver Cromwell, having defeated his enemies in Britain, turned to Ireland and ruthlessly crushed this rebellion in 1650.

Plantations followed, along with a move of the dispossessed Catholics to the province of Connaught. At that point Catholic ownership of land in Ireland was reduced to one-fourth of the total. In the century to follow, this total would be reduced to less than 5 percent.

In 1688, and not for the last time, English political rivalries played themselves out on the Irish stage. James II, a Catholic, had become king in 1685. His pro-Catholic convictions and the fact that his heir was Catholic prompted the British Parliament's decision to depose him and install the Protestant William of Orange on the British throne. James sought his restoration through the back door of Ireland, where he knew he would have Catholic support. James's efforts were to fail at the siege of Londonderry and on the banks of the Boyne River where his forces were defeated by the army of William III. The Catholic forces held out until 1691, when William offered the besieged Catholics in Limerick promises that they would be free to practice their religion, their property would remain secure, and they would be free from reprisals. Although William may have concluded the Treaty of Limerick in good faith, his coreligionists in Ireland and England wanted the Irish Catholics punished.

THE PENAL LAWS

Antipopery was the prevailing prejudice among the Protestants of Ireland and England. They believed that the Catholics were subversive since their primary loyalty was to the pope. Catholics were seen as superstitious, ignorant, irrational, and dangerous. Although anti-Catholicism prevailed in England with respect to Ireland, it was coupled with a stereotyped view of the Irish as subhuman, brutish, ignorant, drunken, violent, and lawless.[3] Clearly few barriers existed to prevent the politically, economically, and religiously dominant Protestants from translating their prejudice into law. The resulting penal laws enacted by the British Parliament and the Irish Parliament were a series of statutes, imposed from 1695 to 1727, that punished Catholics for their beliefs and prevented their participation in public office, the army, and civil employment.

Such persecution was not new—under Cromwell it had become law that to produce the head of a wolf or of a priest would earn one £5. What made the penal laws different was their comprehensiveness. They were, in fact, so comprehensive as to be unenforceable. The principal elements included banishment of bishops and religious orders from the country, and what priests remained were to register and disclaim loyalty to the Stuart pretender to the English throne. Catholics were excluded from Parliament and from the practice of law; they could not found schools or send their children to Europe to be educated. Leasing of property to Catholics was limited to thirty-one years, and purchase was not allowed. Any property owned by Catholics could not be left to one son but had to be divided among all sons. If an eldest son converted to Protestantism, the entire family estate became his. These laws were to last in various forms until 1829.

The penal laws failed in that they were so far-reaching that enforcement was uneven. Catholicism was not eradicated. On the contrary, it was strength-

Dromoland Castle: a symbol of the wealth of the ascendancy in Ireland. (Courtesy, Irish Tourist Board)

ened to the degree that it provided for the dispossessed masses a means of defining their identity and a source of succor in the midst of oppression. Rome continued to appoint Irish bishops; missionaries came from different religious orders to serve the Irish; and young men went abroad to study for the priesthood. Thus the institutional church was sustained. The penal laws brought the linkage between political dissent and Catholicism even closer, although the hierarchy during the period supported the English crown in the hope of receiving grants of religious toleration. The penal laws were successful in that they did prompt conversion to Protestantism among the Catholic aristocratic descendants of the Anglo-Irish. They were also successful in assuring the dominion of the Protestants over the Catholics. Lawrence J. McCaffrey suggests, in fact, that the real purpose of the penal laws was not to extend Protestantism but rather to terrorize Catholics.[4]

The effect then of the defeat of the Gaelic earls, the plantation system, and the penal laws was to reduce the dispossessed Gaelic majority to a dependent, oppressed status. The Anglo-Irish, always in an ambiguous position, caught as they were between their adopted nation and their British affinities, became increasingly dispossessed. The Anglican and Presbyterian planters and administrators were the new class of landlords and overlords. Since the first group was Catholic, the second predominantly so, and the third wholly Protestant, the fundamental pattern of religious conflict was set. As the Protestants owned the land the pattern of Protestant ascendancy over the landless Catholics was to prevail for the next two centuries.

THE PROTESTANT NATION

Catholic political action in the latter part of the eighteenth century was limited to pressure for improvement of rights. Sporadic peasant violence, often organized by secret societies, was the only reaction to Protestant rule. Seeking to halt the evictions, high rents, and other abuses of the tenants and peasants, the secret societies mounted violent attacks against property, livestock, and landlords.

Irish political impulses with respect to Britain in the late 1700s shifted to the Irish Parliament, as it represented the Irish Protestant nation. More secure in their position within Ireland, the Protestant aristocratic minority began to express dissatisfaction with its relationship with Britain. The discontent was directed at two main issues. The first was the political restrictions placed upon the Irish Parliament with respect to enacting legislation, as the Irish Parliament was a subordinate political entity. The second issue was the imposition of economic restraints upon Ireland by England. Exporting woolen products to England was restricted, to say nothing of other manufactured products. Restraints on the export of livestock, wool, and glass were designed to protect English farmers and manufacturers. (Linen manufacture in Belfast was the exception to this policy.) These restrictions discouraged the development of Irish industries and fostered Irish dependence on agriculture. These two issues brought the Irish Protestant elite into opposition with Britain. Although the majority of the Irish Parliament was pro-English (their seats were provided as patronage from the lord justices who were appointed by the king), a group developed that was infused by the ideas of John Locke, and it fostered a form of Irish patriotism not unlike the American patriotism of the same period. The patriots condemned absentee landlords as parasites who drained Ireland of needed investment and leadership. Like the American claims about the injustice of being ruled by an unrepresentative Parliament, the Irish patriots stressed the need for the more representative quality of an independent Irish Parliament.

The British were now confronted with a war in North America and Anglo-Irish patriots agitating for Lockean rights. Moreover, Catholics now were able to accumulate some wealth and social status because some of the penal laws had fallen into disuse or had been repealed. Although Catholics were seen as less treasonous, they were still a source of concern as Catholic France and Spain sided with the American revolutionaries against England. Under these pressures London passed a bill removing the restrictions on Irish trade. The leader of the Anglo-Irish patriots, Henry Grattan, was a liberal who believed in Catholic civil rights, repeal of the penal laws, equality of Catholics and Protestants, and an independent Irish Parliament. The liberal Whigs came into power in England in 1782 and, under Irish and international pressure, granted the Irish Parliament independence.

Although Grattan had championed the rights of the Catholics, he did not represent the sentiments of the Anglo-Irish aristocrats. In fact concessions made to Catholics in the period of 1782 to 1800 came at the instigation of the British rather than of the Irish. Fearing the political tumult that was sweeping Europe as a result of the French Revolution, the British urged the Irish Parliament to discourage Catholic disloyalty by limiting the harshest edge of "no popery." Ceding to this pressure in 1792, the Liberals granted Catholics access to civic positions and the legal profession and the right to open schools, to vote, and to bear arms. Britain also encouraged the opening of a Roman Catholic seminary at Maynooth in 1795. Clearly not motivated by an over-

Currently the Bank of Ireland, this building was the home of the Irish Parliament prior to the Act of Union. (Courtesy, Irish Tourist Board)

whelming devotion to Catholicism, Protestant British and Irish leaders feared that the radical ideas of the French Revolution would flow into Ireland through the seminarians trained in Europe. The Irish bishops were in full agreement about creating a seminary at Maynooth as that action was consistent with their long-run interests in controlling education.

Although the bishops and political elites were interested in quarantining the ideas of the French Revolution, there were others who were swept up in the ideas of Tom Paine, Jean Jacques Rousseau, and the American and French Revolutions. In 1791 middle-class dissident intellectuals formed the Society of United Irishmen in Ulster. Adopting the ideas of republicanism, they advocated a democratic Ireland and the elimination of sectarian strife. As the Ulster Presbyterians had suffered religious oppression under the Anglicans, the idea of a nonsectarian state appealed to the nonconformist Protestants as well as to those Catholics who joined the society. Although the society united Ulster Protestants and Catholics in a common cause, the appearance of unity belied the reality of sectarian relationships in Ireland at that time.

The sectarian bitterness forged by the eradication of Gaelic Ireland, the confiscation of property, and the imposition of the penal laws was too durable to be swept away by rhetoric about the rights of man. The clashes between Catholic secret organizations such as the Defenders and the Protestant Orange Order were more representative of the hostile division between Catholics and

Protestants than was the unity of the United Irishmen.

The rebellion of the United Irishmen was a sporadic affair with a prelude in 1795. Wolfe Tone, the guiding light of the United Irishmen, was from Dublin, a Protestant educated at Trinity College. He had a vibrant personality and a keen mind and was totally devoted to applying the ideas of republican France to Ireland. He had persuaded the French, then at war with Britain, to send a force of 15,000 men to join the society's forces in rebellion. The expedition never landed. In 1796 the Irish Parliament, reacting to the tension in Ireland, instituted a series of coercive measures and created an armed Protestant yeoman corps. In March 1798 the government arrested most of the leaders of the society in Dublin. In May of the same year peasants in Wexford rose up and fought bravely for about a month before they were defeated. In June the United Irishmen rose up in Antrim and Down and were quickly defeated. In August a small French force under General Jean-Joseph Humbert landed in Mayo and for a month fought alongside local peasants, but Humbert surrendered when he ran out of supplies.[5] In October Wolfe Tone was captured off the coast in a futile attempt to invade Ireland. Rather than be hung as a traitor, he took his own life.

The motivations of people who participated in the "rising of 98" varied widely. For the United Irishmen the rebellion was an act of modern revolution to achieve a democratic republic. For the Catholics of Wexford it was a peasant revolution motivated by religious oppression and landlord abuses. For others it was merely an attempt to strike out at the Protestant landlords as the secret societies had been doing for several decades.

The results of the uprising were both immediate and long term. The immediate impact was the dissolution of the Irish Parliament after 500 years of existence. British Prime Minister William Pitt decided that Ireland would have to be integrated into the United Kingdom. The factionalism of the Irish Parliament, the demands of Catholics for rights, and the vulnerability of Ireland to revolution and foreign influence were too threatening to English elites. The persuasive skills of Charles Cornwallis and Robert Stewart Castlereagh were turned loose on the Irish parliamentary members. These advocates of union with Britain stressed the need for internal and external security. The Protestants had come to recognize that the maintenance of their power was dependent upon Britain. If the 1798 rebellion had not been successful, the next one might be. Thus a significant segment of the Protestant elite supported union. The Protestant patriots, however, argued that union would subordinate Ireland's interests to Britain's and relegate Ireland to the status of a mere province. The bishops and upper-status Catholics favored union as they were persuaded that the English Parliament would grant Catholic emancipation. This possibility was precisely what the more "antipopery" Protestants feared, and thus they disliked the idea of union with Britain. Their arguments, in the end, proved less persuasive than the mixture of pressures and payoffs to the Irish parliamentarians engineered by the king's lord lieutenant, who handed out peerages and pensions to get the vote. Ireland was now to be represented in the British Parliament by 100 members of the House of Commons and 32 peers in the House of Lords. The Irish Parliament ceased to exist in 1800.

The enduring heritage of the 1798 rebellion was to provide intellectual fuel and emotional ardor to the development of Irish nationalism. Tone's vision of an independent republic free of sectarian privilege provided a new, modern foundation for the Irish independence movement. No longer was the ideal the restoration of a Gaelic Catholic ascendancy free of English domination, but rather the continental and U.S. doctrines of individual freedom, democracy, and representative government.

In the emotional sphere the heroic struggle of the Wexford peasants' meeting British muskets with farmer's pikes provided ample material for the creation of revolutionary myth and lore to be retold, sung, or recited. Finally, the failure of the rebellion was not seen as stupid or fruitless but rather as a heroic sacrifice, the worth being in the act itself and not in its outcome. Thus the pattern of heroic failure was set for numerous Irish revolutionary outbursts, some plausible, others foolish, but all revered with the same ferocity in the collective folk memory. David Thornley notes: "The year 1798 with its curious blend of the political republicanism of the intellectuals and the agricultural suffering of the dispossessed, better perhaps than any other date marks the birth of modern Irish nationalism."[6]

Absorption of Ireland into the United Kingdom may have been seen by Pitt as the answer to British security problems, but he could not foresee that Ireland was to prove to be politically hard to digest. In the course of the next century Irish political energies focused on Catholic emancipation, repeal of the Act of Union, reform of the rights of peasants on the land, and home rule. The skill of some Irish members of Parliament—such as O'Connell, Parnell, and Redmond—cast Irish interests as the political balance weight in the partisan political conflicts of Britain. Two other threads were to accompany Irish political agitation for home rule—new organizations favoring violent revolution and an emerging sense of nationalism. These threads were to weave together in the early years of the twentieth century to bring Britain to the brink of civil war and Ireland into open rebellion.

The British policy of restricting Irish trade in the eighteenth century, modified only after 1782, had the effect of preventing the development of Irish shipping, manufacturing, and textiles, despite the fact that Ireland was not rich in resources and was unlikely to become a significant threat to British trade. Thus the Industrial Revolution took place in Ireland only in Ulster, where the British had encouraged the linen and shipbuilding industries. Southern Ireland, however, dependent upon agriculture, had no outlet for the surplus of workers that were the result of a rapid population growth. Although census figures are somewhat imprecise, the growth was clearly enormous. In 1800 the population of all of Ireland was over 4 million; in 1821, almost 7 million; and by 1841, over 8 million. This population was putting intense pressure on the land, which was increasingly subdivided into ever-smaller plots, creating a layered system of rents from the poorest peasant up to the, often absentee, landlord. Avarice contributed to the desperate plight of the peasant as the pressure for land pushed rents far beyond the real value of the land. Not only was agriculture becoming more and more inefficient, but the rents were becoming increasingly exorbitant as well. The Irish peasants' diet consisted almost exclusively of the potato; the people seldom ate bread, eggs, poultry, meat, or fish. What a peasant could produce other than the potato was sold to pay the rent. A potato famine in the 1740s, when the population was only slightly more than 3 million, ominously foreshadowed the famine of the late 1840s.

After the Union the established church was the Church of Ireland. To this alien church the Catholic peasant paid a tithe (although altered in 1838, it was not removed until 1869), which was one-tenth of the land's produce. This tithe went to support 4 archbishops, 18 bishops, and 1,400 clergy who ministered to approximately one-tenth of the island's population. If the tenants improved the land through their own efforts, higher rents were charged, and a bill passed in 1816 made capricious eviction easier.

The British politicians in Westminster were either ignorant of, or indifferent to, these conditions as few of them ever visited Ireland. The British leaders perceived the conditions as being the fault of the slovenly Irish. Some politicians personally harbored anti-Catholic, anti-Irish prejudices or were sensitive to British public opinion, which was characterized by anti-Catholic nativism.

The Act of Union did not integrate Ireland into the United Kingdom as an equal component. Ireland continued to be treated as a province whose economic interests were to be subordinated to Britain's, and whose population was to be subjected to law and order. An army of 25,000 men was garrisoned in Ireland, and in 1813 the Peace Preservation Act created a Peace Preservation Force. In 1822 a special constabulary was established, and in 1836 it was reorganized into the Irish Constabulary, an armed paramilitary force directed at suppressing agrarian discontent.

Within Ireland the liberal Protestant patriots faded away, and the Orange Order became the spokesmen for the Protestant community. Founded in 1795 to counter Catholic secret societies, the Orange Order soon grew beyond its Ulster origins. Characterized by antipopery of a particularly vivid variety, the Orange Order was now dedicated to the Union as Ulster's economic prosperity was seen to be tied to the Union. The Irish unionists allied with the Tory politicians in Britain because they shared religious, property, and class interests with the Irish Protestant ascendancy.

This political environment had a deadening effect on Catholic aspirations and activities for two decades after the Act of Union. One notable and tragic exception was the futile "rebellion" in 1803 of Robert Emmet and his followers. The uprising was less a harbinger of the future than a remnant of 1798, as Emmet had absorbed the ideas of his brother, one of the founders of the Society of United Irishmen. After attempting to seize Dublin Castle, Emmet was arrested and convicted for treason. Before he was hung he delivered an emotional speech from the dock, a zealous condemnation of British oppression and a clarion call for Irish revolution. Emmet joined Tone in the hagiology of Irish martyrs whose acts were more important than their consequences. Emmet became a heroic figure and thus a contributor to the revolutionary tradition.

THE CATHOLIC EMANCIPATION

A far more important figure in the development of political organization among the Catholics and in the achievement of Catholic emancipation was

O'Connell Bridge in the heart of Dublin. (Courtesy, Irish Tourist Board)

Daniel O'Connell. O'Connell was born in 1775 to a well-off Catholic family who could afford to send him to Europe for his education. Attracted to radicalism in his youth, he was a sometime member of the Society of United Irishmen. He had extraordinary success as a barrister, which established his reputation in Ireland. In his youth he had opposed the rebellion of 1798 as he feared it would provoke bloody reprisals from the British army. This nonrevolutionary approach to the liberation of Ireland was to characterize his efforts throughout his life (despite his conviction by the House of Lords on a trumped-up charge of sedition in 1843). Two great issues shaped O'Connell's career: the first, Catholic emancipation; the second, repeal of the Union with Britain. In the pursuit of these objectives O'Connell enjoyed success on the former and suffered failure on the latter.

The quest for Catholic emancipation hardly benefited the Catholic peasants. They were mired in a poverty that would scarcely allow exercise of the privileges of Catholic civil rights. The middle- and upper-class Catholics in Britain and Ireland, however, would gain in social status, political influence, and economic opportunity. Although civil rights had been virtually promised to Catholics at the time of the Act of Union, Pitt was unable to deliver as King George III refused to agree. Catholics, however, through the Catholic Committee, continued to petition the House of Commons for emancipation.

In pursuit of this goal O'Connell welded the Catholic community together in 1823 through the Catholic Association. O'Connell created a mass-based organization using priests as his local organizers. He recognized the strength of the relationship between priest and parishioner as well as the literacy and social eminence of the clergy. The emancipation movement sparked mass enthusiasm and was supported by small contributions collected at Mass on Sundays. Because the movement gained such strength, grievances beyond emancipation were discussed. The power of the association was dramatically demonstrated in 1878 when O'Connell defeated a Tory landlord in an election in County Clare. The message to the British government was clear. It was faced with a choice between extremely unpleasant alternatives. Either O'Connell's demands were met, which might provoke anti-Catholic sentiment in England, or they were denied, risking, as O'Connell warned, insurrection in Ireland. The Peel government chose Catholic civil rights and passed the Relief Act in 1829. This gain was not without costs to the Irish Catholics as the Catholic Association was outlawed and 180,000 Catholic voters lost their franchise.

The benefits of emancipation were to assist the Irish elites in gaining access to power and wealth over the remainder of the century. Irish nationalism was advanced through the demonstrated political impact of Catholics when they were welded together in pursuit of a goal.

The second issue to which O'Connell devoted himself was that of repeal of the Act of Union. Having opposed the Union in 1800, O'Connell remained steadfast in that position until his death. Echoing Grattan, O'Connell argued that Ireland could never be justly governed from London as British politicians could never respond to Irish needs. Repeal, however, had hardly any adherents in Parliament, and O'Connell was forced into parliamentary cooperation in order to bring about advances in Ireland. In some instances this cooperation worked. Lord Mulgrave, the viceroy, and his undersecretary Thomas Drumond brought decent, impartial rule to Ireland and outlawed the Orange Order in 1837 (it was revived in 1845). In virtually all other instances, however, O'Connell was frustrated. He hoped for an increase in Irish representation from the reform bill of 1832; none was forthcoming. He expected elimination of the tithe in 1838, but it was simply incorporated into land rents. He expected relief for the poor of Ireland, but Parliament passed a Poor Law that was inappropriate for Irish conditions and added taxes to pay for it.

Mass agitation had worked for emancipation, and O'Connell now believed it was the only road to repeal of the Union. As with emancipation, O'Connell formed a mass-based Catholic organization, the Loyal National Repeal Association, by building upon hostility to the Poor Law. O'Connell had an enormous following, which he excited with promises of freedom, their own parliament and courts, tenants' rights, democracy, and prosperity. As in 1828, he confronted Prime Minister Peel with the alternative of granting repeal or risking Irish revolution. Emancipation had been costly for the Whigs in 1828, and what they had then conceded was certainly less than Irish self-government. Peel sent troops to Ireland and told O'Connell flatly that he would crush an insurrection rather than grant repeal. The Union clearly was more crucial to British interests than emancipation. O'Connell backed down as he believed the costs of violence would be too high.

Peel, however, decided to take a route toward quelling Irish nationalist aspirations other than the traditional strategy of suppression. He decided to divide and conquer by keeping the church, the Catholic middle class, and the tenant farmers from coalescing around the embryonic nationalist movement. He asked Rome to curtail the political activity of the clergy and promised that charitable bequests could be given to the church and to increase support for the Catholic seminary at Maynooth. He created the Queen's University colleges at Belfast, Galway, and Cork, which would open up university education to middle-class Catholics, especially in Galway and Cork. Finally, he proposed a tenants' rights bill, which would improve the security of tenants in Ireland. The plan might have worked as it did split the Irish nationalist movement by revealing the differences between the interests of the church (which accepted the Maynooth support but undermined the colleges), O'Connell (who rejected the colleges and the charitable bequests act), and young nationalists (who accepted the colleges). However, the whole scheme floundered upon the advent of the famine, which caused the Peel government to fall. The Tories came to power, and their policies toward Ireland ultimately fostered the rise of Irish nationalism that Peel had sought to thwart.

O'Connell's commitment to nonviolent means had come under sharp criticism in the Repeal Association from a group of agitators who called themselves Young Irelanders and who split away and formed the Irish Confederation in 1847. This movement had sprung up after 1842 and was encouraged and molded by the newspaper *The Nation.* Founded in 1842 by Thomas Osborne Davis, Charles Gavan Duffy, and John Blake Dillon, *The Nation* advocated an anti-industrial cultural nationalism as well as demanding Irish independence. The movement's nationalism flowed from the romantic movement in Europe at the time, which influenced leaders such as Giuseppe Garibaldi in Italy. Its adherents admired Wolfe Tone, Grattan, and liberal political principles but infused them with ideas from the Irish, Gaelic, and Norman past. Lamenting the retreat of Gaelic before the English language, they urged people to preserve the Irish language and culture.

The Young Irelanders had split with O'Connell over the issues of O'Connell's cooperation with the Whigs and the question of revolutionary violence and on general differences of philosophy and ideology. The Young Ireland movement itself then split on the question of whether the central issue in Ireland was landlordism and the pursuit of peasant proprietorship, as proposed by James Finton Laylor, or national independence, as proposed by Charles Gavan Duffy. The Young Irelanders chose the latter and hoped to extract repeal of the Act of Union from the British Parliament. The Young Irelanders themselves held out little hope for a revolution on the part of famine-wracked peasants, but the British government was convinced that insurrection was imminent. Parliament passed laws against treason, sent troops to Ireland, and applied martial law to Dublin, Waterford, and Cork. The government began to arrest the leaders of the Young Ireland group and provoked the remainder to "revolution." The constabulary crushed the minuscule attempt at insurrection with little difficulty, and the leaders were deported. Young Ireland, however, contributed poetry, songs, and failure to the accumulating tradition of violent rebellion.

NOTES

1. *Oxford Dictionary of Quotations* (Oxford: Oxford University Press, 1959), p. 209.

2. Pope Adrian IV was English, and no traces of the bull have been found, thus leading to speculation that it never existed. The Irish Catholic church, however, was considered to be in need of reform at the time, and Adrian IV was interested in the assertion of strong government in Ireland to bring order to the Irish church.

3. See Richard Ned Lebow, *White Britain, Black Ireland* (Philadelphia: Institute for the Study of Human Issues, 1976).

4. Lawrence J. McCaffrey, *Ireland: From Colony to Nation State* (Englewood Cliffs, N.J.: Prentice-Hall, 1979), pp. 14 and 15.

5. For an excellent treatment of these events in the form of a novel see Thomas Flanagan, *The Year of the French* (New York: Holt, Rinehart and Winston, 1979).

6. David Thornley, "Historical Introduction," in Basil Chubb, *The Government and Politics of Ireland* (London: Oxford University Press, 1974), p. 15.

2

From the Famine to the Rising

THE FAMINE

The middle of the nineteenth century brought an unparalleled human disaster to the Irish, the potato famine. Simply put, the single, crucial staple food of 8.5 million Irish people was struck by a blight that destroyed the crops of 1845, 1846, and 1848. By 1851 approximately 1 million Irish had died of starvation or famine-related causes. Over 1 million emigrated, only to perish in large numbers from the ghastly conditions aboard disease-ridden ships on transatlantic voyages.

The response of Britain ran the gamut from generous humanitarian concern to governmental ideological rigidity and even cruel abuse of the suffering human beings. Peel responded to the famine by purchasing maize from the United States and distributing it in Ireland. Charitable contributions were generous for famine relief, and the government supplied relief and public works projects. When the Tories replaced the Whigs in 1846, the government's policy lapsed into laissez-faire dogmatism blended with more than a little religious and racial prejudice. The doctrines of laissez-faire economics portrayed the famine as some inexorable law of nature that was tragic but about which little could be done as the government could not interfere in the economy. The persistent anti-Catholic, anti-Irish prejudices allowed some British politicians to explain the disaster in terms of Irish laziness and popery. Finally, some Protestant organizations, in a bizarre form of proselytism, would give food to the starving Catholics if they would convert to Protestantism.

The effects of the famine were far-reaching. In the social sphere the famine prompted a tide of emigration from Ireland that did not stop until more than a century later. From a high of 8.5 million people, Ireland's population declined to approximately 4.5 million before it began to rise again after 1960. The Irish unwillingly provided unskilled labor to Britain, Australia, the Continent, Canada, and the United States.

The famine also dealt a deadly blow to the Gaelic language and cultural tradition. The people who suffered most under the famine were those Irish peasants who had the least to do with the rise of industrialism and commerce. They lived in Irish-speaking regions and were driven to death, or to the docks, by the famine. Their demise also signaled the demise of the Gaelic language and the still-vital Gaelic stories, songs, poems, traditions, and legends that had been transmitted by these people across the generations. The people

23

remaining for economic reasons saw no alternative but to send their children to the national schools created by the British, with, of course, English as the language of instruction. Already in decline, the number of people speaking Irish (Gaelic) after the famine dropped rapidly, and by 1871 less than 20 percent of the people could speak Irish, and most of those were concentrated in Connaught.

The effect of the famine on the Irish economy was profound. The famine drove the poorest of the Irish farm workers, peasants, and tenants off the land and halted the pattern of increasing subdivision. In fact, the Encumbered Estates Act of 1849, which allowed the courts to sell the land of bankrupt landlords, prompted the eventual sale of one-third of the cultivated land in Ireland by 1880. The purchasers were predominantly Catholics who had been allowed to purchase land since 1793. The period from 1847 to 1853 produced over 60,000 evictions, which consolidated holdings into much larger units and meant that the docks continued to receive waves of emigrants. Over the next twenty years the process continued, and the fact that the population was reduced by over 2 million people meant that more economically viable farms were created. Not only was Irish agriculture now more efficient, but it shifted from producing grains to supporting livestock. Industrial Britain provided a ready market, and meat, butter, and eggs were exported. The years 1850–1880 saw an economic upsurge for farmers in Ireland. Prices and sales rose, providing the tenant farmers with a much more varied diet and a generally higher standard of living. As rising expectations more often produce agitation for change than does destitution, the Irish peasants still clamored for better guarantees of tenants' rights with respect to rents and security of tenure, and ultimately, for ownership.

The political movements that had culminated during the famine period were all moribund. Peasant support of O'Connell's Repeal Association dissolved into sporadic agrarian violence and famine-induced misery. The alternative Young Ireland movement was in dissolution.

After the famine an independent Irish group appeared in Parliament, but it was not very effectual. This effort was generated by Charles Gavan Duffy of Young Ireland fame, who formed the Tenants League in 1850. This organization was to be the focal point of agitation for tenants' rights. Although electorally successful in 1852, it quickly shattered as some members were altogether too willing to serve in the British government. A more telling blow was the lack of support for the Tenants League from Paul Cullen, the archbishop of Dublin, who saw agitation for tenants' rights as the leading edge of Irish revolution. Cullen curtailed the political activity of the clergy who supported tenants' rights at the grass-roots level, so the league lost any chance of building up a mass base in the O'Connell fashion.

Cullen pulled the church in Ireland away from supporting the nationalist movement. He was more interested in extracting concessions from Parliament with respect to disestablishing the Anglican church, and thus eliminating the tithe, and establishing Catholic control over education. In these objectives he was successful. In 1869 the Church of Ireland was disestablished, and by 1883 the elementary education in Ireland was denominational. Cullen was also interested in a restoration of devotion to the church and an extensive building program. In these objectives he was immensely successful as the more prosperous tenant farmers contributed to an explosion of churches, rectories, convents, and schools. In the clergy there was a tightening up of authority, and in the laity, a sharp increase in the practice of faith.

The collapse of the parliamentary road to Irish reform and independence in 1859 left a gap that was not to be filled until the rise of Charles Stewart Parnell twenty years later. But people who believed that the liberation of Ireland had to come through force were building a new organization on the crumbled ruins of Young Ireland. Three exiled veterans of the 1849 insurrection came together in New York. That an organization to instigate a revolution in Ireland should be created in the United States is another reflection of the impact of the famine. The United States absorbed hundreds of thousands of immigrants into its northeastern cities, and those immigrants had a powerful hatred for the British and a burgeoning sense of Irish nationalism. Michael Doheny had come directly to the United States in 1849, but John Mahoney and James Stephens had drunk deeply of the revolutionary theories and tactics profferred by European revolutionaries at the barricades and in the cafes of Paris.

In 1858 these three founded the Fenian Brotherhood in the United States, and Stephens formed a similar secret, oath-bound society in Ireland that later became the Irish Republican Brotherhood (IRB). A newspaper called *The Irish People* accompanied the movement, and it featured the writing of two extremely talented men, John O'Leary and Charles Kickham. The society and its spokesmen came under immediate attack from the church, which disliked the existence of clandestine organizations, especially those devoted to violent revolution. Cullen led the attack, and he was backed by Rome, which issued a papal condemnation of the Fenians in 1870.

U.S. money, military expertise provided by veterans of the American Civil War, and peasant discontent were to be the ingredients of a successful Fenian rebellion. In Ireland the government was aware of IRB activities through informers, and in 1867 it cracked down on the IRB and provoked the leaderless organization to a modest uprising. The Irish Constabulary put down the Fenians with ease and earned the sobriquet "royal" in front of its name. The people who were arrested were sentenced to long prison terms, and some were tortured. The IRB, although battered, did not disappear and remained on the back burner while the battle for home rule held the stage. Later, in 1916, the IRB emerged to play an important role in that insurrection.

Despite clerical condemnation, the Fenians had captured the nationalist imagination, perhaps even more strongly than Tone and Emmet had, and certainly more than Young Ireland. People flocked to amnesty associations that demanded the release of the Fenians from British prisons. The failed rising provided an array of martyrs for song and story and fresh inspiration to some members of the Irish middle class who were disenchanted with the pallid politics of the Irish parliamentarians. The Fenians revealed the degree to which U.S. support was to play a part in the Irish nationalist struggle. Finally, the Fenians, in their conflict with the church, revealed that the quest for political independence did not require clerical sanction and that church interests were not identical to nationalism.[1]

THE STRUGGLE FOR HOME RULE

The weight of Irish efforts to change the country's political status within the United Kingdom shifted to the home rule party. This movement was played out in two stages, the first of which was under Parnell; the second, under Redmond.

Isaac Butt, a Protestant lawyer, had developed a reputation in Ireland for his defense of the Young Ireland rebels and later the Fenians. He felt that the British control of Ireland had hampered Irish economic development, and his nationalism was directed toward a constitutional form of independence for Ireland modeled on U.S. federalism. He appealed to the Protestants to recognize their interest in an independently governed Ireland and stressed the importance of their participation lest they be left in the lurch as Catholic efforts brought about home rule. In 1870 he founded the Home Government Association and in 1873 drew a broader base of support into the Home Rule League. Butt was able to attract diverse elements into this league. His Protestant background, defense of the Fenians, and constitutional approach could appeal to landlords, the Catholic middle class, clerics, and rebels. The league formed the Irish Parliamentary Party, which was to be committed to home rule. In the election of 1874 this party elected fifty-nine members to Parliament. Their performance, characterized on the one hand by Butt's lack of leadership and equivocation on agrarian issues and on the other by rock-hard opposition from British politicians, was less than dazzling. Responding to the criticism of more militant Catholics, Butt promised to be more aggressive. The task of challenging the British Parliament, however, fell to two members, Joseph Biggar and, more importantly, Charles Stewart Parnell.

Parnell was an astute Protestant landlord who had a deep commitment to Irish self-government. Biggar and Parnell chose to obstruct the work of Parliament rather than to cooperate with the British politicians. The members of Parliament were furious with Parnell, the English press ridiculed him, and finally Butt, still committed to a conciliatory approach, censured him. A split ensued in the movement, and it polarized around Butt's and Parnell's approaches to advancing Irish interests, though most members favored Parnell's confrontational approach.

Although the Irish Parliamentary Party centered on home rule, the nationalist movements also built upon agrarian discontent. In the late 1870s a depression hit Irish agriculture and raised again the issues of rent, security of tenure, and eviction. The response, as it had been so often before, was evictions on the one hand and unorganized, sporadic violence on the other. The crystalization of this peasant anger into political action was engineered by Michael Davitt.[2] In 1879 he created the National Land League, which aborded the various forms of discontent, agitation, and violence and channeled them into a coherent strategy of militant confrontation and rent strikes. Parnell, impressed by Davitt, more and more supported the position of the league and its tactics, and Parnell assumed the presidency of the league when Davitt stepped aside to allow Parnell's luster to add to the agrarian cause. Parnell now led both the home rule and agrarian movements.

In the years 1880–1882 a virtual land war took place that could not be contained by the constabulary. Funded by U.S. money, it swept the Irish peasant into enthusiastic support of land reform and home rule. William Gladstone, the British prime minister, responded with the Land Act of 1881, which granted the demands of the peasants. At the same time, however, Gladstone cracked down on the Land League, outlawing it and arresting the leaders, including Parnell. Of course, Parnell's stature increased among the Irish—one of the few benefits of serving in a British prison. Agrarian violence increased, and Gladstone made a bargain with Parnell according to which Gladstone could compensate evicted tenants if Parnell would support the Irish policies of his government. Parnell was released.

Parnell now turned his energies to home rule. He established a new organization, the Irish National League, to build electoral support for his party. He made a pragmatic accommodation with the hierarchy of the church under which it would support his constitutional efforts for home rule and he would support the effort to create a publicly financed Catholic educational system. Parnell improved the quality of the members of his party and demanded absolute discipline.

The British Parliament unwittingly aided Parnell's cause by passing reforms that extended the franchise. In 1885 the Irish Parliamentary Party sent eighty-six members to Parliament and held the balance of power between the Liberals and the Conservatives. Gladstone introduced a home rule bill in 1886, but his Liberal Party split on the issue, and the government fell.

The split in the Liberal Party in Parliament sent the Irish pro-Union members running to the Conservatives. They stood for an anti-Catholic, anti-Irish, pro-empire position. This split cast a beam of light on the split within Ireland between the Ulster unionists and the Irish Party. In the 1886 debate Lord Randolph Churchill had highlighted the degree to which the Conservatives were in harmony with the industrialized Protestant Ulstermen, symbolized by the influence of the Orange Order. The slogan Home Rule Is Rome Rule reflected the nativist prejudice, and Ulster Will Fight and Ulster Will Be Right gave warning of the depth of the Ulster Presbyterians' commitment against home rule.

Parnell did not gain the leverage to get another home rule bill introduced before a messy divorce scandal brought pressure on him to resign as leader of the party. Originating with the British Protestants and later picked up by the Catholic clerics, condemnation of Parnell grew to such a point that it split the Irish Party. Parnell fought to regain power but failed, his health broke, and he died in 1891.

The home rule party was a shambles over the next decade. John Redmond took over the Parnell wing, the anti-Parnell wing split into feuding factions, and the entire movement stagnated. Ironically enough, while the Irish Parliamentary Party languished, the Conservatives (now called Unionists) adopted a policy of Irish reform in the hopes that it would, as Arthur J. Balfour said, "Kill home rule with kindness." In the periods 1886–1892 and 1895–1905 the Unionists encouraged public works projects, technical schools, and democratized local government in Ireland.

In 1869, when the Church of Ireland was disestablished, church lands were offered for sale to the tenants with loans to aid in the purchase. This act began the process of transferring ownership of land to the tenants, and further acts weakened the landlords' grip on property and made loans available to the tenants at low rates. The Unionists completed this process with the Wyndham Act of 1903, which offered incentives to landlords to sell their estates. The cumulative effect of these acts was to increase the base of ownership from 3 percent of the Irish people in 1870 to 64 percent by 1916. Conservatives, though traditionally the ally of the landlords, had created a peasant proprietorship.

In 1900 the two wings of the Irish Party came together under John Redmond, and the two constituency organizations were merged into the United Irish League. Redmond had over eighty members in Parliament and solid electoral support. Gladstone had introduced a home rule bill in 1893, but under Conservative pressure, it had been vetoed by the House of Lords. This tactic had been used to check other Liberal legislation, and the conflict came to a head in 1910. It became clear to the Liberals that getting their legislation enacted, including home rule, would require restraining the veto of the House of Lords. After the second election of 1910, during which home rule had been a central issue, Redmond demanded that the Liberals curb the House of Lords and introduce a home rule bill. Herbert Henry Asquith did so, although it required a threat from George V to pack the House of Lords with Liberal peers to persuade the lords to accept the act. As the combination of the Liberals, House of Lords, and Irish Party votes were more than enough, home rule passed in the spring of 1912. Its passage was the signal for the conservatives to unleash a torrent of opposition.

The chief opponents of home rule were Sir Edward Carson and Sir James Craig. They immediately went to Ulster and fanned the already bright flames of anti-Catholicism into a pledge by 471,000 Ulster Protestants to resist by all means the imposition of home rule. If it were enacted, they pledged to not recognize the authority of the home rule Parliament. Pledges were the fashion as 2 million British signed a covenant in support of Ulster. The people of Ulster organized a "provisional government" and an Ulster Volunteer Force to resist home rule. Arms began to pour into Ulster for the Volunteers. Notable conservative spokesmen spoke out against home rule to the point of accepting civil war to preserve the Union.

Irish nationalists were not blind to these developments, and they set out to create a force to offset the intimidation of the British government by the Ulster Volunteers. In 1913 the Irish Volunteers were created under the tutelage of the Irish Republican Brotherhood. When the government banned the import of arms into Ireland in late 1913, it touched off an arms smuggling race between the Irish and Ulster Volunteers in 1914.

When the British army officers stationed in Ireland indicated that they would rather resign their commissions than fight their compatriots in Ulster, Asquith bowed to threat of civil war and offered Redmond home rule with the exclusion of Ulster. Redmond refused, but he was caught between the Scylla of Irish nationalist wrath at partition and the Charybdis of bringing down the Liberal government and perhaps losing home rule altogether. Redmond offered to accept partition if there were plebiscites in the counties of Ulster on home rule. The impasse was never resolved, as World War I broke out in August and the British government put the Home Rule Act into law but suspended it for the duration of the war.

With this ambiguous evasion the saga of home rule ends. For thirty years this effort had commanded the allegiance of some of Ireland's most notable political leaders. The prize was denied them, however, when British politicians who had urged parliamentary constitutional processes on the Irish, and crushed the rebels, would not do the same when the Irish won constitutionally and the unionists were the rebels. To the observant nationalist the message was clear: Tone, Emmet, Young Ireland, and the Irish Republican Brotherhood were correct; violent revolution was the only road to Irish independence.

THE RISE OF IRISH NATIONALISM

Militant nationalist sentiments also were fueled by a mixture of organizations and ideas that emerged at the end of the century, interlocked with the political movement, and ultimately swept away Parnell and Redmond's Irish Parliamentary Party. The elements were the revival of Gaelic culture, the Sinn Féin movement, the revived Irish Republic Brotherhood, and the creation of citizen armies by the IRB and James Connolly.

The impetus to search for Irish identity in the heritage of the Celtic past actually began in the 1840s when the writers of Young Ireland turned to the Celtic tradition to assert the distinctiveness and superiority of Irish culture over the materialism of the Anglo-Saxon heritage. However, two organizations brought great energy to this movement. The first, the Gaelic Athletic Association (GAA), was founded in 1884 by Michael Cusak. Cusak wanted to revive Irish games and to discourage the playing of English games. The movement had great success, and Gaelic football and hurling had a substantial following. Although encouraging Irish sports would seem to be a marginal contribution to cultural nationalism, in fact it was more. The GAA grew powerful with strong support from the church. Moreover, it drew its support from, and encouraged, local patriotism in the rural areas of Ireland. Finally, the GAA had a loose connection with the Irish Republican Brotherhood that gave a tone of militancy to its attitude toward sports. The expulsion from the GAA of people who played English games indicates the degree of intense commitment this organization had to things Irish. The mixture of Catholicism, sports, and cultural nationalism in the GAA contributed to the growth of the broader movement.

In 1893 Eoin MacNeill created the second organization, the Gaelic League. Restoration of Irish as the language of Ireland was his goal, as well as studying and preserving Gaelic literature. At the turn of the century the league became very popular, and people began to learn Irish and visit the Irish-speaking areas in the west of Ireland. Schools were founded to teach Irish, and the enthusiasm for the language spilled over into enthusiasm for Irish music, dance, and literature. Proselytizers such as Douglas Hyde expanded the organization and by 1908 had achieved some major objectives—including the teaching of Irish in the elementary schools and secondary schools and, in 1909, in the new National University. The links with Irish nationalism were obvious as the Gaelic League strove to de-Anglicize Ireland and retrieve from the past customs, names, games, and, of course, the language. The emphasis on an Irish-Ireland was a clear step beyond the home rule or independence movement in that it sought the creation of a Gaelic nation, not merely a politically autonomous Ireland. Patrick Pearse expressed this difference succinctly when he demanded, "Ireland, not merely free, but Gaelic as well, not Gaelic merely, but free as well."[3] The GAA and the Gaelic League nurtured virtually every revolutionary who emerged in the period from 1916 to 1921.

The third leg of the Celtic revival was a literary movement in Dublin, which not only contributed to the growing Irish cultural awareness but brought forth some of the greatest writers of modern literature. Unlike Young Ireland writers, who stressed native cultural emphasis in their writings but subordinated it to their political aspirations, the Dublin literary movement was composed of artists who placed their expressive gifts above their politics. The major figures were William Butler Yeats, John Millington Synge, James Joyce, and Sean O'Casey. The collected work of these writers and lesser lights drew upon Celtic mythology, folk tales, and peasant life to create a romantic vision of Irish culture. This vision could have a powerful emotional impact, as did Yeats's play *Cathleen ni Houlihan,* in stirring up intense feelings of nationalism and love of country. Synge and, later, O'Casey went beyond the romantic image, and their plays caused uproars at the Irish National Theatre as some people in the nationalism movement could not accept a less than glorified vision of the Irish. Nevertheless the literary renaissance, bubbling as it was with controversy, injected the nationalist movement as never before with a vision of Irish culture that was portrayed by talents as great as those in other nations. Artistic independence, affirmation of Celtic heritage, and political sensitivity were woven together by the literary renaissance writers in such a way as to promote the Gaelicization of Ireland and also produce enduring works of art.

In the years after Parnell's fall there arose all over Ireland a spattering of small groups, clubs, and societies that were engaged in nationalist political discussions of Irish independence. Partially joined together by a loose national association, they formally organized in 1905 into the group Sinn Féin ("ourselves"). The Irish Republican Brotherhood, still a secret oath-bound society, had a quiet hand in this group, as it had in the GAA and the Gaelic League.

The mentor of the new Sinn Féin group was Arthur Griffith, who had been offering his own ideas on Irish independence since 1898 in his paper, *The United Irishman.* Griffith had mixed an interesting cocktail of ideas in his version of the independence movement. Convinced that Ireland had to be independent, but also convinced that a violent revolution would be crushed, Griffith suggested that the tactics for achieving separation from Britain should be withdrawal from Parliament and the setting up of an Irish assembly that would make policy for Ireland. The objectives would be to create an Ireland that was infused with the values of Celtic culture. Economically, Griffith wanted protectionism, as advocated by the German economist Friedrich List.

The Irish Republican Brotherhood had languished in the years since 1858—its leaders old, and its sparkle gone. Three men regenerated the organization after the turn of the century: Denis McCullough, Bulmer Hobson, and Sean McDermott. McCullough was a vigorous organizer and recruiter for the IRB in Belfast. McDermott was an organizer for Sinn Féin after it had absorbed the smaller political clubs. Hobson was a journalist in Dublin. Together with Thomas James Clark, an IRB veteran who had served fifteen years in prison in Britain, the new leaders quickly moved onto the Supreme Council of the IRB. The IRB was small and financially supported from the United States but now was ready to capitalize on political opportunities for revolution as the home rule situation deteriorated in 1912 and 1913. Ironically enough it was the Ulster Protestants who gave the IRB impetus when they formed the Ulster Volunteer Force. In 1913 the IRB was behind the scenes in getting the Irish Volunteers organized under the prestigious name of Eoin MacNeill, head of the Gaelic League.

The Ulster Volunteers and the Irish Volunteers were not the only citizen armies in Ireland. The Irish Citizen Army, an adjunct to the labor movement, was created in 1913 under tumultuous circumstances. The nationalist movement in Ireland at that time converged with the land agitators and at times with the Catholic church, but never with the urban workers. The task of uniting nationalism and socialism fell to James Connolly. Connolly, a self-educated Scotsman forced by poverty to emigrate, went to Dublin in 1894. Connolly was convinced that the nationalist issue and socialism were complementary and that Ireland needed both freedom and collective ownership of property to prevent class exploitation.

Connolly's position was subordinate to that of James Larkin, the most dynamic figure in the labor movement in 1910. Larkin, a charismatic, energetic, ferocious labor organizer, had been attempting to organize workers in Belfast and Dublin. He faced severe difficulties as the poverty of the workers in Dublin was absolutely appalling, the worst in the United Kingdom. The workers, Catholic and nationalist, were hardly receptive to socialist doctrines. The owners were well organized and had their own strikebreakers, as well as the police, to quell labor disorders. Larkin made inroads with his agitation, called strikes, improved wages, and had gained about 10,000 members for his Irish Transport and General Workers Union by 1913.

In that year Larkin took on a formidable foe, William Martin Murphy, owner of the Dublin United Tramways Company. Murphy was determined that he was going to break Larkin and not recognize his union. Murphy was able to gain the support of the other employers in a lockout, and by the autumn of 1913, 25,000 men were out of work. Both Larkin and Connolly were arrested. The Irish Parliamentary Party did nothing for the workers, and the Catholic hierarchy opposed the strike because of its radical doctrines of socialism. Thus the strike ultimately failed, and the men drifted back to work in the winter of 1914. Larkin left for the United States that same year, and Connolly took over the union. After the strike Connolly inherited the Irish Citizen Army, which had been created during the strike to protect the workers but had virtually withered away. Its regeneration was the work of young Sean O'Casey, at that time working as a laborer, not yet as a playwright.

The socialist side of Connolly gave way to the nationalist side as World War I progressed. He plotted an insurrection with his 200-man army. The outbreak of World War I was a benchmark in the movement toward Irish independence. At the outset of the war Redmond decided that the importance of defeating Germany was greater than the Irish question, and he encouraged members of the Irish Volunteers to serve Britain in the war. His suggestion that the Volunteers enlist in the British army was simply too much for the IRB. The Volunteers split into two factions, with the majority going with Redmond and about 12,000 of the 180,000 taking the position that Irishmen should not die for British interests. This latter group, still called the Irish Volunteers, was under IRB control. In 1914 the Irish republican leaders and the Clan na Gael in the United States decided that they would undertake revolution during the war in line with the dictum that "England's difficulties are Ireland's opportunities." Thus two movements were committed to violent revolution in Ireland—Connolly and his Citizen Army and the IRB with its Irish Volunteers. The prospects for success in each movement depended upon certain conditions. For Connolly success would come when his men in Dublin ignited a general rising in the whole country. Britain, bogged down in the war and unwilling to commit troops to Ireland, would withdraw. Connolly also harbored the peculiar belief that capitalist Britain would be unwilling to destroy property in quelling a rebellion.

For the IRB the plan depended upon U.S. money, German arms, and a mobilization of the Irish Volunteers, who would decapitate British authority in Ireland. What would follow was more vague but included the idea that after the war, Ireland would participate in the peace conference.

Patrick Pearse, Thomas MacDonough, and Joseph Plunkett were notable not only for the critical roles they played in the 1916 rising but also for their vision of the purpose of 1916 and their conception of success. The three were members of the IRB, having shifted, in the years from 1912 to 1914, from home rule to revolution as the answer to Ireland's independence. All were steeped in the cultural nationalism of a Gaelic Ireland. Pearse was a poet, a playwright, and an orator of some ability. He shared with his two poet friends a nationalist vision shot through with mystical religious overtones. The revolution needed a messiah, and more than that, said Pearse, it needed a blood sacrifice. Only such a sacrifice could redeem the corruption of Irish culture and politics. This redemption would generate a purer nationalism, which would ultimately liberate Ireland. Clearly this vision of nationalism brought to a breathtaking extreme the romance of failure. In the veneration of Tone, Emmett, and Young Ireland, the failure had been ignored and the act admired. Pearse asked that the failure be admired (as long as it was a bloody failure), for only in this redemptive act would success ultimately come.

Pearse, MacDonough, and Plunkett were members of the Central Executive of the Irish Volunteers and, with Thomas Clark, were involved in the planning of the 1916 Easter Week rebellion. The two revolutionary movements joined in 1915, when Connolly was brought in on IRB planning, so the mystical nationalism of Pearse was linked with the socialist revolution of Connolly.

THE EASTER RISING OF 1916

Not unlike earlier Irish revolutionary efforts at violence, the 1916 rising was a shambles. The head of the Irish Volunteers, Eoin MacNeill, was hoodwinked by Pearse into giving orders for a general mobilization on Easter Sunday. When MacNeill found out the mobilization was for an insurrection, he canceled his orders, changed his mind, countermanded the cancellation, then changed his mind again. Thus many Volunteers simply did not show up for the revolt. A German ship, carrying obsolete weapons to the Volunteers, was scuttled when it was challenged by a British ship off the coast of Munster and escorted to Cork harbor.[4]

Pearse and Connolly were not deterred, and on Easter Monday approximately 1,000 members of the Volunteers and the Citizen Army took up their planned positions at various locations in Dublin. They held out for a week against the police and the army until, hopelessly outnumbered, Pearse surrendered. The British, contrary to Connolly's belief, did not hesitate to use artillery against property, and 179 buildings in Dublin were destroyed.[5] The Proclamation of an Irish Republic had been read by Pearse the first day to a small, uncomprehending crowd gathered in front of the General Post Office. The document drew on the historical tradition of rebellion, affirmed the republican commitment, and rejected sectarianism.

The insurrection was seen by the relatively content Irish people, some with sons fighting in the British army, variously as a nuisance, a foolish suicidal act, or treason. When the captured rebels were marched through the streets, they were abused and jeered by the people in Dublin.

Most of the rebels were shipped to prisons in England. The leaders, however, were kept in Dublin, and military trials were begun. Of the 160 sentenced, 97 were to be executed. General Sir John Maxwell began the executions as the trials were going on and had 15 men shot in twos and threes over a period of ten days. Among them were 7 men who had signed the proclamation—Thomas Clark, Sean McDermott, Thomas MacDonough, Joseph Plunkett, Eamonn Ceannt, Patrick Pearse, and James Connolly. Connolly, having been wounded in the revolt, was propped up in a chair to be shot. Although the rising was unpopular, the executions were considered a particularly brutal response and outraged prominent Irish and British figures such as George Bernard Shaw and the bishop of Limerick. As some of the events of Easter Week became clear, opinion grew even more negative, and the executions were stopped.

Thus, during the period from the fall of Parnell to the 1916 insurrection, two broad approaches to Irish independence crossed. The home rule movement under Redmond, which seemed to have achieved what O'Connell and Parnell could not, was being replaced by the aggregation of cultural and political forces represented by Sinn Féin, the IRB, and the Irish Volunteers. The transformation was to be extremely rapid, taking place from 1916 to 1918. John Redmond's death in 1918 symbolized the death of the home rule movement and the degree to which the Irish Party was slipping out of touch with the Irish people.

NOTES

1. F.S.L. Lyons, *Ireland Since the Famine* (London: Collins, Fontana, 1973), p. 133.

2. Land agitation was one arm of a strategy called "the new departure" advocated by John DeVoy, a U.S. spokesman for Clan na Gael, the successor organization to the Fenian Brotherhood in the United States. The other arm of the strategy was parliamentary agitation for home rule. Together these strategies would lead to an independent Ireland by 1882, either conceded by the British or established by the Irish and backed with guns and money from the United States. Parnell accepted the strategies of the plan—agrarian agitation and parliamentary pressure for home rule—but rejected the leadership of the Americans and the idea of ultimate revolt.

3. Lyons, *Ireland Since the Famine*, p. 635.

4. Sir Roger Casement, an Ulster Protestant committed to the Irish rebellion, was to arrange for arms to be smuggled to the Irish Volunteers in 1914 and to attempt to enlist German aid in the rising of 1916. The latter assignment was a comedy of errors in which Casement first tried to recruit Irish POWs to fight for Ireland and succeeded only in designing uniforms for a bunch of brigands who never left Germany. Casement was also to enlist Germany artillery and expertise in the rising; instead he received 20,000 obsolete Russian weapons. Casement returned to Ireland to try to call off the rebellion as it did not have adequate German support. He was arrested three days before the rising, after having made no contact, and he was hanged for treason in August.

5. For a particularly vivid and sympathetic account of that week, see Thomas Coffey, *Agony at Easter* (London: Penguin, 1969).

3

From Guerrilla War
to Independence

THE RISE OF SINN FÉIN

The 1916 rising was like a crack in a dam. At first slowly, then increasing into a great cascade, Irish opinion began to support the rebels. The initial negative reaction to the executions was followed by a growing appreciation of the heroism of the outnumbered rebels and their commitment to their cause.

As the British were under pressure from the United States because of the Irish issue both before and after U.S. entry into World War I, David Lloyd George, prime minister of Great Britain, made two offers of home rule to Redmond. The first offer, in 1916, provided for a "temporary" exclusion of six Ulster counties, but Lloyd George, at the same time, was assuring the Ulster Unionists the exclusion would be permanent. The offer collapsed. In 1917 Lloyd George tried again, offering home rule with the permanent exclusion of the six Ulster counties. Redmond initially refused the offer but agreed to try to work out the differences in a conference. Redmond apparently was willing to accept further constraints of home rule, but he died during the conference.

Another British move to placate Irish and U.S. opinion was to release people who had been interned after the rising. From Britain's point of view this decision was a mistake that was to come back to haunt the government because the released prisoners were welcomed as heroes. The prisoners were to provide the backbone of a rebuilt Irish Volunteers as well as to become committed activists for Sinn Féin. Political activity blossomed despite the imposition of martial law in Ireland. The IRB was rebuilt under the direction of released internee Michael Collins, who was to play a great part in the war with England and the treaty to end it. In 1917 leaders of the Irish Volunteers rapidly took over Arthur Griffith's Sinn Féin and used it as the political arm of the republican movement.[1] Griffith remained president.

The event that revealed the strength of Sinn Féin and the weakness of the Irish Party was an election in early 1917 in which Count Plunkett, father of the poet who had been executed in 1916, ran against an Irish Party candidate and won handily with Sinn Féin support. Plunkett declared that he would not take his seat in Parliament. This pattern was followed by three other Sinn Féin victors, including one Sinn Féin candidate who was still in jail. The culmination of this policy occurred in June of 1917 when Sinn Féin put up

35

Eamon de Valera as a candidate. De Valera's leadership emerged in this election, a leadership more influential on Irish politics than any other in the next forty years.

De Valera was born in the United States, the son of an Irish mother and a Spanish father. He grew up in Ireland, however, and became a mathematics teacher. As a young man he became involved in the Gaelic League, and he joined the Irish Volunteers in 1913. His enthusiasm and talent landed him the rank of commandant, and his was the last unit to surrender in the Easter Rising. De Valera emerged as an informal leader of the men who were imprisoned in England after the rising. Although personally aloof and spartan in temperament, de Valera evoked great loyalty as a leader. One of the last prisoners released, because of his rank, de Valera went back to Ireland in June and won an election in County Clare in July by a more than two-to-one margin. As de Valera was now seen as a hero of 1916, his victory was a victory for the Easter Rising. In October, at a party conference in Dublin, de Valera was elected president of Sinn Féin. Two days later he was elected president of the Irish Volunteers, so De Valera now held the reins of leadership of the republican movement.

The British in 1918 undertook two actions that first, infuriated all of Ireland (save Ulster) and second, created great sympathy and support for Sinn Féin. It is an overstatement to say that the British never remember Irish history and the Irish never forget it, but clearly few lessons had been learned in Westminster. In April 1918 Parliament passed a bill authorizing the draft in Ireland. The reaction was immediate and explosive. The Irish Party walked out of Parliament, and Sinn Féin, the Labour Party, the Irish Party, and all other parties condemned conscription. The Catholic hierarchy joined in the condemnation and the Irish Congress of Trade Unions called a general strike. Sinn Féin used the anticonscription activity to build political support and legitimize its existence in the political arena.

The British authorities also aided Sinn Féin through wholesale arrests of Sinn Féin leaders. The British claimed the arrests were a result of Sinn Féin's plotting with Germany. The "evidence" was scanty at best, but it provided a justification for the arrest of hundreds, and Sinn Féin was outlawed. For Irish nationalists it must have seemed that to ensure election to Parliament, one must be in a British prison as in May, Arthur Griffith won another election for Sinn Féin from a cell. The British plan backfired as Sinn Féin gained popular support and, while outlawed, expanded under the leadership of Michael Collins.

The scene was set for the December 1918 general election, which was to select 105 members of Parliament. The outlawed Sinn Féin movement ran candidates who were in jail or on the run from the police. The program put forth to the people consisted of four points: withdrawal from the British Parliament, resistance to British authority, the creation of an Irish assembly, and recognition at the postwar peace conference of Ireland's independence. Sinn Féin swept the election.

A change in the electoral laws had increased the Irish electorate from approximately 700,000 to approximately 2 million, and a significant number of the young voters were new to elections. The Irish Parliamentary Party entered the election with sixty-eight seats; Sinn Féin, with seven. The former came out of the election with six seats; Sinn Féin, with seventy-three. The Ulster Unionists increased their strength to twenty-six seats, but outside the Ulster area Sinn Féin gained 65 percent of the vote.[2]

The winners of seven by-elections throughout 1917 and 1918 had vowed not to take their seats in Parliament. In January 1919 those who had been elected in the general election went further and invited all elected, including Unionists, to a meeting in Dublin to set up a new assembly. All except Sinn Féin members refused to come, and Sinn Féin could only produce twenty-seven members—the rest were in jail or in hiding. The members who showed up designated themselves as the Dáil Éireann (Assembly of Ireland) and issued a declaration of independence that stated that the Dáil was an affirmation of the Republic declared in 1916. A government was set up, and a "Message to the Free Nations of the World" was enunciated, which looked to Irish participation at the postwar peace conference.

The Dáil created courts, a land bank, and an Industrial Disputes Board, essentially setting up a parallel government to the British administration. Its efforts to get recognition at the Paris peace talks failed, however, as the delegates there were unable to persuade the United States to support the Republic. The second session of the Dáil elected de Valera president. He immediately left for the United States after a daring jail break to seek money and political support. In his absence the power of Sinn Féin centered around Michael Collins.

Collins was born in Ireland in 1890 and emigrated to London at sixteen. He became involved with the GAA and Gaelic League and went on to join the IRB. He fought in the 1916 rising and was interned. Like de Valera, he emerged as a leader in prison. Returning to Ireland he set out to rebuild the IRB and the Irish Volunteers. He was a bright, powerful, and efficient leader whose influence permeated the politics of the Sinn Féin movement. In September 1919 the British government outlawed the Dáil. De Valera was in the United States, and the success of the provisional government very often depended upon the ability of Collins as minister of finance. Moreover, in his IRB role, his responsibilities increased as the Republic slowly slid into guerrilla war with the British authorities in Ireland.

THE WAR AND THE TREATY

At the outset the war (as seen by the Irish) or civil disturbances (as seen by the British), Irish Republican Army (IRA) actions were directed at the Royal Irish Constabulary,[3] and for a little more than a year the police fought a losing battle. Large numbers of them resigned, and new recruits did not clamor for a dangerous job that had no future. The decay of the police aided the Dáil government in extending its control throughout Ireland, so the British government decided to respond to the attacks with force in 1920. Bringing in a specially created armed force (the Black and Tans, a name derived from the color of the uniform) and recruiting ex-army officers to serve as auxiliaries to the police only served to increase the amount and brutality of the terror. Bombings, shootings, executions, and torture were rampant. Public opinion in

Britain and the United States was negative toward the "war" against the Irish and critical of the repressive policies of London. The death of Terence MacSwiney, the mayor of Cork, after a seventy-four-day hunger strike in a British prison, stirred public opinion for the Irish cause and released a great wave of protest throughout the world.

The latter part of 1920 saw some of the most brutal acts and reprisals of the period. For instance, the IRA murdered fourteen Englishmen thought to be intelligence agents, and the Black and Tans responded by shooting into the crowd at a Gaelic football game, killing twelve people and wounding sixty. In December auxiliaries were killed in an ambush, and the Black and Tans looted and burned down the center of the city of Cork. For another six months the savagery continued until a truce was established in July 1921.

In 1920 an election took place that displayed Sinn Féin at its greatest strength but also created an insurmountable barrier to its objective. Lloyd George had enacted a bill in 1920 titled, no doubt by someone with a sense of humor, the Better Government of Ireland Act. It was home rule and partition again. Six counties in Ulster were to have their own parliament, as would the remaining twenty-six counties. To deal with matters of concern to both North and South, the bill created a Council of Ireland. The act went into effect, and elections were held. In the South the results were a massive landslide for Sinn Féin as it took 124 out of 128 seats in what was supposed to be the new parliament. Sinn Féin, however, used the election to select the Second Dáil Éireann, held to its position of abstention from British-created assemblies, and continued the war. Partition was now a fact as the Unionists swept forty out of fifty-two seats in the Ulster election. The Parliament of Northern Ireland began to function, but it was dominated by Presbyterian Unionists with strong overtones of the Orange Order.

Partition was to be the rock upon which the Sinn Féin movement shattered. In 1921 de Valera and Lloyd George met, and the prime minister set out his conditions for Ireland. They provided for dominion status but included partition and a number of other conditions primarily directed at British military security, such as air and naval bases in Ireland and the recruitment of soldiers in Ireland. De Valera flatly rejected these conditions but reported them to the Dáil. Lloyd George wanted to continue negotiations, so de Valera and the Dáil appointed five men, among them Arthur Griffith and Michael Collins, to return to London to negotiate a treaty. The treaty would require final approval from the Dáil. De Valera's decision not to attend is perplexing in that, to a certain degree, he was sending lambs to slaughter. Lloyd George skillfully persuaded the Irish delegation to accept partition by offering the promise that the boundaries would be open to later negotiation, implying that they would shrink and ultimately disappear. Lloyd George persuaded the Irish delegation to accept dominion status, with its oath of loyalty to the crown, by threatening resumption of the war. The delegates signed the treaty establishing the Irish Free State and returned to Dublin.

Debate on the treaty in the Dáil, ironically enough, focused more on the dominion status and less on partition, military facilities, and compensatory payments to Britain. The hard-line republicans, de Valera included, argued that a partitioned semisovereign Ireland and the requirement of making an oath to the crown were not what men had died for since 1916. The pragmatists, notably Collins, argued that the Free State was a beginning, that the IRA could not continue to fight against the full might of Britain, and that the treaty was the best that could be obtained. The Dáil, on a narrow vote of sixty-four to fifty-seven, accepted the treaty. De Valera resigned, symbolically setting the stage for the next confrontation—that of Irishman against Irishman over acceptance of the treaty.

The British began to dismantle the administrative machinery in Ireland, and Collins and Griffith began to set up the government of the Free State. The antitreaty members of Sinn Féin were ready to continue the fight and established headquarters around the country, including one in the Four Courts in Dublin. In this tense atmosphere an election was held, which resulted in thirty-five seats in the new Free State Assembly for the protreaty wing. An additional thirty-one seats could also be considered protreaty as they went to parties that were going to accept the Free State. The Irish people, it appeared, were ready to put an end to bloodshed and accept the new state.

The tension could not last, and the new government eventually attacked the IRA "irregulars" in the Four Courts in Dublin. The flames of civil war burned for a year in Ireland, with the same ugly brutality displayed earlier against the Black and Tans. The Free State was tough on its old compatriots, executing seventy-eight IRA irregulars. The antitreaty republicans could not spark public support, were condemned by the church, and eventually called the armed struggle off in May 1923. In August of 1923 there was a general election, and the antitreaty forces, despite open hostility from the church and press, managed to win forty-four seats. The Free State government supporters, now called Cumann na nGaedheal, took sixty-three seats. The remaining forty-six seats were split among the Labour, Farmers, and other smaller parties. Even as it was holding to the position that the government was illegitimate, Sinn Féin could still muster the second-largest block of seats.

THE FREE STATE

Sinn Féin members would not take their seats in the Free State Assembly and adopted the position that the Second Dáil Éireann, elected in 1920, was the true government of Ireland. Although satisfying their commitment to political principles, this position left Sinn Féin politically powerless because the Free State, under William Cosgrave, slowly built up the machinery of government. De Valera had been jailed by the government in 1922 but had been released about a year later, and he watched as the Free State negotiated the border issue in 1924. Cosgrave's efforts on this matter seem to deserve less than a standing ovation. The Ulster Unionists were absolutely intransigent, and when a commission finally began its work the chairman, a South African judge, interpreted the effort as one of a "correction of irregularities." The Free State delegate, Eoin MacNeill, resigned when it appeared that there would be no significant adjustments, especially in heavily nationalist/Catholic areas such as County Derry, but that Northern Ireland would, in fact, gain some territory. Cosgrave hastily agreed to revoke the commission and in 1925 signed an agreement to leave the border as it was in exchange for relief of debt to

London. Certainly not a victory, it was not even a very good fight. De Valera and the republicans pounced on this agreement with intense criticism, and de Valera announced that he would enter the Free State Dáil if the oath of allegiance were removed.

In 1926 de Valera formed a new party out of his Sinn Féin followers, called Fianna Fáil (Warriors of Ireland), as a result of his growing impatience with the wilderness of Sinn Féin republican abstentionism and his attraction to the reality of power in the Free State government. The IRA, Sinn Féin, and the Second Dáil all repudiated de Valera as an apostate for his willingness to participate in the Free State. There remained only the question of de Valera's opposition to the oath to the crown.

In the first general election of 1927 Fianna Fáil won forty-four seats and the government, forty-seven. Labour held twenty-two seats and smaller parties, the remainder. Cosgrave, the prime minister, forced de Valera's hand when he sponsored legislation that would require the oath in order to run for office as well as for membership in the Dáil. De Valera and his party signed the book containing the oath and entered the Dáil. De Valera's explanation of his signing the oath but not taking the oath raised equivocation to an art form, but at least he was a participant in the real power of the state.

During the next five years Fianna Fáil was the opposition to the government, always threading its way through the maze of participation in the Free State government while trying to preserve the posture of viewing the Free State government as not quite legitimate. Sean Lemass aptly summed up this position when he described Fianna Fáil as a slightly constitutional party. At the grass-roots level Fianna Fáil still had strong ties to the IRA, and thus its entry into the Dáil was accompanied by an increase in IRA violence. The IRA had not withered away after 1923; on the contrary, it had become convinced that acceptance of partition had revealed the true colors of the Cosgrave government. The IRA bitterly opposed the Free State, sometimes with violence, throughout the 1920s. Moreover, the IRA became convinced that partition would never end in a peaceful manner and that only physical force would liberate the province of Ulster, a position that is, in part, a foundation of the present difficulties in Northern Ireland.

Upon assuming power, the Cosgrave government had a full plate of problems. Required to fight a civil war, the government also had to build a government that would be credible to the Irish people. The achievements of the Cosgrave years from 1922 to 1932 cannot be lightly dismissed. In the economic and social spheres the government was timid, hesitant, and conservative. Unemployment was not lowered; agriculture, not improved; and industry, hardly developed. Emigrants still filled the docks as the population of Ireland declined in the Free State to under 3 million in 1926. However, taxes were not raised, and debt was kept to a minimum. To be fair, the last years of the Cosgrave government were a time of worldwide depression, which affected Ireland. Overall the record was one of stability rather than progress. In the social sphere Cosgrave did little as both his lack of a social policy or ideology and the basic conservatism of his supporters did little to encourage social welfare policies.

In the international sphere the Free State government achieved successes that were inadequately appreciated by people who were preoccupied with the treaty-antitreaty split in Irish politics. In many ways Cosgrave set out to dismantle the treaty a full decade before de Valera's more dramatic new constitution. The Free State took an active role in the League of Nations, appointed ambassadors, and took a foreign policy position that was different from that of the United Kingdom. Within the empire Ireland worked with Canada to pass resolutions that gave the member states equal status. In 1931 these efforts were acknowledged by the United Kingdom in the Statutes of Westminster, which granted the dominions the right to reject the legislation of London. The "empire" became the "commonwealth," and the dominions were sovereign and equal states.

Perhaps the most difficult task the Free State government faced was that of civil order. The government took a hard line concerning the rebels in the civil war. Shortly after the war the IRA followers of Michael Collins in the Free State Army demanded that the government cease postwar demobilization and move more rapidly toward becoming a republic. This mutiny was rapidly crushed by Minister of Justice Kevin O'Higgins. O'Higgins held extensive powers under a 1923 Public Safety Act and did not hesitate to use them to control the lawlessness and violence that was rampant at the time. O'Higgins renewed the 1923 act in 1926, but an even more draconian law came about as a result of his own death. O'Higgins was gunned down in the street in 1927. The government reacted by outlawing associations designed to overthrow the state by force and by authorizing special courts and extensive powers of search and detention. This legislation lapsed a year later in 1928, but when violence surged in 1930 and 1931, Cosgrave responded with the harshest law of the decade. Under this act military tribunals could impose the death penalty on members of illegal organizations. The IRA and other republican groups were soon declared illegal, and the law drove many republicans underground and out of Ireland. The law was also quite unpopular, and along with high unemployment, widespread poverty, and the accumulation of past blunders, it exhausted the Cosgrave government's political support among the Irish electorate.

In 1932 Fianna Fáil won seventy-two seats and Cumann na nGaedheal, only fifty-seven. With Labour Party support Fianna Fáil then undertook a limited program of social reform, an area Cosgrave had left untouched, and allocated money for housing, pensions, and welfare benefits. In the economic sphere de Valera imposed tariffs on foreign goods and enlarged the subsidies to farmers and to industry.

Two of de Valera's major efforts touched off conflict with Britain. The first was the refusal in 1933 to pay the land annuities that were due Britain as a result of land purchases by tenant farmers after the Wyndham Act of 1903. The British response was to put a tariff on Irish imports. De Valera responded with tariffs on British imports, and the result was "the economic war." As a war it was no contest. Ireland's fragile economy was so dependent on Britain that the burden fell far more heavily on Ireland as imports dropped by one-half and exports by three-fifths. For five years this state of affairs continued until Neville Chamberlain concluded a treaty with de Valera in 1938, which not only ended the economic war but transferred to Ireland the naval bases Britain still had as a result of the 1921 treaty. Additional trade agreements were predominately to the advantage of Ireland.

The second provocation to Britain was a series of steps de Valera took to dismantle the treaty. Beginning in 1932 de Valera informed Britain he was dropping the oath to the king on the grounds that it was a domestic matter for the Irish people to decide. The same year de Valera, through a series of petty embarrassments and political pressure, forced the dismissal of the governor general and replaced him with an insignificant political lackey. In 1933 the Irish government removed the right of appeal from Irish courts to the Judicial Committee of the British Privy Council and in 1936 eliminated the king from the Irish constitution (except in a very limited way in foreign affairs) and abolished the position of governor general. All of these actions were a prelude to the development of a new constitution for Ireland (discussed in Chapter 6), which was a mixture of various political and social doctrines with a large dose of de Valera.

In the new constitution the political doctrine of liberal democracy and Catholic social thought coexisted in an uneasy blend. The structure of the state was democratic and parliamentary, and liberal principles of tolerance, civil rights, and liberties were guaranteed. However, Catholic thought was manifest in the special position of the family and the Catholic church. When presented to the people for ratification the vote was 685,105 for the document and 526,945 against it. Thus the new constitution took effect in 1937.

In power de Valera was not exempt from the inexorable fact that the people who govern are responsible for civil order, and he found himself, as had Cosgrave, in the position of trying to crush the IRA revolutionaries he had associated with only a few short years before. Upon taking office de Valera had removed the restraints on the IRA enacted by the Cosgrave government. The result was a rapid escalation of IRA drills and meetings, which, on occasion, took the form of intimidation of the supporters of Cumann na nGaedheal.

An innocuous organization of veterans of the Free State Army, concerned primarily with veterans' benefits, was quickly transformed from the Army Comrades Association into a semifascist political organization. This group pulled together the anti-IRA supporters in defense of free speech and assembly, which they perceived were threatened by the IRA. Right-wing intellectuals provided some doctrines on the corporate state and warnings about the dangers of communism from leftist IRA groups. In early 1933 the organization turned its leadership over to General Eoin O'Duffy, recently dismissed by de Valera from the position of commissioner of police. Under O'Duffy the members took to wearing berets and blue shirts (black and brown having already been adopted in Italy and Germany) and giving fascist salutes; they also adopted the name "National Guard." After the group had engaged in some violent clashes with the IRA, the government outlawed the organization. In September of 1933 the banned National Guard, Cumann na nGaedheal, and the Centre Party merged to form Fine Gael (Tribe of Gaels) and reconstituted the Blue Shirts as the Young Ireland Association. The government banned this group as well, and by 1934 the Fine Gael movement was disintegrating under O'Duffy's irrational leadership. The movement was quite unlike continental fascism in content if not in symbol. Supported mainly by farmers hurt by the economic war, it lacked a broader base of support. Its doctrines were in part derived from Catholic social thought, and its greatest fear, a communist Ireland, was so implausible as to be amusing.

The IRA, however, was another matter. Continuing violence and some brutal murders caused the government to declare the organization illegal in 1936, and its chief of staff was arrested. The IRA turned its attention to Britain and began a campaign of bombing. In 1939 de Valera responded with the Treason Act and the Offenses Against the State Act. The former prescribed the death penalty for treason; the latter reconstituted military tribunals and internment without trial. Both acts were directed at the IRA.

THE EMERGENCY AND AFTER

The most crucial test, however, came at the outset of World War II when de Valera held that while partition existed, Ireland would be neutral in the war. Terming this an "emergency," the government adopted powers to censor, control prices, and regulate resources. Under the circumstances imposed by geography Ireland could hardly be as scrupulous in neutrality as de Valera would have liked, and the neutrality was clearly benevolent to Britain. Over 50,000 Irishmen volunteered to fight in the British army, allied pilots downed in Ireland were returned to Northern Ireland, and downed German pilots were interned. On the other hand, neutrality could not have been a policy at all without British forbearance in the use of Irish ports during the battle for the North Atlantic. At the end of the war Winston Churchill could not resist taunting de Valera about Irish neutrality and British patience:

> However, with a restraint and poise to which, I venture to say history will find few parallels, His Majesty's government never laid a violent hand on them, though at times it would have been quite easy and quite natural, and we left the de Valera government to frolic with the German, and later Japanese representatives to their hearts content.[4]

De Valera replied a few days later, pointing out that Churchill had elevated Britain's necessity to a moral plane superior to Ireland's rights. But de Valera went on to remind Churchill just how deeply the Irish felt about those rights.

> Could he not find it in his heart to acknowledge that there is a small nation that has stood alone not for one year or two, but for several hundred years, against aggression, that endured spoilations, famines, massacres in endless succession, that was clubbed many times into insensibility but each time, on returning to consciousness took up the fight anew; a small nation that could never be got to accept defeat and has never surrendered her soul?[5]

Neutrality was for Ireland the ultimate display of its independence and its sovereignty.

After the war the program for economic recovery bogged down, and Ireland slipped into a deadened political and economic state. Fianna Fáil had been in power continually since 1932 and was suffering from hardening of the arteries, ineffective economic policies, and a weariness on the part of the electorate. Fine Gael on the other hand was a rather anemic competitor, having lost considerable support over the previous sixteen years. The electorate, and the political arena, were brought to life by the creation of a new party, which in some ways resembled the Fianna Fáil of twenty years earlier. Led by Sean McBride, a veteran of the antitreaty forces, Clann na Publachta (Republican Family) was formed in 1946. The party's program combined a fresh emphasis on the republican tradition with social and economic reform. The party drew its support from the republican veterans of the 1930s and 1940s but broadened its appeal to disillusioned Fianna Fáil and even Fine Gael supporters. Clann na Publachta seemed to be a new wind in politics with the promise of having a fresh impact on policy. Contesting many seats in the 1948 election, the Clann won ten—a good showing but disappointing in view of the high expectations of its partisans. Although Fianna Fáil still had the largest number of seats in the Dáil, it had lost eight in the election, and the opposing parties formed a coalition government. It was a strange mixture, but one that managed to last over three years in power.

Since Wolfe Tone the idea of an independent republic of Ireland had burned brightly. As of 1948 Ireland was clearly an independent sovereign nation, but it still did not bear the title "republic" in de Valera's constitution. The realization of Tone's dream came about in a manner that no doubt would have amused him; John A. Costello, the prime minister of Ireland, announced the fact at a press conference in Ottawa, Canada. Some people have suggested that Costello did this because he was insulted by the governor general of Canada, but the matter had been discussed in the cabinet of the coalition government. However, a matter as important as the final severing of ties to the Commonwealth would seem to have warranted some discussion and debate among the Irish people before being announced to Canadian journalists. The reticence de Valera had shown in 1937 displayed more wisdom than Costello's act. The British government responded with the Ireland Act of 1949, which was an explicit guarantee that Northern Ireland was part of the United Kingdom and it would not cease to be so without the consent of the Parliament of Northern Ireland. What little bridge had existed in the Commonwealth between Ireland and Northern Ireland was broken.

Although far greater attention had been directed toward social welfare policy since the Cosgrave years, there were still enormous gaps in the support people received from the government. The coalition government appointed Dr. Noel Browne of Clann na Publachta as minister of health, and his initial success included an imaginative use of finances to create a collection of sanitariums, which virtually eradicated tuberculosis from Ireland. Browne, however, was to flounder on the rocks of Catholic social doctrine in his notable endeavor to provide maternal education and medical care for mothers and children up to the age of sixteen. Drawing upon a plan developed by Fianna Fáil, which had already attracted clerical hostility, Browne began to implement the scheme and ran into a blizzard of opposition. The medical profession considered the plan unwarranted interference into its area of concern and reacted negatively to the idea that there would be no means test, or test of poverty, and thus be free to all comers. The most powerful opposition, however, came from the church. Noting that the constitution stated that the family was the basic unit of society, the church maintained that the bill was an invasion of family rights and that provision of health care to children was a family responsibility. Browne made efforts to bridge the gap between himself, the Irish Medical Society, and the bishops. All efforts failed, and Browne lost support within the government and eventually resigned from the cabinet. Under the next government Fianna Fáil enacted most of the provisions of Browne's plan.

The election of 1951 brought Fianna Fáil back into power for several years, but the government was confounded by the economic problems of stagnation, unemployment, and emigration. An election in 1954 resulted in a coalition government of Fine Gael, Labour, and Farmers parties—Clann na Publachta had disintegrated and won only two seats. The coalition had no more success with the depressed economy than had the previous government and was burdened also by an increase in IRA activity, which it had difficulty controlling.

In 1957 Fianna Fáil came back to power with a much stronger majority of seventy-eight seats. De Valera was seventy-five years old, and it appeared that the wheel had come full circle as the young revolutionary now presided over a cabinet of old men in a government that lacked luster and a country that was socially, economically, and politically stagnant. Appearances were deceptive, as the old leadership was being augmented or replaced by a rising generation of politicians who were far less influenced by the treaty debate and the events of the twenties and thirties. Molded in a rapidly changing postwar world, they were more concerned with economic and social issues than with the traditional concerns of nationalism and partition. In Fianna Fáil the names included Jack Lynch and Charles Haughey, both later to become prime minister. In Fine Gael the names included Liam Cosgrave and Garrett FitzGerald, also both later to become prime minister.

In 1959 Sean Lemass became prime minister. De Valera retired to the presidency of Ireland, serving two seven-year terms. De Valera's death in 1975 ended one of the most extraordinary careers in modern political history. Only a day or so from a British firing squad in 1916, de Valera eventually made a greater mark on Irish politics than O'Connell or Parnell. His dedication to his values, to Catholicism, to the Irish language, and to simple Irish life was combined with a pragmatic toughness that carried him through the rough and tumble years of 1916 to 1932. His astute leadership carried him from 1932 to 1959. De Valera once remarked that when he wanted to know what the people of Ireland thought, he had only to look in his own heart. Such hubris from anyone else would be intolerable. In the case of de Valera, it was, for most of his life, a simple statement of fact.

The stage was set for the post–de Valera era of Irish politics with the rise of Lemass, the initiation of the Whitaker Plan in 1958, a new generation of leaders in Ireland, and a new generation of voters more interested in looking forward to living in a modern society than backward to events that formed less and less a part of their personal experience.

NOTES

1. Not long after Sinn Féin was created it became the name the British press, the British military, and even the Irish Party used to lump together those people who were more militantly nationalist. The rebellion of 1916 was also erroneously labeled a Sinn Féin action. The secret IRB, of course, was most important in stimulating revolutionary republicanism and in undertaking the 1916 revolt. Only after 1917 did the popular label and the political reality coincide as Sinn Féin became the broad political front for all nationalists and republicans.

2. The Irish Parliamentary Party, ironically enough, did not lose much voting strength compared to the 1910 general election, but the majority of the new voters clearly supported Sinn Féin.

3. The Irish Volunteers were in somewhat of an ambiguous position with respect to the Dáil, which produced a great deal of tension between the minister of defense, Cathal Brugha, and Michael Collins, who was adjutant general, director of intelligence of the Volunteers, and to complicate matters, president of the IRB. Brugha tried to assert authority over the Volunteers and eventually persuaded the Volunteers as individuals to take an oath to the Dáil. Thus the Volunteers became the Army of the Irish Republic, or the Irish Republican Army (in this chapter, the IRA).

4. Quoted in Tony Gray, *The Irish Answer* (London: Heinemann, 1966), p. 114.

5. Ibid.

4

Economic and Social Transformation

In a speech in 1943 Eamon de Valera portrayed his vision of family, society, and economy in Ireland.

> The Ireland which we have dreamed of would be the home of a people who valued material wealth only as a basis of right living, of a people who were satisfied with frugal comfort and devoted their leisure to things of the spirit; a land whose countryside would be bright with cozy homesteads, would be joyous with the sounds of industry and with the romping of sturdy children, the contests of athletic youth, the laughter of comely maidens; whose firesides would be forums for the wisdom of serene old age. It would, in a word, be the home of a people living the life that God desires men should live.[1]

Although God may desire that people should live that way, Irishmen decided otherwise. The Ireland of the 1950s, which de Valera presided over, was characterized by massive emigration, social stagnation, parochial insularity, and economic decay. The practice certainly fell short of the ideal, and in the late 1950s Ireland opted for a different form of economic order, which, in conjunction with a number of other developments, whisked Ireland into a process of social modernization.

THE WHITAKER PLAN

The Irish economy in the 1950s was predominantly agricultural and essentially unchanged since the thirties. The economic growth rate for the period 1922–1938 has been estimated at 1.2 percent per year, zero during the war years, and only 1.8 percent per year after the war.[2] This rate of growth was considerably slower than that of other European nations and was stimulated not by investment in industry and rising employment but by government spending to provide social services. In fact the number of people who were employed in agriculture dropped 218,500 in the years from 1947 to 1951, and manufacturing lost 8,200 during the same period.[3]

The tide of emigration from Ireland continued at a record rate in the 1950s, as 408,766 people chose to live and work abroad, and emigration during the period 1951–1961 was greater than at any other period since 1900.[4] Obviously the stagnant economic conditions were pulling the Irish to the

47

opportunities available in Britain, Canada, the United States, and the Continent. Most of the young people emigrating were from the west of Ireland, and the economic atrophy in the whole country was accompanied by an acute decline and demoralization of the people in the west.

Emigration to other countries was accompanied by internal migration to the cities of Ireland, especially Dublin. The rapid urbanization of Ireland continued in those dismal years as people sought the opportunity to work in the city. In fact, if emigration abroad had not drained off large numbers, the Irish government would have had to deal with a more serious unemployment situation than it did.[5]

The emigration and economic stagnation were accompanied by a feeling among the people, especially in the west of Ireland and among the intellectuals, that Ireland had no future. The mother and child welfare plan proposed by Dr. Noel Browne had revealed that the church was willing to cast its weight against government activity in the social sphere. The church preserved a high degree of control over the devotion of the people, and ineffective governments, made timid by the church's opposition and imprisoned by the protectionist doctrines of de Valera, were less than bold in addressing social and economic issues in the 1950s. The deadening hand of the Censorship Board gave aspiring writers little creative room and drove them to emigrate as well. The values for which Sinn Féin fought—an independent, autonomous, Gaelic, Catholic Ireland—seemed to be betrayed as thousands of young people left their land upon completion of their education.

In 1955 a Capital Investment Advisory Committee urged that a greater amount of public money be directed at increasing productivity. The secretary of the Department of Finance, T. K. Whitaker, undertook this task and presented his conclusions in a report, *Economic Development*, in 1958.[6] Of this report, historian F.S.L. Lyons notes: "It is hardly too much to say, indeed, that even today it can be seen as a watershed in the modern economic history of the country."[7] The report cited a cascade of failures in the protectionist policies of the Irish Free State since 1921. Agriculture oversupported by public money was backward compared to other countries; industry was feeble, lacking private capital or bold capitalists and hampered by a small domestic market. Emigration drained the youth of Ireland, the people who remained found no employment, and finally, government expenditures on socially valuable construction projects such as schools, houses, airports, hospitals, and roads were unproductive in terms of economic growth.

The Whitaker Plan proposed that public money be concentrated on encouraging productive investment, especially industries keyed to exporting goods. The development of industry would come through foreign capital, which was to be attracted by generous incentives. The attractions in Ireland were a plentiful supply of labor at relatively low wages and a convenient location, not only with respect to Britain and Europe, but also, within Ireland, with respect to water, power, and transportation. For some British and U.S. investors the fact that Ireland is an English-speaking country was an advantage, and certainly the political stability and administrative sophistication of the Irish government attracted investors who felt that the risk of investment in third world nations was too great.

The principal incentive, however, was the promise of generous grants and loans to companies willing to locate in Ireland and generous tax breaks on their earnings for years after their initial investment. For the first ten years profits were to be tax free, and taxes were to be kept at a reduced level for five years thereafter. The government would also underwrite up to two-thirds of the costs of building factories and purchasing land and equipment. In addition the government would assist in the training of workers needed for specific industries. The plan also set aside grants for Irish firms in order to increase their efficiency and improve their prospects for export sales. Agriculture was not to be ignored as grassland farming was to be improved so as to increase exports, and the government was to improve marketing, disease control, and agricultural education so as to maximize agricultural management.

Clearly the old policy of protectionism was to be abandoned, and industry and agriculture were going to have to compete without special tariff protection. Import quotas and protective tariffs, some as high as 60 percent, were to be gradually eliminated. Much of the planning was done with an eye on the eventual possibility of Ireland's entering the European Common Market. Ireland, in fact, applied for membership in 1961 but did not actually enter the Common Market until 1973.

The Industrial Development (Encouragement of External Investment) Act of 1958 instituted a five-year plan to last from 1959 to 1964 and set the relatively modest goal of an increase in the gross national product (GNP) of 2 percent per year. The results were more impressive as the rate of growth was 4.5 percent per year and industrial exports doubled. During the same period about 200 new factories were built and approximately 27,000 new jobs were created. The GNP had increased by 15.5 percent by 1962, and production, personal expenditures, and imports had all jumped accordingly. The incentives to foreign investors had manifestly paid off. Of the 200 factories established during the period, the British accounted for about one-half and the Germans for about one-fourth. The remaining one-fourth was spread among U.S. (later to rise sharply), Dutch, Italian, French, Belgian, Swiss, Danish, Canadian, and Japanese investors. Products manufactured in Ireland by these firms included everything from chewing gum to airplane parts.

During this period the government did not neglect the domestic sector. Among the efforts to revise the west of Ireland and to keep Irish business competitive was the Shannon Free Airport Development Company set up in 1959 with government support. Designed to prevent the slow death of Shannon Airport as long-distance jets began to bypass that stop, the Airport Development Company undertook to create an industrial area within the customs boundary. Thus no duty was paid on raw materials entering the area, and there were no export duties on finished products that were flown out. Tax incentives were granted to firms setting up at Shannon as well as assistance in building plants. The idea was successful as foreign light industry flowed in and took advantage of both the financial incentives and the obvious access to air transport. The Airport Development Company also undertook the responsibility of promoting tourism and generated a significant tourist business in the area around Galway and County Clare.

The economic indicators told a story of rapid economic expansion, but the impact on Irish life was even more marked than simply punts (the Irish pound) and pence. The country acquired a vibrancy that observers noted had been absent in the 1950s. The affluence generated by this growth was modest by European standards but promptly generated those consumer values characteristic of industrial societies. The consumer values in turn generated pressure on social values. The traditional features of modernization having been achieved during the last 100 years, the economic transformation was in a sense the last step in the modernization of Ireland. Although a culmination in that sense, it was a commencement in another for a generation of Irish used to deadening emigration, a stagnant economy, an authoritarian church, an arid cultural climate, and widespread rural and urban poverty. The new possibilities of a good job, good pay, and travel seemed to encourage the idea that change might be worthwhile in a wide variety of social institutions. The confrontation with modern, secular pluralist pressures was beginning and was going to be more far-reaching than simply improvement in economic prosperity. For the first time in a century the flow of emigration decreased, and in the period from 1961 to 1966 the population in Ireland grew by 62,000 people. Those who stayed or returned to Ireland were in the lower age bracket, and thus began a demographic shift that led to an Ireland in 1981 in which 50 percent of the population was under thirty years of age.

Struck by the success of the first plan Sean Lemass proposed a second plan that was to run from 1963 to 1970 and was more ambitious than the first. It was difficult enough to meet the ambitious targets for growth in GNP and employment, but the task was made more difficult by the British imposition of a tariff on Irish imports in 1964. A treaty between Dublin and London in 1965 eased some of the damage as the agreement removed restrictions on Irish goods in 1966 and Ireland's restrictions on imported British goods were gradually reduced by 1975.

The second plan did not stem the flow of emigration as planned. The number of people leaving remained high in the middle 1960s, with a jump to over 20,000 in 1965. From 1966 to 1971 the overall flow diminished, however, and by the 1970s emigration had virtually ceased.

Lemass was faced also with greater costs in sustaining the levels of government expenditure for increasing social services and also financing development. Thus the government had to increase taxes, cut the amount targeted for capital investment, and borrow from Irish and U.S. banks in order to have adequate revenue. The pattern of foreign debt and the high cost of debt servicing was initiated, and it continues up to the present day.

In 1968 the second plan was abridged, and a third plan was devised for the years 1969 to 1972. This plan was to be more realistic in light of the experience of 1964 to 1968. The targets of the third program were not achieved although, to be sure, Ireland's economy was far more prosperous than in 1958. The rate of growth in the economy by 1972 was only 2.5 percent, and labor costs had jumped considerably. Overall growth for the period 1969–1972 was still near 12 percent, however. Ireland was now on the brink of two separate and major economic changes that were to come: entry into the European Economic Community and the skyrocketing cost of oil.

ECONOMIC GROWTH

The economic success of the years 1961 to 1968—increases in the GNP, greater employment, and more export industry—was accompanied by relatively low inflation, 4.2 percent, and a solid growth in agriculture and tourism. From 1968 until 1972 the success of the prior decade continued but less dramatically. The average rate of growth in the GNP was 3.7 percent per year, not substantially lower than during 1961–1968, but this growth was accompanied by a population growth rate of 1 percent per year. This latter rate was, on average, twice as high as in the prior seven years and meant a slight drop in the GNP per capita.[8] The decline in emigration meant, of course, more people to employ, and total employment dropped during these years as the nonagricultural unemployment rate rose from 6.7 percent in 1968 to 8.1 percent in 1972.

During this period some problems emerged that foreshadowed those of the contemporary period. As affluence prompted consumption, the amount of imports increased and the rate of growth in exports declined to create a balance of payments deficit that amounted to 3.6 percent of GNP, over twice as high as during the prior seven years. The years 1968 to 1972 also saw the rapid increase in inflation that has bedeviled the Irish economy from 1972 to the present. The rate of inflation roughly doubled to 8.5 percent in the period 1968 to 1972, more than in other European countries. Manufactured products for the domestic market lost out to imported goods during this period. Notable in terms of the traditional problem of a politically divided Ireland was the decline in tourism during this period, which coincided with the explosion of violence in Northern Ireland. Receipts from British visitors dropped by one-fourth, and the traditional attraction of Ireland for tourists from the United States also diminished.[9]

On January 1, 1973, Ireland entered the European Economic Community (EEC). This step was not only an economic milestone for the Republic of Ireland, but a politically important and symbolic step toward placing Ireland in a European partnership in addition to the de facto economic and cultural partnership with Great Britain. The Irish negotiated for a transition period of five years for elimination of trade restrictions and agricultural adjustment to the Common Agricultural Policy, which covers all EEC members. In addition the Irish received special dispensations to continue their policy of industrial development and promises of EEC support to raise the standard of living in Ireland to that of the other members.[10]

The expected benefits from membership in the European Community included direct grants from the Social Fund, the Regional Fund, and the European Investment Bank; extensive direct support for agricultural development; guaranteed floors for agricultural prices; and access to the extensive European market for Irish exports. The disadvantages were the loss of some economic autonomy and vulnerability to a wave of manufactured products from Europe, which might sweep aside domestic producers.

By and large the expectations on entry into the European Community have been borne out. The net flow of contributions from Ireland to the EEC rose from £6.1 million (about $9.5 million) in 1973 to £60.3 million (about

The rural beauty of Connemara, which is also famous for its marble. (Courtesy, Irish Tourist Board)

$91 million) in 1979, and the EEC funds paid to Ireland rose from £43.8 million (about $66 million) to £500.6 million (about $752 million), with the greatest amount being in the area of agriculture. Moreover, in 1979 Ireland negotiated a ten-year development grant for the west of £300 million (about $455 million) and a five-year drainage scheme for the west at £40 million (about $62 million). In the future, however, the bulk of the regional funds are likely to go to Greece, Portugal, or Spain.[11]

The encouragement of investment in Ireland, with access to the European market without the EEC tariff barrier, has been successful. The combination of the Whitaker Plan incentives and access to EEC nations has brought over 200 firms from the United States, with a total of £650 million (about $100 million) invested by 1976. In fact, from the initiation of the Whitaker Plan to 1976, the United States contributed 50 percent of the foreign investment.[12] Agricultural prices rose at a rapid rate, making the farmers in Ireland the most rewarded beneficiaries of EEC membership. The prices on farm products rose 64 percent from 1973 to 1977, although there was a bad slump in the cattle market in the mid 1970s.

The expected importation of manufactured products from Europe did not occur, and thus the industrial sector was spared some of the expected losses. Imports have steadily risen but reflect increased demand for consumer goods, especially cars. The traditional dependence on Great Britain as a trading partner has been diminished to a limited extent. Although Ireland imported approximately 51 percent of its goods from Britain in 1972, by 1977 the figure had dropped to about 48 percent. Concomitantly, in 1972 Ireland exported over 61 percent of its goods to Britain; by 1977 this figure had dropped to approximately 47 percent, with the difference going to the other members of the EEC.

The most obvious break with the economy of Britain was the severing of the Irish punt from the British pound in 1979. Traditionally the currencies had held the same value, as it was advantageous to link the Irish currency to a trading currency that had worldwide acceptance. The disadvantages of this policy began to surface when Ireland underwent rather rapid economic development at the same time that the British economy was slipping and the British pound was constantly being devalued. In April 1979 Ireland decided to join the European Monetary System (EMS), which stabilizes the European currency values in terms of each other and prevents wild gyrations in exchange rates. As Great Britain did not join, the Irish punt was detached from the pound for the first time since 1826. This change allowed greater flexibility in setting interest rates and in developing an independent monetary policy. The risk, however, is a sharp decline of the punt against the British pound as the pound is not locked into the EMS. Since Ireland imports more from the United Kingdom than it exports, more punts must be used to purchase goods, and thus the balance of payments suffers.

Evaluation of the performance of the Irish economy after entry into the EEC is hindered by the advent in the mid-seventies of massive jumps in oil prices and a worldwide economic recession. Ireland was particularly vulnerable to the increase in oil prices as the country was 70 percent dependent on imported oil. When the price quadrupled in two years, 1974 and 1975, the effect on all forms of production was severe. Ireland's balance of payments suffered as the flow of currency to pay for oil soared. The rate of inflation, which had been increasing in the early seventies, escalated rapidly, hitting an appalling 25 percent in 1975. It dipped again in the late seventies, but hit 18 percent in 1981. Exacerbated by the increase in population, the rate of unemployment increased, and the steady growth in the economy, which had begun in 1961, stopped in 1975.

Although oil prices were an obvious element in the inflationary spurt, they were not the only factor. Since 1970 the government, the employers, and the trade unions have concluded national pay agreements. The first was designed to last eighteen months; those concluded thereafter were to last two years. Although not including all workers, the agreements do include the major industrial unions and thus provide some stable element in planning the degree of wage inflation and labor costs. The agreements of 1972 and 1974 themselves contributed to the ascending inflation rate as they granted wage increases in excess of the rate of economic growth.

The pressure for higher wages was not surprising, of course, as inflation was eroding the pay of the workers. In addition the rate of taxation increased, which constrained the purchasing power of the punt. The psychological effects of a decade of increasing prosperity cannot be discounted as workers sought to gain what they saw as a fair piece of an ever-widening pie, and the pressure for improved wages and benefits led to labor unrest and strikes by both private and public sector workers. Bank employees, for example, struck for six months in 1970; bus drivers, in 1977; telephone workers, in 1978; and post office workers struck in 1979 for four and one-half months. Private sector strikes are also the cause of a disproportionate loss of productive time compared to the situation in other EEC countries.

In 1977 it was decided that the national pay agreements would not increase wages more than 8.5 percent, which in part contributed to the improved performance of the economy in the years 1977 and 1978. However, in 1980 government workers achieved a 30 percent increase in pay, which clearly added to the inflationary spiral.

The Fianna Fáil government elected in 1977 put forth a white paper in 1978: "National Development 1977–1980." The plan set economic targets to be met by 1980 in what has emerged as the four crucial areas in the Irish economy: unemployment, inflation, growth, and government borrowing. The plan in the employment area was enormously ambitious as it projected the increase in new jobs to be 5,000 in 1977 with an additional 75,000 thousand by 1980. Inflation was to fall from 11 percent to 5 percent by 1980, and real growth in the GNP was to be 7 percent per year for 1978, 1979, and 1980. The amount of borrowing, as a percentage of the GNP, was to fall from 11 percent in 1977 to 8 percent by 1980.

The actual state of affairs in 1980 was something less than what had been portrayed by "National Development 1977–1980." The Lynch administration, and the subsequent Haughey administration, wanted to ignite the economy to meet the growth objectives. The campaign promises made had the effect of reducing government revenues, i.e., cutting taxes, while increasing spending to a substantial degree. Investment incentives, social welfare benefits, and capital expenditures for transportation and communication all increased public spending. The effect on the economy was good as the rate of foreign investment continued undiminished, the unemployment rate fell to a low of 8 percent in 1978, and the real growth of the economy in the late seventies was the highest in the EEC. Return on investment was higher than anywhere else in Europe.

But all of the expenditures had to be paid for. The government had used foreign borrowing in the past, but by 1981 the government had run deficits for nine years running. The deficits, moreover, had reached a figure that was increasingly unacceptable to lenders, and Ireland faced a severe credit squeeze.

As recently as 1978 the balance of payments deficits were manageable, but by 1981 the balance of trade was expected to be £1.3 billion (approximately $2 billion) in the red. Moreover, the government's expenditures were expected to produce a deficit of £800 million (about $1.2 billion). Together these figures constituted about 15 percent of Ireland's GNP, and even these grim figures did not include the existing government debt of £3.2 billion (about $4.8 billion), which had to be funded at high interest rates.

In mid-1981 public sector borrowing shot up to £1.97 billion (about $2.9

billion), an amount equivalent to 20 percent of the GNP. The FitzGerald government undertook austerity measures at that point, but the overall problem remains staggering. Britain, for example, adopted severe austerity measures to control government borrowing that represented only 5 percent of GNP, one-fourth the Irish figure.[13] The interest payments on Ireland's debt alone could require sharp tax increases, to say nothing of increases needed to achieve a balanced budget.

The increase in the public debt has not been accompanied by the favorable projections of "National Development 1977–1980." The rate of unemployment rose from a low of 8 percent in 1978 to 12 percent in 1981, although that figure is not entirely the result of government economic policy as a 10 percent increase in population has required that the process of job creation must not only absorb the historically high unemployment of a stable population but also an increasingly larger employable population. However, the rising costs of labor and the inflation rate have caused layoffs in current jobs, as well as difficulty in creating new ones, and both of those problems are a function of government policy. The projected inflation rate for 1980 was 5 percent; in 1981 the rate was 18 percent. Finally, the growth rate targets were not met as the economy grew at a slower rate after 1978.

The oil crisis of 1979, prompted by the revolution in Iran, displayed again the vulnerability of Ireland to energy-induced inflation. Ireland pays more for oil as international oil payments are made in dollars, and the appreciation of the dollar in 1981 demanded a greater expenditure of punts to purchase the same quantity of oil. Energy conservation measures have been implemented, and the use of peat has increased, but at present the cost of oil is a substantial drain on the Irish economy. Efforts to develop nuclear power have encountered the same opposition as has developed in other European countries, especially after the accident at the Three Mile Island plant in the United States. Promising finds of oil have been discovered off the coast of Galway, but as yet the finds have not been the bonanza that North Sea oil has been for Britain.

The cumulative impact of the pressures of inflation, unemployment, and massive foreign debt has brought not only economists but also politicians to the realization that sharp measures are in order for the Irish economy. Both the current prime minister, FitzGerald, and the former prime minister, Haughey, have stated that tough deflationary measures are required. Without such measures the government faces the curtailment of loans by foreign banks.

The public, however, has elevated expectations with respect to pay increases commensurate with or greater than inflation and with respect to the availability of consumer goods. The demand for imported goods has increased, which continues to fuel the downward spiral in the balance of payments. Promises by both parties in the three elections in 1981 and 1982 concerning job creation have created greater expectations in regard to employment.

Governments are notorious for avoiding electorally unpopular choices, and those choices are exactly what is required if Ireland's economy is to improve. Austere budgets, caps on pay increases, increased taxes, and reduced public expenditures must be introduced in order to bring the debt level down within the next few years. To an Irish electorate grown used to twenty years of economic growth and election promises of more social services, lower taxes, and more jobs, this message may have the effect of killing the messenger—a problem the current government faces.

The problems of the Irish economy at present are serious. Yet a more positive picture emerges if we take a longer look. In the two decades since the initiation of the Whitaker Plan over 300 foreign firms have invested a total of £2.4 billion (roughly $3.6 billion) in Ireland. These firms, coupled with the development of Irish industry, have created over 100,000 jobs. The Irish shifted the number of workers in agriculture from 36,000 in 1961 to approximately 20,000 in 1981, and the industrial and service sectors have grown accordingly. The increase in real income for the people of Ireland has nearly doubled, and the growth rates measure favorably with those of the most sophisticated of the European countries.

Entry into the EEC brought special funds for agricultural improvement and development, a sharp increase in the income of farmers, and the access to the extended market of Europe that is necessary for an economy based upon exports. The entry into Europe also brought Ireland out of the shadow of the United Kingdom and into contact with diplomats, bureaucrats, and economists from nations that have much in common with Ireland's size and economy. Potential resources within Ireland are under exploration or development, including zinc, uranium, timber, fish, and oil.

Human resources are also being developed at a rate necessary for a competitive economic posture in the future: High technology, agronomy, accounting, management, European Community law, and foreign languages are being taught to young men and women at the established universities as well as at the Limerick National Higher Education Institute.

Ireland will suffer the costs of the current debt crisis and the general depression of Western economies. However, the foundation is in place for a modern, productive, adaptable economy that can provide the economic well-being necessary to keep the Irish at home and give them a decent standard of living by European standards and an affluent life-style by global standards.

SOCIAL CHANGES

Sean Lemass presided over the emergence of a new leadership in the political arena and rapid growth in the economic sphere. Lemass rejected the doctrines of protectionism associated with republican Gaelic cultural nationalism and embraced free trade and a concept of Ireland-in-Europe as the means to genuine political independence. The sense that a new Ireland was in the making was prevalent, and an impulse toward social modernization arose, prompted in part by the economic regeneration and in part by the wave of self-awareness and receptivity to changes in Ireland. The country increasingly measured itself against the standards of contemporary European life as opposed to the bucolic visions of de Valera. On one such measure, education, the Irish system was clearly ripe for reform as the rising tempo of Irish economic change raised the question of the need for people who were educated and trained for the future.

Education

The Irish educational system had been essentially unchanged since the nineteenth century with the exception of the Irish language question (discussed in Chapter 5). The three levels of Irish education are primary, secondary, and higher education, and most schools were run by the church and supported by the state. The curriculum was rigidly prescribed, and the teachers were sternly authoritarian, not only in classroom discipline but also in their teaching of social and religious values. The Christian Brothers came to be identified with secondary education in Ireland as they ran so many of those schools. Their educational philosophy included rigid segregation of the sexes, substantial doses of corporal punishment with leather straps, a classical curriculum, including Irish and Latin, and, of course, extensive religious indoctrination.

Those students who continued beyond the secondary level went to the National University of Ireland with its three branches at Cork, Galway, and Dublin or to Trinity College (University of Dublin), the traditionally Protestant institution. In fact few students from the Catholic secondary schools attended Trinity College as it was forbidden by the church, under pain of mortal sin, unless the bishop of Dublin gave permission. Thus Trinity College remained somewhat out of touch with the mainstream of Irish educational life while the predominantly Catholic National University of Ireland absorbed that small number of secondary graduates who had the examination grades and the money to attend a university.

In 1966 a commission that had been charged in 1962 with the responsibility of investigating Irish education published a report entitled *Investment in Education*.[14] The conclusions of the report were supported by careful research and constituted a severe indictment of the Irish educational system and a call for substantial reform. The litany of deficiencies was extensive and included the ramshackle condition of school buildings that had been built in the previous century; the failure of the national schools to sufficiently educate even one-half of the students so they could attain the minimum standard of the primary certificate; the failure of the educational system to educate a significant number of students at the secondary level; and the failure of the universities to educate more students at a time when specialized training was needed more than ever. Not only was secondary education limited to small numbers of students, but not surprisingly, those students came from the more populous areas and affluent strata. Of 57,000 students leaving the national schools in 1957, under 2,000 ended up in the universities. Those students who did attend a university were also predominantly from the more advantaged sectors of Irish society.

The government, beginning in the mid-1960s, was galvanized into legislating educational reform. The area of secondary education was thoroughly revamped as legislation increased the age of leaving school, eliminated fees for the vocational schools, paid fees to secondary schools to take students, and provided transportation to students. The effect was dramatic as the number of students enrolled in the secondary schools rose about 118,807 in 1967-68 to 167,309 in 1973-74.[15] In rural areas schoolhouses were consolidated, and comprehensive schools (primary and vocational) were established in areas where there were few traditional secondary schools. By 1975 there were over

Trinity College, Dublin, the oldest university in Ireland, founded in 1591. (Courtesy, Irish Tourist Board)

thirty such comprehensive schools, and vocational education was invigorated by free secondary education and the establishment of nine regional colleges of technology.

Primary education was not untouched as a revised curriculum was introduced in 1971 as well as changes in school management. The boards of the primary and secondary schools had been traditionally composed of religious people, but in 1975 these boards were broadened to include parents and teachers. The church in some cases did not accept this change graciously as control of education had traditionally been a primary concern of the church.

The highest level of education, the universities, was the subject of an intensive examination by the Commission on Higher Education. Their report called for making the universities at Galway, Cork, and Dublin independent and for leaving Trinity independent, among other things. This recommendation was drowned in a torrent of controversy as the then-minister of education, Donogh O'Malley, suggested that Trinity College and University College Dublin be merged in order to integrate Trinity into Irish life and eliminate the duplication of costs and efforts.[16] The furor eventually died down, and the two universities have remained independent, although some efforts have been made to eliminate excessive duplication. Trinity College has become less isolated from the mainstream of Irish educational life in the past decade. An effort on the part of Trinity to have fewer British students, coupled with the removal in 1970 of the ecclesiastical ban on attendance of Catholics, has created a different mixture of students and less of a "cricket and cucumber sandwiches" image for that institution.

As the number of students in secondary schools increased and more scholarships to the universities were offered by the government, the population at the universities exploded. University College Dublin virtually doubled in size and moved from the city to a modern campus in the suburbs, indistinguishable from any branch of the University of California. The sharp increase in the number of university graduates in the 1970s coincided with the sharp decrease in emigration and the diminution of the period of rapid economic growth. Thus the government has been faced with the problem of providing employment not only for secondary school graduates but also for well-educated university graduates with higher expectations.

Since 1964 a virtual revolution has occurred in Irish education in the realms of accessibility, levels of completion, curriculum, management, and quality. The effects of such rapid changes in such a crucial sphere of social life will be felt increasingly in the years to come. Education has become a less incandescent transmitter of the social claims of Irish language, Irish Catholicism, and Irish nationalism in both content and style. People educated in the 1970s will perhaps come to view the national question, the church, and the traditional authoritarian values of Irish society differently. The Ireland of the future will be determined by the young students, beneficiaries of the transformation in Irish education.

Social Life

The social life of Ireland has felt the pressures of change as well. The Irish marriage, so often stereotyped in literature, has fundamentally altered, and the problems of alcoholism, mental illness, and drug abuse have grown or emerged.

The Irish marriage after the famine was a union of two older people, steeped in sexual puritanism, who, ironically, produced extremely large families. The number of people who did not marry at all was higher than in any other European country. The stereotype of the old Irish bachelor was rooted in the reality of an Ireland bound by a traditional family structure, religion, and pattern of land ownership that discouraged early marriage or, for that matter, marrying at all.

The average age of marriage for Irishmen in 1960 was thirty-one and for Irishwomen, twenty-seven, four years higher than the averages in Great Britain. Ireland had the highest percentage of unmarried males in Europe as well as the lowest marriage rate.[17] Despite these characteristics the Irish also had larger families, which meant higher degrees of infant and maternal mortality due to the women's extended age of childbearing.

All of these patterns have changed swiftly since 1960 as the impact of decreasing emigration, urbanization, and economic prosperity not only drove down the age of the population, but also drove more of the people to the altar. The average age of marriage dropped to twenty-six for males and to twenty-four for females, and the rate of marriage accelerated by over 40 percent between 1958 and 1970. By 1977 the rate of marriage had reached

Bachelors Walk in Dublin along the River Liffey. (Courtesy, Irish Tourist Board)

that of other European states. The number of children born to these younger couples has been decreasing, and there has been a drop in the number of births after two or three children as well. That rate has dropped to such a degree that demographer Brendan Walsh noted that a one-third decline in fertility had occurred from 1961 to 1977 in Ireland.[18]

The effect of these demographic changes has been a challenge to the traditional patterns of family structure and authority, especially in urban areas, and the marriage pattern is coming closer and closer to that of the more economically prosperous European states. Thus tensions of modernization have permeated and altered not only education but also the family.

Irish people may be marrying at a younger age, but they still face the pressures that have always bedeviled Irish marriages—sex, drink, and deterioration. William G. Shade cites a number of reports that indicate that two-thirds of the Irish women do not find sex satisfying, that Irishmen do not have an adequate interest in sex, and that they suffer from premature ejaculation.[19] Whatever the validity of these reports, commentators note that a specter of guilt, contributed by the church, and socially reinforced sexual repression make for a less-than-robust interest in sex among Irishmen. There is no question that alcohol (discussed below) and a social life centered on male groups have contributed to immature attitudes among men toward women in general and the partnership of marriage in particular. Moreover, the general attitude toward women in Ireland, both within marriage and in the society at large, has been that their proper role is one of subservience. Married women have been unlikely to get jobs, and unmarried women have been seen as likely to get married so little effort has been made to advance their careers or salaries. In the home the woman is to clean, cook, and procreate. This de facto subordination has been coupled with a rhetorical reverence for women and motherhood derived, in part, from reverence for the Holy Mother.

Alcohol abuse, sexual immaturity, male chauvinism, large numbers of children, economic hardship, and the lack of divorce have made marriage stressful in Ireland. A high incidence of wife beating, especially in the less-advantaged social classes, is a result of this stress, and an alarming number of battered children is another tragic consequence. The stability and strength of Irish marriages are hard to determine as there are no official divorce statistics. There are forms of Irish divorce, however, such as a husband's going to Great Britain and simply leaving his wife and children to seek social security benefits as a deserted wife and family.

The lack of a divorce law hides the problems in Irish marriage, but the number of bad marriages that would instantly dissolve were divorce granted is estimated by psychologists at 25 to 40 percent, and the remaining 60 to 75 percent are hardly idyllic unions. Tim Pat Coogan notes that 80 percent of one prominent Dublin psychiatrist's cases were the result of marital problems.[20]

Psychiatrists have been busy, not only with marital problems, but with a rate of mental illness that is higher than in most Western European countries. The rate of hospital admission for mental health problems had been high as early as 1960 but took a rapid jump of 30 percent between 1970 and 1975.[21] Readmission for mental illness is over 50 percent. The incidences of anxiety, stress, and depression are such that the use of tranquilizers, such as valium and librium, is extensive. Although serious mental illness and neuroses are not solely attributable to the rapid advent of new values in Ireland, there is little doubt that the pressures have accentuated anxiety.

The image of the Irish as heavy drinkers is one portrayed in song and story and reinforced by events such as Brendan Behan's appearing on a BBC television interview drunk and making no effort to hide the fact. The pub and the pint traditionally have been the solace for the worker and farmer seeking some relief from a hard life of sometimes desperate poverty. Poteen, a potent and illegal homemade brew, was an escape from hard, rural drudgery. The pub in more recent times has come to be the center of social life in Ireland, associating drink with good company and conversation.

In fact, however, the average amount of consumption of pure alcohol per person in Ireland, 7.64 liters, is below that of virtually all European countries and less than one-half that of the French (24.6 liters) and the Italians (18 liters).[22] Moreover, the Irish death rate from cirrhosis is well below that of other European countries. The benign impact of these statistics is belied, however, by several others that indicate a sharp rise in drinking and alcoholism. The average consumption figures include, in Ireland, an older generation of Pioneers, an organization whose members pledge to abstain totally from drink, and thus the figures imply a greater amount of drinking among the relatively young. Moreover, numerous other indicators provide evidence of an existing alcohol problem and a sharp rise in the consumption of alcohol. The Irish spend more of their disposable income on drink than other Europeans, approximately one-eighth of all personal spending. The first-admission rates for alcoholism and alcohol-related problems are the highest in Europe and have increased fivefold in the past twenty-five years. Drinking is involved to a great degree in automobile accidents, and drunk driving convictions were very difficult to obtain until very recently. Alcohol consumption has steadily risen, jumping 60 percent in the 1960s and 43 percent in the 1970s. Not only has drinking increased by over 100 percent, but hospital admission records show that the alcohol increase includes a far greater rate for women than in the past. Altogether, a substantial increase in drinking has accompanied the surge of prosperity and social change in Ireland. The young, especially the young women, are drinking more and spending more to do it.

Informal indicators are also revealing. New lounges, less spartan than the traditional pub, dot the cities and the countryside. The Irish are encouraged to drink through the habit of "buying rounds"; that is, to be with a group means drinking as many drinks as there are group members as each buys a round for the table. The acceptance of drunkenness at social and business functions is greater in Ireland than in other countries. A shift has occurred in drinking habits as hard liquor, and some wine, have increasingly supplanted the drinking of beer.

The government's policy on alcohol has been characterized by ambivalence. The members of the Dáil, themselves reared in the Irish drinking ethos, have tended to see the social pattern of drinking as normal. The industries that manufacture and sell drink, such as Guinness, are large employers and politically influential. Finally, the revenues from the taxes on alcohol are substantial, totaling approximately £250 million (about $375 million). However, the rise in drink-related automobile accidents, the pressure of doctors' and clerics' testifying to the damage done to Ireland by alcohol-related hospital costs, and work lost through employee alcohol problems prompted the government to crack down on drunken driving in 1978 and to urge the media to regulate the advertising of alcohol in 1980.

Alcohol is not always the preferred drug of the young, especially since the 1960s, and Ireland is not free of the problem of illicit drug use. The use of marijuana, as well as other stimulants and depressants, is certainly not as widespread as on the Continent, but nevertheless use has grown in popularity along with the other symbols of youth culture: punk and new-wave rock music, jeans and the general panoply of counterculture attire. In the early seventies arrests for use of illicit drugs more than doubled in Ireland, and shipments of marijuana and heroin were confiscated by the authorities.

Marriage problems, mental illness, alcoholism, crime, and teenage drug use did not all emerge contemporaneously and were not driven at the same rate or to the same degree by the celerity of the economic prosperity and new winds blowing across Ireland. Some people believe that the roots of such problems lie in Irish cultural patterns: "Anxiety or fear, stemming from deprivation of love, and punishment, are the dynamics which are predominant in virtually all our human relationships in Ireland."[23] Although this statement is no doubt true, the degree and rapidity of expansion of these social phenomena have been stimulated by the changes in the last quarter century and, in turn, have become part of the stimulus to change. The process of modernization is likely to accelerate rather than abate, and whatever social patterns emerge, Ireland will surely not be the pastoral paradise of de Valera's dreams.

Welfare

Tony Gray, writing in 1966 on the increase in prosperity in Ireland as a result of the Whitaker initiatives, noted: "At the other end of the scale, there is no longer any real poverty in Ireland."[24] This preposterous statement was clearly the triumph of naiveté over research. Poverty has been in the past, and continues to be, a tragic problem in Ireland. Whether one looks at the agrarian poverty of the nineteenth century, the pestilential slums of Dublin at the turn of the century, or the current manifestations of misery among the unemployed, poorly housed, disabled, and elderly, real poverty certainly has been and is present in Ireland.

As a relatively poor, predominantly agricultural country, Ireland's indigence, relative to more affluent European countries, is not surprising. Poverty was coupled with the conservative social welfare doctrines, which were prevalent for half a century after independence, and the antistatist ideology of the church. Not only were there few resources to distribute to the disadvantaged, but few people were inclined to undertake the task. Thus poverty was a persistent part of the Irish social scene.

Historically the response of the government to social welfare was a laissez-faire attitude with the provision of minimal facilities for the indigent and ill. Workhouses, county homes, dispensaries, and general hospitals, all less than adequate, served people who had to prove their lack of means in order to gain admittance. Essentially unchanged from the nineteenth century until 1945, this service, as F.S.L. Lyons notes, "was scanty, old fashioned and frequently humiliating to those whose poverty left them with no other alternative."[25] After World War II, and despite the setback of the mother and child health plan, expenditures for health care on the part of Dublin, local governments, and private enterprises increased substantially. The degree of economic stagnation in the decade of the 1950s is revealed, however, in the number of people entitled to the increased medical services. In order to qualify for a "blue card," which granted free medical care, people had to meet a rather stringent means test, i.e., prove they were very poor. In 1958 over 28 percent of the population qualified for a blue card. The remainder were entitled to medical services at reduced cost if they met certain qualifications, which, in fact, were met by another 50 to 60 percent of the population.[26] The services under the 1953 Health Act were slender when compared with other nations and burdened with serving a poor population, which, measured by fairly severe means tests, composed about 85 percent of the country.

In areas other than health service Ireland has had a patchwork of both contributory and noncontributory plans for pensioners; allowances for children, widows, and orphans; and sickness insurance. In 1952 Fianna Fáil unified these plans into the Social Welfare Act, which covered national health insurance, unemployment insurance, and benefits for widows and orphans. The legislation was, with respect to the past, fairer and more generous. The state contributed 40 percent of the costs and the contributors, the remainder. The deficiencies were the low level of payments as compared to say, Britain—less than two-thirds—and the exclusion of certain categories of workers. The desperate, who could not even contribute to an insurance plan, were assisted by the state, which assumed complete responsibility for certain elderly people, widows, and orphans.

The local governments in Ireland have provided subsidized housing since the end of the nineteenth century, and approximately one-fourth the housing built in Ireland up to the advent of the Whitaker Plan was built by local authorities. As that housing deteriorated over the course of a half century, and as the rate of new building diminished, the decrease in emigration began to create an enormous demand for housing. The estimated need for new houses from 1966 to 1971 was 9,000 units a year and destined only to go up, so a combination of increased government expenditures and private contractors' entering the housing market created a housing boom in the 1970s. The costs however, were high, and the advantage of home ownership went to the more affluent middle class. In 1979 less than 20 percent of new housing was built by local authorities, a drop of 13 percent since 1975. The four-fifths of the new housing that is private is very costly, so there are 35,000 families on lists waiting for local-authority housing, unable to afford a home and forced to live in substandard housing while they wait over two years for an assignment. The result is severe overcrowding, both outside of and in public housing, and an attendant increase in problems of marital discord, mental illness, crime, child abuse, and alcoholism.

In the other realms of social welfare the governments since 1960 have increased the benefits available to the Irish. The benefits, however, have had to chase the inflationary spiral, which in 1980 was over 18 percent. Moreover, when the economy slumps, as it did in the mid-1970s, the unemployment rate rises, which puts more pressure on the social insurance plans and squeezes more people into the margins of poverty.

Poverty can be measured in various ways, but however measured, in the Republic of Ireland the conditions of old age, unemployment, and single parenthood virtually always mean poverty, especially for women. An assessment of poverty in Ireland done by the magazine *Magill* in 1980 estimated the number of poor in Ireland at nearly one-third of the population.[27] This group included all people whose income fell below two-thirds of the national average. The current upper limit on income to qualify for medical cards is an income of £57 (about $87) per week for a couple and two children. About 40 percent of the population of the Republic is in this category, a figure of well over a million people. The same number is either fully or partially dependent upon some form of welfare support. The welfare support has been increased, but the amounts received still deny the recipients extensive access to goods and services. The small size of the payments, plus the lack of available housing, leaves some deserted wives and elderly people living in what could only be termed squalor. Although conditions in the cities are bad, the countryside is not free of older people, remnants of urban migration, living in poverty on small farms and in cottages.

The effects of poverty on children are well known as they tend to repeat the social patterns of their parents—unsuccessful marriage, low education, high unemployment, and dependency on state welfare. Poverty, of course, breeds social tensions, such as crime and prostitution, and interpersonal tensions, which lead to child beating, wife beating, alcoholism, and desertion.

The governments since 1960 have faced the problem of poverty with a dual response. The first response is a continuing emphasis on overall economic growth so as to provide jobs, which help alleviate poverty. Economic growth alone, however, cannot eliminate poverty, and thus the second response has been to extend and increase social welfare benefits. This response, however, has suffered a decline—dropping from 16 percent of the total government expenditures in 1975 to 13 percent of that total in 1979—a time during which the population and unemployment rates increased. The Haughey government made efforts to repair this gap in 1981 by proposing a 25 percent increase in social welfare benefits. The total cost to the government was in the order of £110 million (about $170 million), which, of course, creates pressures on the government's deficits and tax policy. The dilemma for Ireland is to provide acceptable levels of social welfare, a burden on government expenditures, and at the same time attempt to combat unemployment, generate investment, promote exports, preserve a favorable balance of payments, and avoid excessive debt. Until the advent of Greece into the European Community, Ireland was the poorest country with the lowest GNP and the lowest level of social welfare. The task of providing minimal decent standards of health, housing, and welfare is expensive and yet is one of the most visible manifestations of a modern government's measure of concern for the least advantaged of its people.

NOTES

1. Quoted in Thomas J. O'Hanlon, *The Irish: Portrait of a People* (London: André Deutsch, 1976), p. 167.

2. F.S.L. Lyons, *Ireland Since the Famine* (London: Collins, Fontana, 1973), p. 623.

3. Ibid., p. 624.

4. Ibid., p. 625.

5. Terence Brown, *Ireland: A Social and Cultural History, 1922–79* (Glasgow: Fontana, 1981), p. 212. Brown points out that in 1957 there were 54,000 emigrants and yet 78,000 were still unemployed in that year.

6. Department of Finance, *Economic Development* (Dublin: Stationers Office, 1958).

7. Lyons, *Ireland Since the Famine*, p. 628.

8. Kieran A. Kennedy and Brendan R. Dowling, *Economic Growth in Ireland* (Dublin: Gill and Macmillan, 1975), p. 256. The ensuing assessment of the Irish economy draws substantially from this book.

9. Ibid., pp. 275–276.

10. The original six members were Belgium, the Netherlands, Luxembourg, Italy, France, and West Germany. The Republic of Ireland, Denmark, and Great Britain joined the EEC in 1973, Greece became a member in 1981, and Portugal and Spain were to become members in the early 1980s.

11. Figures are from Brian Donaghy, "Will the Goose Lay a Wooden Egg?" *Magill* (December 1980), pp. 39–41.

12. H. Hermann Strohmeyer, "Ireland: Problems and Opportunities of a Small Country on the Fringe of the European Community," *Euro Cooperation* (Paris) no. 21 (1978), p. 72.

13. Stewart Dolby, "The Millstone of Public Debt," *Europe* (September–October 1981), p. 11.

14. Department of Education, *Investment in Education* (Dublin: Stationers Office, 1966).

15. Brown, *Ireland,* p. 252.

16. Lyons, *Ireland Since the Famine,* p. 657.

17. William G. Shade, "Strains of Modernization: The Republic of Ireland Under Lemass and Lynch," *Eire-Ireland* 14 (Spring, 1979), p. 36.

18. Cited in Brown, *Ireland,* p. 260.

19. Shade, "Strains of Modernization," p. 40.

20. Tim Pat Coogan, *The Irish: A Personal View* (London: Phaidon Press, 1975), p. 102.

21. Shade, "Strains of Modernization," p. 32.

22. Sean O'Donnell, "Curing the Habit," *Eire-Ireland* 16 (Fall 1981), p. 134.

23. Dr. Noel Browne, quoted in O'Hanlon, *Irish Portrait,* pp. 219–220.

24. Tony Gray, *The Irish Answer* (London: Heinemann, 1966), p. 340.

25. Lyons, *Ireland Since the Famine,* p. 661.

26. Ibid., p. 664.

27. Brian Trench and Pat Brennan, "Poverty in Ireland," *Magill* (April 1980), pp. 10–31.

5

Cultural Change

The economic development of the Republic has had direct repercussions on the structures of Irish society, and the changes in the society and the economy have had repercussions on elements of Irish cultural values. Irish language and culture, the media and their modern messages, and Catholicism and the church are arenas in which old and new tangle in Irish modernization.

THE IRISH LANGUAGE

From the time of the founding of the Gaelic League in 1893 the policy of Irish language revival was to haunt Ireland. The Gaelic League became associated with Sinn Féin in the early part of this century as its members associated the quest for an independent Ireland with the creation, or restoration, of a Gaelic Ireland. The crux of the Gaelic revival was the revivification of Gaelic, or Irish. Douglas Hyde, the first president of the league, argued that the authentic Ireland was a Gaelic Ireland and that the central facet of that authenticity was the Gaelic language. Through the increasing Anglicization of Ireland the nation had lost its true cultural identity. Ireland without its own language, as Hyde and others saw it, was spiritually deficient as the prevalence of English corrupted Ireland's cultural uniqueness. Restoration of Irish would, for the language revivalists, allow individuals to flourish within their native culture and allow that culture to flourish among other cultures.

In the years from 1916 to 1921, when Sinn Féin became politically predominant, the political thrust for independence from Britain was inculcated with the cultural quest to be Catholic and Gaelic. When the Cosgrave administration took power in the Free State it undertook to revive the Irish language in the hope, at least for the most extreme partisans of Gaelic, of replacing English with Irish as the vernacular language.

In the schools the government mandated that the Irish language be the medium of instruction for at least one hour a day and that history and geography by taught in Irish. In 1926 a policy was introduced that indicated that Irish should be the medium of instruction in as many subjects as possible and that the time spent on other subjects should be reduced to allow more time for the teaching of Irish. In effect, a movement of nationalist rebirth was to be realized through the education of the children in the Irish language. The difficulties of this policy were lost in the often dogmatic and authoritarian efforts of the language revivalists. The policy ignored the degree to which English had become widespread, and thus reinforcement of the Irish language at home or in the everyday world was lacking. The country had become part of the orbit of Great Britain, however much resisted or denied.

Along with instruction in the schools, the preservation of the language depended upon the preservation of the regions in which Irish still prevailed as the native tongue, the Gaeltacht. As it was, the number of Irish speakers was in steady decline, first from the pressure of pragmatic accommodation to an English-speaking country and second, from emigration. From 1881 to 1926 the number of Irish-speaking persons dropped 41 percent.

The problem then, as now, involved making a choice between ineffective alternatives. To preserve the language in the Gaeltacht the best policy may have been to leave the region alone. This choice, however, simply meant continuing the disproportionate emigration from the depressed rural areas of the declining west. Development schemes, however, invariably meant introducing commercial ventures, improved management of fishing, and programs to train people for new forms of employment, which directly or indirectly would stimulate the use of English. As this result was the end to be most avoided, the development projects could be productive in economic restoration but counterproductive in linguistic preservation.

Eventually the people began to object to the amount of teaching in Irish and to feel that all other educational values were being sacrificed at the altar of a nearly impossible task. The economic decline of the western areas and the increasing use of English in Ireland persuaded a majority of the teachers to oppose the policy of using Irish as the sole medium of instruction for children of English-speaking families. In fact, the decline of the west was a crisis for the language revivalists who saw the authentic Ireland in the Gaelic-speaking, Catholic people of the land. Emigration was not only an economic necessity but a cultural crisis as the national and cultural ideal was turning out to be no more than a labor pool for the factories of Leeds, Birmingham, and London.

The 1940s and 1950s brought about little change in the language situation as the overall number of Irish speakers continued to decline. By 1966 there were fewer than 70,000 native speakers of Irish as rural disintegration took its toll on the Gaeltacht. A government commission reporting five years earlier in 1961 and a government white paper in 1965 both detailed the dismal situation and indicated that Irish could die out as a spoken language in a few decades.

Both in the schools and in the handling of the Gaeltacht the governments since the 1960s have oscillated on the language question. In the face of the persistent decline of Irish speakers and the desire for a future in Europe, the goal of restoring the Irish language and creating a dual-language state has shifted to preservation of the Irish language. In 1969 Commairle na Gaelige, a council to advise the government on the preservation and extension of the Irish language, was created.

The mid-seventies brought about some setbacks to the language revivalists as in 1973 it was no longer necessary to pass an exam in Irish to achieve the secondary school leaving certificate (diploma) and thus the requirement that civil servants pass Irish in their leaving certificate was eliminated. The rapid changes in Ireland since the early sixties had dealt the language movement

A gathering of musicians for an evening of traditional Irish music. (Richard Finnegan)

a blow as people thought they should be learning French and German, not Irish. The ambivalence of the people was revealed in a survey done by the Committee on Irish Language Attitudes. Approximately two-thirds of the respondents believed that the Irish language was important for Irish cultural identity, that the Gaeltacht should be supported, and that children should still be taught the language. At the same time the respondents indicated they were not convinced the language could be passed on to the next generations, that they did not know or use much Irish, and that they thought the language inappropriate for modern commercial life.[1] By 1975 the number of native Irish speakers had declined to approximately 32,000, and the regions in which Irish was the first language diminished.

By the late 1970s partisans of the Irish language, however vigorous or imaginative their efforts, were seeing the decline of Irish in the schools, the government, and the Gaeltacht.[2] Recently Irish speakers have taken to demanding that their civil rights be respected as they believe they are being discriminated against in the educational realm, the media, and the development of the Gaeltacht. This demand differs substantially from Douglas Hyde's call for a de-Anglicized Gaelic-speaking Ireland.

Irish-language pressure groups operating in a very sympathetic public and governmental environment were unable to overcome the inexorable pressures that resulted in a diminishing of Irish and an expansion of English usage in the first four decades since independence. In the next two decades Ireland underwent substantial economic modernization, a communications explosion, and entry into the European economic and political arena. The probability of a Gaelic revival has scarcely been improved by these changes. Nollaig O'Gadhra wrote of the first direct elections to the European Parliament: "The most significant thing about all this, from a language point of view, was the almost total lack of debate about Irish language matters in any of the contests."[3] A supporter of the Irish language, O'Gadhra reveals more than she intended in juxtaposing the new door to Europe and an utter lack of concern for the Irish language. Other than in formalities, scarcely a word of Irish is heard in the Dáil, and if it were used, most members would be at a loss to comprehend what was said—even though the legislature is empowered by a constitution that declares Irish to be the national language.

The Irish language appears to have more vitality in traditional Irish music and poetry than it does in the day-to-day life of Ireland. Modernization both creates and destroys, but no society ever abandons its old culture completely. The Irish language will live on, probably more sung and recited than spoken, but it will be preserved as an important symbol more by conservators of culture than by government policies.

THE MEDIA AND CENSORSHIP

There are a host of influences on people's information, attitudes, and values. The impact of television, coming as it did at the same time as other changes, has been especially important in Ireland. Radio broadcasting, under government authority, had existed in Ireland since 1926. In 1960, when the government decided to engage in television broadcasting, radio and television were placed under a single board; Radio Telefis Éireann (RTE). Television broadcasting began in 1962, and from the start it was the subject of controversy. The RTE was dependent upon U.S. television shows at the outset as there was an insufficient number of Irish shows to fill the viewing hours, and almost immediately the RTE was accused of presenting too many U.S. programs. This criticism, though weakened as Irish-produced shows have increased, still has merit as "Dynasty," "Lou Grant," "Dallas," and "Hill Street Blues" are seen regularly on Irish television. Another divisive issue was the number of Irish language broadcasts, almost invariably seen as too few by advocates of the preservation of Irish. The church also felt mistreated, and on more than one occasion it has criticized the RTE because the subjects of sex, marriage and divorce, and birth control have been discussed on the screen.[4]

The history of radio and television in Ireland is one of firm government control and censorship. Thin-skinned politicians chaffed at criticism and also exerted control over programming, which resulted in a politically sanitized, purportedly impartial approach to public issues on the radio. In fact, the control was a pallid concession to political and ecclesiastical pressures. Television has fared somewhat better in that political events are reported and investigated, but it falls far short of the degree of independence of British and American television.

In terms of the changes in Ireland, television has contributed to, and accelerated, changes in attitudes toward consumerism, social values, and the west of Ireland. Advertising, both on the British channels available in the east of Ireland and on the Irish channels, opened the world of material goods to the Irish people as the first wave of prosperity hit Ireland. After 1962 more and more Irish people bought television sets, and by 1978, 83 percent of the households in Ireland had a television set—92 percent in greater Dublin where one-third of the population resides. Television urged people to purchase more and more, and new styles of dress, new places to go, new trends in music, new household goods, and a new way of life were presented to the Irish people on the persuasive little screen. De Valera's vision of frugal asceticism was not highly regarded by the people of Ireland once they had the opportunity to opt for something else. Calls from the pulpit to reject materialism and the hedonistic ways of Britain and the United States were not so compelling as they had been in the past when the Irish had little choice in the matter.

Not only consumer values have been encouraged by television. British television was accessible in the east of Ireland before 1962 and was, obviously, free from the Irish censor's hand. Thus a way of life that was characterized by critics as the "permissive society," and by others who were less critical as a modern liberal society, was presented in Irish homes. Values that had been taken for granted in domestic life, work, and religion were now open to examination as television portrayed far more fluid values related to family, sex, religion, drugs, and pornography. Although the Irish censor laboriously worked at condemning books and snipping flims, the British Broadcasting Corporation (BBC) was showing those same films uncut, and more, night after night. Programming from the United States—portraying the California life-style, gaudy cars, lavish restaurants, flashy homes, and trendy clothes—contributed to this phenomenon as well, though often the shows had as little to do with the authentic United States as they did with Ireland.

The impact of television on the west of Ireland was most acute as that area was already suffering depletion from emigration. Television not only introduced the young people to the world beyond Galway but, in fact, treated rural life with derision. There is little place in the values of the sophisticated urban world for rural life. Although occasionally romanticized, more often rural life is portrayed as a world of tedium filled with bumpkins and fools. Television brought both the allure of the new and a disdain for the old to the west of Ireland. As Thomas J. O'Hanlon notes, the outside world rules the destiny of children: "And that world, however unreal and idealized it may appear on the screen, pulls like a powerful magnet on the imagination of the young. The normal dissatisfaction of teenagers with the lack of social amenities has been replaced in conversation by a tangible hatred of country life."[5]

Although television is repeatedly condemned as superficial, violent, and vacuous in Ireland, as well as in Britain and the United States, it has replaced the newspaper as the principal source of news and has become the center of entertainment for the family. The effects of television on the Irish will continue to reinforce the other changes in the country and to contribute its own shallow luster to contemporary Irish values.

Television is not the only realm of communication subject to government control. Censorship of periodicals and books has persisted in Ireland to the dismay of civil libertarians and the disgust of artists and writers. Censorship, like family law, is an area in which the ideal of the liberal state and the ideal of a Catholic nation collided and the Catholic ideal prevailed. The law was originally generated by a committee appointed in 1926 to examine "evil literature," mainly British newspapers because of their lurid treatment of sexual matters. The Censorship of Publications Act passed in 1929 included books as well as newspapers and also included a prohibition of any treatment of birth control. The legislation had strong clerical support, and the conservative, puritanical thought of the time prevailed. Ireland set out to isolate itself in the name of one of the nation's social pillars, Catholicism, from the contaminating influence of secular cultures. A five-member Censorship Board began to assess not only periodicals and paperback novels but also the works of some of the world's greatest literary figures, including Simone de Beauvoir, John Steinbeck, Arthur Koestler, Ernest Hemingway, Somerset Maugham, Alberto Moravia, André Gide, Jean-Paul Sartre, F. Scott Fitzgerald, Doris Lessing, and George Orwell. Also embarrassing was the banning of Irish writers such as George Bernard Shaw, Frank O'Connor, J. P. Donleavey, Sean O'Casey, Brendan Behan, and Edna O'Brien, which denied these artists the audience of their own countrymen.

The operation of the censorship process placed the exercise of literary and moral judgment in the hands of the disgruntled. People who were offended by something had merely to underline the passage and send the book to the board. The board members were volunteers and could hardly have read the avalanche of books sent to them each year. Thus the underlined passages determined the fate of such works as Sartre's *Age of Reason* and Hemingway's *For Whom the Bell Tolls.*

Irish intellectuals fought a lonely battle against the censorship law, indicating that not only was it illiberal, but it also made Ireland look foolish in the eyes of other Western nations. A 1946 act amended the process to allow for appeal, which proved to be rather clumsy and ineffectual. The same act also allowed customs officials to seize books they felt should be reviewed by the Censorship Board. This censorship prior to sale hardly seemed to be a step forward as it expanded the censorship authority to members of the Department of Customs and Excise, who, as Thomas J. O'Hanlon cynically notes, "assign import duties on inner tubes one day and become literary critics the day after."[6]

Liberalization of the practice of censorship came in the 1960s and 1970s. In the early fifties the board banned about 60 books a month (over 80 a month in 1954); in the early sixties about 30 books a month, and in 1970, about 13 books a month.[7] Legislation in 1967 amended the Censorship Act so as to remove all books that had been banned for more than twelve years and limiting new banning to a similar time period. The change released 5,000 books to the Irish people, though books could be banned again by the board. One that was banned again deserves mention: J. P. Donleavy, who lives in Ireland, still cannot purchase his book *The Ginger Man* there.

Film has fared no better in Ireland as the government has appointed a film censor since 1925. Devoid of any film expertise, or background, the practice of the film censor has been to edit out all objectionable scenes until the result is bland enough to pass muster regardless of any artistic mayhem that may result.

Censorship has been excused by some people, such as those who suggest that it is honor for an author to be banned, that the Irish market is so minimal the author does not lose much money, that no intelligent person would want to read most of what is banned anyway, or, finally, that the Irish people want censorship as they are, in fact, rather puritan in outlook. However, the fact remains that the people of Ireland have been deprived of the right to make judgments for themselves under a policy of government and clerical paternalism.

The demise of the type of censorship that was practiced in the 1950s reflects the demise of parochial paternalism and the rise of a more open policy in the areas of books and British television (though film has remained somewhat restricted). In part this new situation is an indication that the church has changed not only in its capacity to control but also by adapting to a new Ireland.

THE CATHOLIC CHURCH

The Roman Catholic faith in Ireland survived the Reformation, penal laws, and independence movement and remained tenaciously bonded to the Irish people. The conjunction of the church's right for religious liberty with the Irish quest for political liberty meant that devotion to the church was devotion to the country. Moreover, the Gaelic Ireland movement associated devotion to the church with Irish cultural identity. The convergence of these forces created a religious institution that was more revered and powerful than any such institution in any other European state.

The historical evolution of the Catholic church created a structure that was profoundly hierarchical, paternal, and authoritarian, and religious doctrines were theologically rigid and absolutist in character. In the framework of the Free State the strength of the church remained undiminished as the Cosgrave administration created legislation in accordance with Irish Catholic principles and dogmas. The 1937 constitution and the de Valera years produced little friction in the realms of censorship, social policy, and family law. Only in the case of the mother and child plan did the position of the church differ from that of the state, and that difference was brought out and debated in public. Reflective of the position of the church during the 1950s was the comment of Bishop Lucey of Cork in 1955: "In a word their [the bishops'] position was that they were the final arbiters of right and wrong even in political matters. In other spheres the State might for its own good reasons ignore the advice of experts, but in faith and morals it might not."[8]

In practice the influence of the Church took the form of enforcing a sexual puritanism, supporting the legislation of church doctrine in family matters, and opposing state intervention into social policy. The church saw the temptations of a secular, atheistic, and modern world everywhere, and these temptations invariably assumed a sexual form. Every conceivable human situation was fraught with the danger of sexual license, and the church sought to extirpate such lures of the flesh. The Irish church's paranoia was enforced in the rigid sexual segregation of the country's school systems as well as in other social settings. Dance halls were deemed particularly dangerous, and the church persistently agitated that they be regulated as they "lent themselves

A graveyard in Roscommon by the ruins of an ancient castle. (Richard Finnegan)

not so much to rhythm as to low sensuality."[9] The support of the censorship law reflected clerical concern with the temptations of the "evil literature" from Britain, which was seen as destroying parental authority and eroding the morals of the young. The censorship law reflects a concern with doctrine as well, in that literature that contained any treatment of contraception, especially a favorable view, was also denied to the people of Ireland. The pressure of the church for sexual purity was reinforced in a thousand direct and indirect ways, from the stern glance of a priest at a young couple holding hands to novenas and retreats filled with preaching against the sins of the flesh.

The second area of church concern is doctrine. The church's position on marriage holds that marriage is an inviolate and permanent union. Thus the church opposes divorce and supported the Cosgrave government's 1922 act that precluded legal divorce. In the 1937 constitution this law was elevated to a constitutional directive in Article 41, which states that "no law shall be enacted providing for the grant of a dissolution of marriage." Thus to legalize divorce in Ireland would require a constitutional amendment rather than simply legislative change. In Catholic doctrine the primary purpose of marriage is the procreation of children; the companionship of the marriage bond is second in importance. Thus contraception is considered a violation of the natural law, so in 1935 legislation was passed that included a ban on the importation and sale of contraceptives.

The church's position on education is reflected in the extensive clerical control of the educational system and the intensity with which the hierarchy preserves that domain. Thus the education of children in the faith is firmly in the hands of the teaching orders, especially the Christian Brothers. Any threat to the transmission and reinforcement of the faith is to be eliminated— the church's ban on attending Trinity College is illustrative of this fact. Trinity, as a Protestant school, was viewed with a jaundiced eye by the hierarchy. In 1927 the National Council of Bishops stated: "Since there are within the Free State three University Colleges sufficiently safe in regard to faith and morals, we, therefore, strictly inhibit, and under pain of grave sin, we forbid priests and all clerics, by advice or otherwise, to recommend parents or others having charge of youth to send young persons in their charge to Trinity College."[10] This ban was made more explicit by the archbishop of Dublin, John C. McQuaid, in 1944 when he forbade attendance at Trinity College by students in his diocese without his permission under pain of mortal sin. In 1956 this position was endorsed by all the bishops in Ireland when they forbade students from any diocese from attending Protestant schools without the archbishop of Dublin's permission. The permission would be granted if there were sufficient "guarantees against the danger of perversion."[11] This ban included not only Trinity College but all non-Catholic schools as the church believed that only it was competent to determine what training augmented or corrupted Catholic education.

Thus in the realms of education, social life, and family law the church's moral vision and doctrine have held sway, which is not to suggest that such positions have been imposed upon a recalcitrant people. On the contrary, the Cosgrave and de Valera administrations, including the Labour Party, embraced these norms wholeheartedly. The devout public offered no resistance, and the only voice of opposition came from a small clique of intellectuals, such as William Butler Yeats and Sean O'Faolain. Their complaints made no dent on the public's attitude, and they were roundly condemned by authoritarian Catholics.

The third area of church influence is in the realm of social policy. The general thrust of the church was antistatist, which is reflected not only in the 1937 constitution, in which the right to private property is enshrined, but also in the vocational emphasis adopted by the church during that period. In 1944 a report was issued from a commission, chaired by the bishop of Galway, that called for diminishing the centralization of bureaucratic control in Irish government as it was inefficient and insensitive. The state, the report declared, should instead operate through the already existing vocational organizations in the society. That same year a report issued by the bishop of Clonfert called for a reorganization of the medical services and other social services into a social insurance scheme supported, not by the state, but by the contributing members. Both reports were either criticized or ignored by the Fianna Fáil government, but they did reflect church thought during the period on the role of the state bureaucracy in the vocational and social spheres. Essentially that thought was to deny the state the role of supplanting the family, or the vocational sectors of society, in the provision of social service. The actual confrontation in the social sphere between church and state came on the matter of providing health care, and the mother and child plan brought the church's doctrinal opposition into the public arena. The position of the church on the state's right to legislate on matters the church considered doctrinally important was reflected in the statements of the bishop of Tuam to the prime minister during the controversy:

> The right to provide for the physical education of the child belongs to the family and not the State. Experience has shown that physical or health education is closely interwoven with important moral questions on which the Catholic Church has definite teachings. Education in regard to motherhood includes instruction in regard to sex relations, chastity and marriage. The State has no competence to give instructions in such matters."[12]

In this case the church was connected with two crucial issues: first, the extension of state services into what the church regarded as the inviolate sphere of the family; second, the potential for those services to introduce ideas that might be at variance with church doctrine on that apparently most compelling of matters, sexual behavior. The fact that the mother and child health plan was to be administered by doctors who were overwhelmingly Catholic did not moderate the church's opposition.

As Ireland stood on the brink of rapid economic and social changes the church was fixed in a mode not substantially different from that of earlier centuries: pervasive, powerful, and puritanical. Just as Cardinal Paul Cullen shaped the Irish Catholic church in the latter part of the nineteenth century, so Archbishop John Charles McQuaid of Dublin put his imprint on the church for thirty-two years. Serving from 1940 until 1972, McQuaid encouraged a wide range of church building and Catholic charitable organizations but coupled his ministrations with a rigid sexual and theological code. Determined to preserve Ireland from the rapidly moving currents of modernization McQuaid imposed his chaste attitude on newspaper advertisements, editorials, films and film advertising, plays produced in Dublin, and sports and social activities engaged in by young people. McQuaid is noted for his oft-quoted remark upon returning to Ireland from a Vatican council: "Allow me to reassure you no change will worry the tranquility of your Christian lives."[13]

McQuaid was wrong, of course, as neither he nor anyone else could hold back the hands of the clock. Not only was Ireland changing, but the church itself, under the impetus of the Vatican councils, was destined to undergo substantial transformation.

The signs of change in the church actually began as a slow trickle. In the early fifties new Catholic periodicals such as *The Furrow* (1950) and *Doctrine and Life* (1951) began to question whether the principal features of Irish Catholicism—anti-intellectualism, dogmatism, and authoritarianism—would serve in a new Ireland that was in extensive contact with a wider, and obviously more secular, European world. John Kelly, a Jesuit, put the matter rather bluntly: "Too many people in Ireland today are trying to make do with a peasant religion when they are no longer peasants anymore. We are a growing and developing middle-class nation, acquiring a middle-class culture and we must have a religion to fit our needs."[14]

External and internal impulses for change produced a series of intended and unintended consequences. The same generational change that had occurred when de Valera passed the torch to Sean Lemass was also occurring in the church, albeit more slowly. The bishops who had worked their will on Irish moral life and social policy in the 1930s and 1940s were giving way to another generation of clerical leaders who were somewhat more flexible than, say, Archbishop McQuaid.

The self-analysis of the church that was begun by clerics in the 1950s took the form of sociological analyses in which writings on the church and Irish society slowly shifted from being accumulated litanies of purported immoral acts to discussions of the empirical foundations of Irish society and Irish religious life. Concomitant with the shifting sociological perspectives was a changing posture of the church on the role of state intervention. As a more realistic portrait of Irish society emerged—the declining west of Ireland with its desperate poverty, poor health conditions, and ramshackle housing—Irish churchmen began to reverse their antistatist doctrines and to call for more state intervention. This volte-face not only called for increased state activism but criticized the government for lapses in its support of decent economic standards of living.

Notable in terms of the church's changing position was a 1977 pastoral letter, "The Work of Justice," that called for alleviation of the problems of poverty and unemployment. Such a reversal of views reflected the impact of Pope John XXIII, who initiated great changes in the Catholic church through his personal actions, through the Second Vatican Council (1962–1965), and through his encyclical *Mater and magistera* in 1961. The Second Vatican Council examined all doctrines that were characteristic of the tridentine, rigid, and dogmatic church and attempted to define the place of the church in the modern world. The encyclical jettisoned vocationalism and accepted the validity of the state's responsibility in the social welfare sphere. These changes were absorbed by the church in all countries, albeit more slowly in Ireland.

Within the church the position on censorship began to change, at least among the younger clergy. Reviews of literature and films banned in Ireland were published in the early 1960s in *The Furrow*. The approach of some authors, such as Peter Connally and John Kelly, was to ignore the argument about censorship and evaluate the aesthetic or artistic merit of the works. This open confrontation with what Father Connally called a juvenile standard of censorship indicated that moral principles need not be compromised in appreciating and learning from modern literature and film. Brian Lenihan, the minister for justice, liberalized the process of censorship for film in 1964 and for books in 1967. The ban on literature discussing birth control was simply overwhelmed by the avalanche of debate on that topic that was spurred by the Second Vatican Council and by the publication in 1968 of Pope Paul VI's encyclical on birth control, *Humanae vitae*. Virtually every magazine and newspaper in Ireland, to say nothing of television, would have fallen under the ban if it had been applied. Archbishop McQuaid and Bishop Lucey spoke out against the liberalization of censorship, of course, but they represented a view many younger clergy were out of sympathy with.

The government undertook an extensive reform of education during the 1960s, and its efforts transgressed on a theretofore sacrosanct area of church control. Surprisingly the transformation of curriculum, management, and state support and the creation of new schools were remarkably free of the acrimony that would no doubt have ensued had such events occurred in the twenties or thirties. Even the ban on Catholic students' attending the Trinity College was removed in 1970, about which John Whyte notes: "When it is remembered how adamant the Bishops had been, only a few years previously, on the subject of Trinity College, the change in attitude is remarkable. It is perhaps the most striking instance of the new flexibility which the hierarchy has been displaying in recent years."[15]

One of the most concrete symbols of the Catholicity of the Irish Republic was Article 44 of the constitution, which gave the Catholic church a special position in the state. A 1967 report of an all-party committee of the Dáil, charged with a review of the constitution, recommended the elimination of this section. The recommendation was based upon a recognition that the article was especially offensive to the Ulster Protestants and thus exacerbated the differences between the North and the South of Ireland. Contrary to expectations, fulmination was not forthcoming from the hierarchy, and, in fact, Cardinal Conway, the primate of Ireland, commented that he would not shed a tear if that section of the constitution were to be deleted. The bishops concurred with that view, and in December 1972 the constitution was amended. By that time, however, the intensity of the conflict in Northern Ireland was such that the constitutional change did little to soften the utterly intransigent attitude of the Ulster Unionists, but the lack of opposition on the part of the church on a matter that on the face of it would seem to have been central to its traditional position was interesting.

The 1967 report on constitutional reform also raised an issue that confronted church doctrine directly—divorce. The committee argued that the blanket prohibition on divorce was unjust to the Protestant minority in the Republic for whom divorce was not theologically unacceptable. Again, the differences between Northern Ireland and the Republic were raised as the ban of divorce was considered by the Protestants in the North to be evidence of discrimination by a Catholic state against religious minorities. The committee recommended that the constitution be amended to allow divorce for people who had been married in a religion that held that divorce was acceptable.

The church responded quickly and sharply to this suggestion. Divorce, Archbishop McQuaid flatly stated, is contrary to the law of God. Cardinal Conway chose to speak for the Protestant community when he noted that "few of them believe in divorce, still fewer of them want it"[16]—a bold presumption on his part to be sure. The brunt of the church's argument, however, was that allowing divorce for Protestants would rapidly expand to allowing divorce for all people in the Republic, which would result in grave evils and suffering for society. In the late sixties the established view prevailed, but in the ensuing decade the pressure for a divorce law accelerated in three ways. The first was a marked shift in public opinion on the acceptability of such a law, from 73 percent opposed in 1971 to 65 percent in favor in 1977.[17] The second was the rise of women's groups that saw the need for a divorce law to provide rights and legal statutes for separated women who currently exist in a legal limbo. The third development was the recognition by the political parties, such as Fine Gael, that the problem must be confronted. The divorce issue will not disappear, and the church will have to make a choice as to whether to mass its power to preserve the constitutional ban on divorce or to withdraw its opposition and cope with the issue as a private matter between the individual and his or her church.

The expected response of the church to removing the ban on divorce may be inferred from its response to the question of contraception. The 1935 act prohibiting the importation and sale of contraceptives was the backdrop for the developments of the seventies. Although forbidden, the use of contraceptives was in fact increasing in Ireland, and in 1969 a family planning clinic opened in Dublin and distributed contraceptives. The first formal challenge to the law came in 1971 when Senator Mary Robinson and two other senators introduced a bill to facilitate the availability of contraceptives. They argued, as with divorce, that a blanket prohibition penalized those people who had no religious strictures against contraceptives. The Lynch government had little interest in dealing with this thorny problem, and the bill was voted down in the Senate—as was a similar bill in the Dáil in 1972. The redoubtable Archbishop McQuaid spoke out against the bill, noting that it was contrary to church doctrine. McQuaid also indicated the deleterious effects contraception would have on that perennial concern, sexual morality: "Given the proneness of our human nature to evil, given the enticements of bodily satisfaction, given the widespread modern incitement to unchastity, it must be evident that an access, hitherto unlawful, to contraceptive devices will prove a most certain occasion of sin."[18]

The introduction of another such bill in 1973 prompted a strong statement from the church hierarchy, which painted a bleak portrait of the ills that would result in the Republic of Ireland from the availability of contraceptives. Infidelity, illegitimate children, abortion, disease, and the destruction of marriages would prevail, according to the bishops. The concern, stated the bishops, was not the moral question of using contraceptives, as the church had spoken on that matter, but the effect such a law would have on the quality of life in Ireland.

The tentative legislative debate on the matter was abruptly accelerated when the Supreme Court of Ireland declared in 1973 that the pertinent sections of the 1935 act were unconstitutional and legalized the importation of contraceptives.[19] The government had to come to terms with the problem of legalizing contraceptives and their availability and sale. The debate ranged from condemnation of the court's decision and pressure for a complete ban from conservative groups, such as the Irish Family League, to pressure for unrestricted availability of contraceptives from such groups as the Contraceptive Action Programme. The thorniest point for most legislators was that of liberalizing availability but restricting that availability to married couples. In 1974 the coalition government under Liam Cosgrave introduced a bill that legalized the importing and sale of contraceptives but encircled their availability with numerous conditions on licensing, advertising, and sale to unmarried people. The Cosgrave government waffled on the issue and after having introduced the legislation, allowed a free vote to the coalition deputies. The result was an embarrassing defeat in which the prime minister himself voted against the bill.

The debate continued over the next five years, with the bishops' reiterating their position in 1978 on the social damage that would follow from legalization. In that statement, however, the bishops outlined some of the legal difficulties that had to be resolved and thus indicated that they were not in support of the absolute-negative position on a contraception law. In 1979 the Fianna Fáil government introduced a bill drawn up by the then-minister of health, Charles Haughey, who had not as yet become prime minister. The bill was quite restrictive and required a doctor's prescription, limited advertising, and banned abortifacients. The bill was opposed by some Labour and Fine Gael deputies because it was too restrictive, but the bill passed into law in 1979.

Thus another tenet of Catholic doctrine was changed by the state. The church had found the courts, legislators, pressure groups, media, and segments of the public increasingly less willing to accept that murky blend of a liberal state enforcing Catholic doctrine. The church then had shifted its position on the question to attacking the immorality of contraception, and the consequences of the law, but accepting the right of the state to pass laws not in accord with Catholic doctrine.

Thus on a wide spectrum of issues—education, state services, the special position of the church, censorship, divorce, and contraception—the church has been confronted with demands for change. The church has had to cede a great deal of ground on many of these matters or to change its views on a number of them.

The winds of change have not turned the Catholic church in Ireland into a hollow presence as recent surveys indicate high levels of devotion among the people in the Republic. Approximately 90 percent of the people attend Mass at least once a week, and among people in the eighteen-to-thirty age group the figure is 85 percent.[20] The amount of property owned by the church is extensive, and the number of church social agencies, hospitals, and charitable organizations is formidable.

Yet a number of indicators foretell of more pressures yet to come. Since 1970 young people have not turned to the religious life as much as they did in the past. Surveys of young people leaving school indicate that the number considering the religious life declined from 80 percent in 1969 to 46 percent in 1974. Of those considering a vocation, a substantial number rejected or postponed that choice because of the vow of celibacy and the allurement of the secular life.[21] This change in attitude resulted in the number of people choosing a priestly vocation declining from 1,409 in 1966 to 547 in 1974, and in the period from 1971 to 1978 the total number of deaths and departures from the priesthood outnumbered the total of new vocations by 3,587.[22] Identity as Catholic is strong among the Irish as 94 percent proclaim their allegiance to the church, but research on university students indicates a lessening of the bond to traditional Catholicism, structure, and doctrine. Not only is church attendance declining, but traditional church dogma is increasingly discarded on such matters as sex before marriage, contraception, and divorce.

The issues discussed above, and the church's response to them, have a direct bearing on the question of Northern Ireland. A number of changes have been advocated in light of the relationship of the North to the South and the view that Ireland is not only a Catholic country but also a Catholic state. The increasing secular pressures in the Republic could someday be coupled with the need to absorb 1 million Protestants who are not at all receptive to a Catholic state. Sooner or later pluralist pressures accentuated by the process of modernization will force the church to redefine its place in the life of Ireland.

The debate within the church, and between the church and the state, on such matters as birth control and divorce was more than an abstract pas de deux on the relationship between Catholic doctrine and a liberal state. That debate was taking place in the context of rapidly changing mores and values in the realms of sexual behavior and family life. The image of Ireland in the middle of this century as an ascetic sexual wasteland permeated by a church ever watchful for the slightest attention to, to say nothing of pleasure in, sexual matters was substantially true, and it was also true that the Irish repressed the sexual aspect of their lives to a startling degree. In tandem with the rapid economic transformation of Ireland came an equally startling new set of attitudes and behavior regarding sexual and family matters.

Students questioned in 1976 on the morality of sex before marriage felt, by a four-to-one margin, that it was not always wrong, and nearly 60 percent thought contraception was morally acceptable.[23] In a report published in *Magill* in 1978, women respondents not only indicated that they felt that sex outside of marriage was far more common than in the past, but over 60 percent felt that sex outside of marriage was right given emotional commitment.[24]

The indicators of changes in sexual behavior are manifold. The joys, such as they are, of paid-for sex seem to be more in demand. Prostitution was not absent from Ireland in the past, but it definitely has increased in recent years. In 1974, 70 women were arrested and charged with prostitution; in 1976 the number arrested escalated to 273.[25] The indoor version of the street corner, prostitutes available in a massage parlor, has appeared in Dublin and other Irish cities. Not surprisingly the incidence of venereal disease has increased in tandem with changing sexual behavior.

The amount of premarital sex has increased from all indications. The number of illegitimate births increased from 2.4 percent in 1969 to 4.5 percent in 1977, and the number of brides pregnant at the time of marriage rose in twenty years from 12 percent to approximately 24 percent.[26] The number of young Irish women seeking abortions in Great Britain increased from 122 in 1969 to 2,183 in 1977,[27] and certainly the availability of contraceptives implies a greater degree of sexual activity than the statistics indicate.

Thus the church has had to give way not only to changing values but also to changing behavior in that most crucial of realms, sexuality. The church will certainly not wither away in Ireland, but it will never again have the control over state policy and personal behavior that it did in the past.

CONCLUSION

In a rapid kaleidoscopic mix the elements of economic and social transformation swept away de Valera's vision of a bucolic Irish society. Each change—whether in the economic sector, education, or the media, especially the advent of television—interlocked with and accelerated the others. Pillars of the Irish system of values, such as Catholic doctrine and Irish language, were battered by the winds of change, and traditional structures of Irish life— such as the family, the church, the farm, and the school—were shaken by the secular European world. Finally, an inefficient, stagnant, agricultural econ- omy was plummeted into a world of offshore oil drilling, the European Agricultural Guidance and Guarantee Fund, and silicon chips.

Such stresses on a relatively traditional society such as the one that existed in Ireland were not without costs. People committed to de Valera's vision see the years from 1959 to the present as a descent into cheap secularism and the eradication of a distinctive Irish culture; those committed to an Ireland free of parochial provincialism see in the same years an awakening and the advent of a new Ireland proud of its present as well as revering its past. On balance, Ireland has dealt with the stresses in a reasonably successful manner.

NOTES

1. Terence Brown, *Ireland: A Social and Cultural History, 1922–79* (Glasgow: Fontana, 1981), p. 273.

2. Numerous organizations are concerned with promoting Irish, but perhaps the most creative is Gael Linn, founded in 1953, which has used films and games to encourage interest in Irish, has supported creative writing in Irish, and teaches courses in the Irish language.

3. Nollaig O. Gadhra, "Language Report: The Fortunes of Irish 1979," *Eire- Ireland* 15 (1980), p. 129.

4. The bishop of Clonfert, Dr. Thomas Ryan, indicated that he would urge people not to watch Gay Byrne's (the Irish Johnny Carson) "Late Late Show" because one guest had said that on her honeymoon she had not worn a nightgown. The bishop regarded the discussion as "most objectionable."

5. Thomas J. O'Hanlon, *The Irish: Portrait of a People* (London: André Deutsch, 1976), pp. 48–49.

6. Ibid., p. 292.

7. Figures derived from Tony Gray, *The Irish Answer* (London: Heinemann, 1966), p. 235; O'Hanlon, *Irish Portrait*, p. 159; and Brown, *Ireland*, p. 198.

8. Quoted in John H. Whyte, *Church and State in Modern Ireland*, 2d ed. (Totowa, N.J.: Barnes and Noble, 1980), p. 312. This section relies heavily on this superb history.

9. Archbishop Gilmartin of Tuam in 1927, quoted in Whyte, *Church and State,* p. 25.

10. Whyte, *Church and State,* p. 305.

11. Ibid., p. 307.

12. Ibid., p. 424.

13. ibid., p. 690.

14. Quoted in Brown, *Ireland,* p. 295.

15. Whyte, *Church and State,* p. 343.

16. Quoted in ibid., p. 348.

17. Ibid., p. 403.

18. Quoted in ibid., p. 406.

19. The case involved one Mary McGee, who would have been in grave danger if she had become pregnant. She could not take the pill, and the rhythm method was too unreliable, so she had to use contraceptives imported from Great Britain. The law prevented the importation, but the Supreme Court disallowed the law on the grounds that married couples had a right to privacy in sexual matters and the 1935 act prohibiting contraceptives violated that right.

20. Whyte, *Church and State,* p. 382, although Brown (*Ireland,* p. 302) reports only 75 percent in the younger age bracket.

21. Report of research by Tom Inglis, "Decline in Number of Priests and Religious in Ireland," *Doctrine and Life* 30 (February 1979), pp. 79–98, cited in Brown, *Ireland,* p. 302.

22. Brown, *Ireland,* p. 301, and Whyte, *Church and State,* p. 383.

23. Brown, *Ireland,* p. 303, citing research by Tom Inglis on university students.

24. "The Sexual Explosion," *Magill* (April 1978), pp. 11–14.

25. William G. Shade, "Strains of Modernization: The Republic of Ireland under Lemass and Lynch," *Eire-Ireland* 14 (Spring 1979), p. 36.

26. Whyte, *Church and State,* p. 383, and Shade, "Strains of Modernization," p. 38.

27. Whyte, *Church and State,* p. 384.

6

Political Structure and Culture

The government of Ireland is a republic and is parliamentary in form, with the party achieving a majority of seats in an election forming a cabinet and undertaking to rule for up to five years. If no party gains an absolute majority, then either a minority government is formed or a coalition with enough votes to assume control of the cabinet is forged, a formula not unlike that of Great Britain and other parliamentary democracies but with elements and flavors that are distinctly Irish. The blend of parliamentary institutions and Irish political values and process produces a system of government that reflects the historical and cultural dynamics that have shaped modern Ireland.

THE POLITICAL CULTURE

Irish political culture is the unique outgrowth of three significant and mutually reinforcing forces of the twentieth century—nationalism, Irish Catholicism, and the influence of Great Britain.[1] Moreover, its political culture illustrates the ongoing and irreversible impact of the process of modernization.

The growth of nationalism in Ireland culminated in the war for independence from 1919 to 1921 under the aegis of Sinn Féin. The dominant claims of Irish nationalism on the Irish mind were Catholicism, Gaelic identity, and political autonomy from Britain, and the growth of this form of nationalism widened and exacerbated the split between the two principal segments of Irish society. The Irish-Ireland movement's commitment to the Celtic Catholic heritage helped to widen the gap between the native Irish and the Protestant ascendancy. The pervasive Catholicity of the nationalist movement stood in distinct contrast to the Protestant faith of the ascendancy. The Sinn Féin commitment to an independent republic of Ireland was contrary to ascendancy commitment to the Union. Thus the somewhat exclusive version of Sinn Féin nationalism tended to intensify the differences between Irish Catholic nationalists and Anglo-Protestant unionists. Clearly nationalism is not responsible for the chasm between the two communities; rather, the Irish nationalism was a reaction to the historical dominance, land confiscation, and religious oppression that had stimulated the polarization. However, the inclusive vision of Wolfe Tone's Irish nationalism shifted to a more exclusive version that included an emphasis on the Celtic and Catholic girders of the Irish cultural structure.

The nationalism that had exacerbated the split between the Anglo and the Irish communities itself split in 1921 over the question of the Anglo-Irish treaty. The question as to whether the treaty should be accepted polarized Sinn Féin into protreaty and antitreaty wings, which ultimately took the form of opposing political parties. Thus the partisan dimension of Irish electoral competition is rooted in the nationalist movement's debate over the strategy of obtaining the objective of an independent Ireland. The more uncompromising antitreaty position, that of de Valera, was itself compromised when de Valera agreed to enter the Free State Dáil in 1927. The people who felt that de Valera had "sold out" to the Free State by accepting partition remained faithful to their position of "pure" nationalism and provided the foundation for the position of the Irish Republican Army. Thus the nationalism of the Sinn Féin movement has continued to be influential with respect to the situation in Northern Ireland.

The intense nationalism of the independence movement might have matured into a less frantic version of pride in Ireland's independence and Celtic cultural destiny had partition not occurred. But the ultimate promise of Irish nationalism was not fulfilled, and it is often advantageous for politicians to fuel the flames of nationalism by reminding the people of Ireland of the problem of Northern Ireland. The effect is to perpetuate a lingering attitude among the Irish that is conducive to mistrust and hostility toward Britain. Politicians in the Republic of Ireland have generally been uncertain about the real strength of Anglophobia, but it remains a subdued yet important element in the political culture of Ireland.

The nationalist sentiment has also contributed to ambivalent governmental relationships with Great Britain. There is hardly any advantage for politicians in stressing the virtue of close ties with Britain, however pragmatic or necessary given the substantial intercourse between the two countries. Irish condemnation of historical British oppression, however rhetorical, is worth more politically as long as Ireland remains partitioned and Irish memories retain their enormous capacity for citing a cascade of British excesses in Ireland. The economic realities of the Irish-British link have not been sufficient to mute the nationalist vision of Irish history.

The nationalist component of Irish political culture has politicized the issue of the Irish language. It is certainly not surprising that Sinn Féin nationalism should elevate the Irish language to a position of importance in the affirmation of the Celtic culture.

Thus Irish nationalism has contributed in the past to a polarization of the two broad communities on the island, to the foundations of electoral partisanship within the Sinn Féin movement, to the language question, and to the preservation of the true flame of the nationalism of 1916.

Catholicism, the second important element of the Irish political culture, pervades the Republic of Ireland. Historically the faith became associated with the nationalist movement and with the Irish-Ireland cultural revival. As such, religion and the church became a focal point in the political development of Ireland as well as an important part of the private sphere of personal convictions. The political influence of Catholic values in the past and the present has been and is substantial. The blending of Irish political and theological creeds, to say nothing of emigration, is nowhere more evident than in the altar mosaic in Galway Cathedral, which displays a large portrait of Jesus and two smaller portraits, one of Patrick Pearse and the other of John F. Kennedy.

The Irish version of Catholicism was cultivated in relative isolation from the ebb and flow of theological currents in Europe and North America. Thus the Irish church remained free of secular intellectual influences and radicalism, which were manifest in, for example, liberation theology. Rather Manichaean and puritanical, the Irish Catholic church has historically stressed the inviolability of established dogma and practice, the purity of the soul, the degradation of the flesh, the authority of the hierarchy, and the value of devotional expressions.

The conservatism of Irish Catholicism has had the historical impact of diminishing attempts to generate radical or socialist doctrines in the labor movement or elsewhere. The leftist movements that did spring up were battered by the conservatism of Irish society and condemnation by the Catholic hierarchy.

The agenda of political and social issues in Irish politics has been shaped by the Catholicity of the people and by the influence of the hierarchy. The constitutional ban on divorce, abortion, and contraception; support for censorship; and control of education are particularly notable manifestations of the Catholic church's influence.

The influence of Britain upon Ireland is so extensive as to defy brief description. The impact upon the political culture has been to infuse Irish political attitudes with British ideas, institutions, and processes even though the Irish were either denying that influence or explicitly rejecting it.

Four manifestations of the British influence are especially notable, the first being language. English is the language of Ireland and has been dominant since the latter part of the nineteenth century. Although Irish is still spoken in the western fringes, and is revered as a manifestation of the distinctly Gaelic heritage of Ireland, Irish is clearly not the language of everyday use in business, education, government, science, or any other sphere of life. The widespread use of English and geographical propinquity contribute to the second manifestation of British influence, the extensive interaction between the two countries. British television is watched in the eastern part of Ireland; books, newspapers, and magazines from Great Britain abound in all parts of Ireland. The massive emigration of Irish workers to Britain creates a constant flow of people between the two countries for personal reasons. The extensive commerce between the two creates another conduit of influence, to say nothing of the professional interactions in law, medicine, architecture, education, and the sciences.

The third type of British influence is the structure and style of the government of Ireland. When the Irish Free State was created in 1922 after ratification of the 1921 treaty, the structure adopted was parliamentary government, and the process of government resembled that of Ireland's neighbor. The British civil service model and pattern of local government were completely absorbed. The inherent legitimacy of such institutions in the Irish political culture is indicated by the acceptance of the Free State government by most of the Irish people, despite the split in the nationalist movement and the rejection of that government by no less a figure than de Valera.

The economic relationship of Great Britain and Ireland has always been extensive and interdependent. When "the economic war" broke out between

Ireland and Great Britain in the 1930s, the exports from Ireland dropped by three-fifths, and the imports to Ireland dropped by one-half. Even since Ireland's entrance into the European Economic Community in 1973, Great Britain has remained Ireland's largest trading partner.

Political, cultural, and economic domination of Ireland by Great Britain isolated Ireland from extensive contact with the Continent. Thus the influence of Great Britain even today is quite strong. Irish nationalism, especially some of the more virulent IRA strains, was and is substantially anti-British, yet the country continues to reflect the coloration of 700 years of the Union Jack over Ireland.

THE GOVERNMENT

Parliamentary government has taken three forms in modern Irish history. The first was the revolutionary Dáil Éireann set up in 1919, the embodiment of the republic declared by the rebels of 1916. The second manifestation of parliamentary government was the Free State Constitution, drafted in accord with the 1921 treaty in 1922 and lasting until 1937. The current structure of Irish government is embodied in the new constitution created under de Valera and put into effect in 1937. This constitution not only defines the formal relationships of the components of government but also is a reflection of the political culture and values of Ireland—a tenuous blend of Irish Catholicism and Western liberal democracy.

De Valera, after ascending to power in 1932, began to shear the 1922 constitution of the elements he found offensive. Legislation introduced in 1932 removed the oath of allegiance to the crown and cropped the powers of the governor general; 1933 saw the end of the right of appeal from Irish courts to the Privy Council in London. In 1936 de Valera abolished the Senate of the Free State Constitution. In the same year the abdication crisis in Great Britain provided de Valera with the opportunity to legislate the elimination of references to the king and governor general in the Free State Constitution—but retaining reference to the king in connection with Commonwealth affairs.

By 1936 the Free State Constitution was in tatters as it had been amended repeatedly in four years. De Valera, however, planned to introduce a new constitution. His efforts were concluded in 1937, and the new constitution, called Bunracht na hÉireann (Constitution of Ireland), was approved by the Free State Dáil in June of that year, approved by a popular plebiscite in July, and went into effect in December. The new constitution blended structures and values that were a manifestation of de Valera's personal vision of Ireland. Committed as he was to liberal democracy, de Valera also was committed to Catholicism and a reunited Ireland.

The document identified Ireland as a "sovereign, independent, democratic state" (Article 5) and stated that sovereignty was rooted in the people of Ireland. In all essential forms the country was a republic, but de Valera refrained from that explicit designation so as to not exclude the possibility that Northern Ireland could again become part of Ireland. A complete break with the Commonwealth of Nations, de Valera assumed, would diminish the possibility of eliminating partition.

The careful abstention from the use of the word "republic" did not preclude, however, a constitutional claim to sovereignty over all of Ireland. This claim is circumscribed by the declaration that the state's laws will not have force in Northern Ireland "pending the re-integration of the national territory" (Article 3). The claim may have strength from moral and historical points of view, but it is less than persuasive from a constitutional-law point of view.[2]

In principle the broad structure of government is liberal—being, of course, a democracy with free elections and majority rule. The civil rights of citizens, free speech and association, habeas corpus, and freedom from discrimination are guaranteed in Article 40.

Elements of Catholic thought pervade the constitution as well, most notably in Articles 41, 42, 43, and 44. The family is defined as the natural, primary, and fundamental unit of society in Article 41 and is seen as antecedent to positive law rooted, as it is in Catholic doctrine, in the natural law. The institution of marriage is protected to the degree that no law can be passed that allows for divorce. Article 42 defines the family as the educator of the child, and Article 43 grants the right to property as a "natural right" and forbids any law to abolish private property. Article 44 was the most explicit in recognizing the state's Catholic nature, yet at the same time de Valera tried to avoid discriminating against other religions and to ensure that were Ireland united and a large group of Protestants incorporated into the state, all religious beliefs would be respected. The result was a prolix mixture of primacy and toleration that stated:

> The State recognizes the special position of the Holy Catholic Apostolic and Roman Catholic Church as guardian of the faith professed by the great majority of the citizens. The State also recognizes the Church of Ireland, the Presbyterian Church in Ireland, the Methodist Church in Ireland, the Religious Society of Friends in Ireland, as well as the Jewish Congregations and the other religious denominations existing in Ireland at the date of the coming into operation of this constitution.[3]

In addition freedom of conscience is protected, and no religion is to be endowed by the state. This article remained controversial until its elimination in 1972, which was prompted in part by the troubles in Northern Ireland. Critics argued that it only exacerbated the Protestant view that Ireland was a Catholic state that had little toleration for other beliefs and constitutionally enshrined the Catholic church in a special position.

The Directive Principles of Social Policy included in Article 45 of the constitution reflect the social values that were to undergird the state but are not enforceable in law. De Valera read widely on Catholic doctrine and consulted Father John Charles McQuaid who provided de Valera with the then-current documents and ideas on Catholic social teaching, such as Leo XIII's *Rerum novarum* and Pius XI's *Quadragesimo anno*. Included in Article 45 are mandates to the state to have a just and charitable social order, to have concern for the disadvantaged, and to protect private property.

The composition of the Senate in the new constitution was also a reflection of the vocational emphasis in Catholic thought during the 1930s. The Senate was to be composed of representatives of the vocational sectors of society rather than partisan groups. Culture and education, agriculture, labor, business, and public administration were allotted seats in the new chamber. This scheme never worked as planned, and partisan competition quickly supplanted the apolitical innovation of vocational voices.

The constitution was hailed by Cardinal MacRory as a "great Christian document" in 1937.[4] The provisions, from the Preamble, which states that all authority flows from God, to the Directive Principles of Social Policy, indicate that Cardinal MacRory could have used the term *Catholic* document. The constitution of 1937, of course, did not make the Irish people Catholic, but it came as far as liberalism would stretch toward making the Irish state Catholic.

The structure of government created by the 1937 constitution has at its head a president (uachtarán). Elected by popular vote for a seven-year term, the president may be reelected only once. For the most part a figurehead, the president appoints the prime minister and may convene the Parliament (Oireachtas) composed of the Assembly (Dáil) and the Senate (Seanád).

The center of power, however, is in the cabinet, which is the policymaking body. The cabinet consists of the prime minister (taoiseach), deputy prime minister (tanaiste), and between seven and fifteen party leaders who are appointed to various ministries by the prime minister. A majority party in the Dáil, of course, has the claim on the right to rule, and the president "invites" the leader of the majority party to form a government. If no party has a clear majority, attempts are made to form a coalition of parties, which then take on the responsibility of forming a government. The cabinet members are at once party leaders and ministers for various government departments such as Foreign Affairs; Health and Social Welfare; Agriculture; Fisheries and Forestry; Defence; Finance and Public Service; Industry, Commerce and Tourism; Justice; Posts and Telecommunications and Transport; Irish Speaking Affairs; Education; Environment; Labour; and Energy.

The general relationship of the components of the Irish government is one of subordination. The cabinet is subordinate to the prime minister; the Dáil is subordinate to the cabinet. The Seanád, finally, is secondary to the Dáil. The structure of the Dáil is such that debate is usually a forum to gain local publicity while strong party discipline ensures that the cabinet will have its way when a vote comes on legislation. Checks on the government ministers, such as the "question time," during which parliamentary members are free to challenge the ministers on the conduct of government, all too often become a capricious exercise in nit-picking on local matters, such as why mail delivery was delayed in Mayo. The members of the Seanád and Dáil are not equipped with the staff or the resources (offices, library, clerical help) to be able to challenge the government in any effective way. The salary is not very large, and a member of the Irish Parliament would envy the resources of a state legislator in the United States, to say nothing of a member of the U.S. House or Senate. The agenda for legislation is controlled by the cabinet, and the introduction of private bills is usually a tactic to gain publicity as they have no chance of passing in the Dáil. The structure of the Dáil is such that there is no strong committee system, and thus no committee chairmen to provide the kind of legislative power exerted in the U.S. Congress.

If the Dáil is a weak chamber in comparison to the cabinet, the Seanád is more pallid still. The debates in the Seanád, while drawing more media attention in recent years, essentially remain ignored by the ministers. The Seanád does serve, however, as a forum for bringing attention to new issues; it has also been a haven for members of the Dáil who have lost elections or for other party faithful. More important is the use of the Seanád by the parties as a place to groom young politicians before they stand for election to the Dáil.

THE ELECTORAL SYSTEM

The electoral system of Ireland is a form of proportional representation, which, although rarely used elsewhere, has been very satisfactory to the Irish voter. Under this system the constituencies have more than one representative; six have as many as five TDs (teachtaí Dála; "members of the Dáil"), ten have four, and twenty-six have three. The size of the constituency varies, and each TD is to represent no fewer than 20,000 and no more than 30,000 of the population.[5]

The selection of candidates is essentially the prerogative of the local party organization, which generally guards it jealously. In the 1977 election the head of the Fianna Fáil, Jack Lynch, was able to add candidates to the selections of the local party organizations, and Garrett FitzGerald did this in 1981 in the Fine Gael Party. This practice is becoming more common and indicates a greater degree of central party control over the local party organizations.

The parties put forth more candidates than there are seats, so members of a particular party are running against each other as well as against opposition-party candidates. The number that is to run in a given constituency is determined by each national party's leadership. Not all seats are contested by the Labour Party and the minor parties, but Fine Gael and Fianna Fáil usually contest virtually all the seats. Concerning the selection between its own candidates, the party does not attempt to guide the voters. Election material urges the people to vote for the candidate of their choice within the party.

The actual voting system is more complicated to explain than to operate. The central feature is the ability of the voter to rank-order his or her preference for the candidates. All the valid votes for a district are counted, and the "quota" necessary for election is determined.[6] The candidates who achieve the quota are declared elected. If the number meeting the quota is less than the number of seats, then the "surplus" votes of the elected candidates are transferred to the other candidates and added to their totals.

The proportional representation system has been praised by some people as being capable of registering voters' preferences with greater sensitivity than other electoral systems. Critics have suggested that it creates splinter parties and an unstable government. The Irish experience has tended to affirm the view of proponents of the system and to confute its critics. The record shows that the Irish government has been stable as Fianna Fáil has dominated the government of Ireland since 1932, ruling for thirty-eight of forty-nine years.

In two periods, 1932 to 1948 and 1957 to 1973, Fianna Fáil has enjoyed sixteen years of unbroken rule. As Basil Chubb has noted, "clearly Ireland has not had unstable government. 'Stagnant' might sometimes have been a more appropriate term."[7] The Irish system has not had the effect of multiplying the number of parties as the rise and fall of minor parties has been generated by periodic discontent with the major parties, which means that the minor parties disappear rapidly.

The duty of the TD to the constituents includes everything from attending wakes, weddings, and retirement parties to solving problems for his or her supporters on matters concerning pensions, land, licenses, and jobs. Although close ties do exist between the TD and constituents, the TD is also expected to be loyal to the party of which he or she is a candidate. Not only does a nomination come from a local party convention, but it must be approved by the national executive of the party, and the candidate is compelled to sign an oath of loyalty and obedience to the party.

The voters in Ireland have powerful parochial loyalties. The successful candidates cultivate that loyalty and reinforce it with constituent service. Ireland is a small country, and the TD returns to his or her constituency regularly to perform the rituals that ensure electoral success.[8] The TDs who perform these services well over time gain the electoral loyalty of the voters and are more likely to be reelected. Thus seniority and service are a difficult combination to defeat at the polls. If the TD is the son or nephew of a man who served in the rebellion in the years 1916 to 1921, this fact increases all the more his chances of being elected or reelected. A final patina adding luster to the candidate would be to have achieved some reputation in sport. The past few prime ministers offer instructive examples of these attributes. Garrett FitzGerald, prime minister in 1981 and at the present, is the son of Desmond FitzGerald, minister for foreign affairs in the Cosgrave government from 1922 to 1932. The former prime minister, Charles Haughey, is the son of a prominent IRA man and son-in-law of Sean Lemass, prime minister from 1959 to 1966. Lemass's successor, John Lynch, was an all-Ireland hurling star from Cork, and Lynch's successor, Liam Cosgrave, is the son of William Cosgrave who headed the Free State government from 1922 to 1932.

The attitude of the Irish voter toward the members of the Dáil is aptly summed up by Brian Farrell:

> Attitudes toward central secular authority swing from continuous demands for grants, services and special treatment for local needs to equally vociferous resistance to what is seen as interference from Dublin. There is a curious casual treatment of office holders reflecting this ambiguity; their power is recognized by a steady stream of supplicants seeking assistance while any aloofness, even a human demand for privacy, is quickly criticized. Moreover in a small homogeneous community the interest in political leaders is easily transferred into personal gossip that can have a reductive effect.[9]

POLITICAL PARTIES

Political allegiance in Ireland, beyond the individual TD, is, of course, to the major political parties. Since the creation of the Irish Free State in 1922, three parties have continually held the loyalty of the electorate, and numerous others have arisen and disappeared. The dominant party is Fianna Fáil, and the role of the opposition party has fallen to Fine Gael. In addition the Labour Party has persisted, though with fewer supporters than the other two parties. The two major political parties in Ireland have their roots in the nationalist movement Sinn Féin, but developments after the treaty of 1921 gave the Irish parties particular characteristics that are somewhat different from those of the social-class-based parties of Western Europe.

Fianna Fáil

Fianna Fáil, the dominant party, has its roots in the defeated wing of Sinn Féin after the civil war of 1923. The defeat of the antitreaty forces did not eliminate that group as a political presence, and in an election in August of 1923 Sinn Féin, under adverse circumstances, achieved forty-four seats. Adhering to the policy of abstention, these representatives did not take their seats as they viewed the Free State government to be illegitimate. Remaining in the shadows of government, however, prevented Sinn Féin from exercising any power other than condemnation. The party's efforts to set up parallel governmental institutions, as had been done by Sinn Féin in 1918, failed. Eventually realists, such as de Valera, recognized that the political wilderness was not the place to be. As the funds and organization of Sinn Féin began to deteriorate, de Valera attempted to lead the Sinn Féin party toward the position of accepting the Free State Dáil while rejecting the oath of allegiance to the crown. The party split on this issue, and in May of 1926 de Valera took his followers out of Sinn Féin and formed Fianna Fáil.

Fianna Fáil founded a newspaper, *The Irish Press*, and consistently developed its organization at the grass-roots level. The combination of Fianna Fáil's growing strength and the conservative, almost inert, policies of the Cosgrave government put Fianna Fáil into power in 1932. The party was to rule without interruption from 1932 to 1948. During this period de Valera's polices on the constitution, the economic war, and neutrality fixed Fianna Fáil as the dominant party in Irish politics, though the ineptness of its opponents was no small help.

After World War II Fianna Fáil began to show signs of old age and an absence of initiative on problems facing Ireland. Challenged by a weak opposition, the position of the party appeared to be that of intolerance and insensitivity to economic decay, and there were hints of corruption. In 1957 de Valera formed his last government, the eighth in twenty-five years, but he resigned two years later and turned over the leadership to Sean Lemass.

Lemass was more receptive to the younger members of Fianna Fáil who had begun to be active in the party after the war. The party had, in fact, a form of intergenerational conflict in the 1950s as de Valera kept the leadership in the hands of the aging chieftains of the revolution. Lemass had reorganized the party from 1954 to 1957 and opened positions to such men as Charles Haughey and Dr. Patrick J. Hillary, and Lemass's resignation from leadership in 1966 provoked a battle within Fianna Fáil among the leaders who had emerged during the prior decade. Charles Haughey, a representative of the "new" entrepreneurial leaders; George Colley, a traditionalist; Neil Blaney, a republican; and Jack Lynch all sought the leadership. Each candidate, except Lynch, was unacceptable to some segment of the Fianna Fáil TDs, so Lynch emerged as the new leader of the party, defeating Colley after the withdrawal of Blaney and Haughey. Lynch led the party in a low-key manner but was caught up in the impact of the violence in Northern Ireland. The leadership of Fianna Fáil was shattered by these events as cabinet members were arrested and tried on charges of arms smuggling to the North. Fianna Fáil at this point went through a crisis that would cause most governments to fall.

Lynch responded to the crisis with a powerful declaration on August 13, 1969, and appointed Charles Haughey, the minister of finance, to head a committee designed to revamp the Irish army, to administer relief funds, and to monitor events in Ulster. This committee set up accounts to disburse money, the manner and amount to be determined by the minister of finance, to provide aid for the victims of the violence. The money eventually was channeled to the North mostly for the purpose of assisting the IRA; little went to the relief of victims. Coupled with the provision of money was an attempt to bring arms into the Republic of Ireland. Unsuccessful efforts were made in London and the United States to obtain guns, but eventually $35,000's worth of machine guns, rifles, grenades, pistols, and ammunition was purchased on the Continent, and arrangements were made to ship the material to Dublin. Although the shipment was called off, the ministers involved in arranging and paying for the arms were arrested and charged with illegally smuggling arms into Ireland.

Haughey as well as Neil Blaney, minister of agriculture, and Kevin Boland, minister of local government, were tried in August of 1970 and acquitted. The prosecution argued that the disbursement of funds and the purchase and importation of arms were illegal, and the defense contended that the cabinet members had acted within their authority. Haughey argued that he was unaware that the funds would be abused and that the provision of arms was a form of relief. The prime minister, Lynch, maintained that he was unaware that members of his cabinet were engaged in the illegal importation of arms.

The episode is a morass of conflicting testimony and evidence, and it is still difficult to obtain a clear portrait of the events. The result, however, was the resignation of Boland, not only as a minister of the government but also from the Fianna Fáil Party. Haughey returned to the back benches to begin his slow climb back to leadership, which culminated in his election as prime minister in 1980 and again in 1982. The arms trial crisis illustrates the degree to which politics in the Republic of Ireland is never totally free of the events and conditions in Northern Ireland.

As a result of the election of 1973 Fianna Fáil became the opposition party. The outcome of the election revealed not so much the loss of electoral support, as the election was quite close, but rather, the threat of a well-organized opposition, something Fianna Fáil had rarely faced. Lynch set out to revitalize the party by adopting a professional approach to organization, the recruitment of young people, and improved relationships with the press.[10]

The sweeping victory of Fianna Fáil in 1977 brought about another change in the leadership as Lynch, who had been on top since 1966, began to be seen as unable to handle the intractable problems of Northern Ireland

and economic growth. In 1980 he stepped down under the pressure of a back-bench revolt within the party, and Charles Haughey was chosen to head Fianna Fáil. In 1981, when a general election was called, Fianna Fáil again went into opposition as a Fine Gael–Labour coalition formed a government. Haughey, however, returned to power in 1982, only to be ousted later the same year. Haughey has retained the leadership of Fianna Fáil despite a sharp challenge from a segment of the party that would prefer a new leader. It remains to be seen if his leadership will be as effective as those of Lemass and Lynch.

The support for Fianna Fáil in the years after 1932 was essentially that of those people who had given their support to Sinn Féin: the areas in the west and south of the Republic of Ireland, which were relatively poor and had a relatively high rate of emigration. These areas also had a greater proportion of Irish speakers. By the forties Fianna Fáil had increased its support to include all sectors of Ireland and all social classes. In a survey of party preference by occupational class taken in 1969, Fianna Fáil was chosen by 45 percent of the middle class, 42 percent of the working class, and 53 percent of the small farmers.[11]

Fianna Fáil has always been able to generate support among the younger voters. In 1977 the combination of a direct appeal to young voters, both in recruitment and in electoral issues, resulted in 49 percent of the people from eighteen to thirty-four indicating their support of Fianna Fáil.[12]

As the dominant party of Ireland for so many years, Fianna Fáil has been able to accumulate support through the distribution of patronage and favors and thus has a distinct advantage over the opposition parties. Moreover, people who wish to seek a future in politics find the potential for reaching positions of power much greater in a party in which ruling is the tradition and opposition only an intermittent role.

Fine Gael

The role of almost permanent opposition in Ireland has fallen to the party that ruled for a decade after the creation of the Irish Free State, Cumann na nGaedheal. When the split occurred in Sinn Féin, the leadership of the protreaty side was in the hands of Arthur Griffith and Michael Collins. However, both died in 1922, and leadership passed to William T. Cosgrave. At that point the protreaty group was not a political party, but by 1923 the formal trappings of party structure had been adopted, and the group took the name Cumann na nGaedheal. Thus Cosgrave set out to restore order after the civil war, disband the army, inspire confidence in the Free State government, and manage the economy. Cosgrave's success was not inconsiderable given the difficulties, but problems such as those over the Boundary Commission damaged the support of Cumann na nGaedheal among voters who still felt strongly about partition.

In the first 1927 election Cumann na nGaedheal's number of seats dropped from sixty-three to forty-seven, and the minor parties and independents won sixty-two seats. The fact that the Fianna Fáil members refused to sit in the Dáil allowed Cosgrave to continue to rule, but when the vice-president, Kevin O'Higgins, was assassinated legislation was passed that forced the Fianna

Fáil representatives to take their seats; that is, it legitimized them even against their will. Unable to govern with the Dáil so fragmented, Cosgrave called another election in 1927 in which the voters expressed their clear preference for either Cumann na nGaedheal or Fianna Fáil, and the two parties won sixty-two and fifty-seven seats, respectively. The greatest loss was suffered by the minor parties, which found the expense of contesting another election too great and their appeal as alternatives to Cumann na nGaedheal stolen by Fianna Fáil. Although capable of ruling until 1932, Cosgrave was incapable of doing any more than continuing the same policies, which, in 1932, appeared inert and lifeless to the electorate.

The 1932 election put Cumann na nGaedheal in the role of opposition, and the Blue Shirt episode caused a further deterioration in support for Cumann na nGaedheal, now called Fine Gael. The party was hollow in the 1930s— weak in organization, leadership, and ideas. The new leadership of Richard Mulcahey did little to strengthen the party, and in 1944 Fine Gael won only thirty seats and did not even contest all the constituencies.

The 1948 election produced a government of all parties that were in opposition to Fianna Fáil. Although the stimulus for this coalition had come from the new Clann na Publachta Party, Fine Gael, with thirty-one seats, was still the largest opposition party and provided the new prime minister, John A. Costello. Although Fianna Fáil went back into power from 1951 to 1954, Fine Gael won forty seats in 1951 and fifty seats in 1954. In combination with the Labour and the Farmers parties, Fine Gael was able to rule again from 1954 to 1957 and be the dominant party in that coalition. Thus a party that was clearly slipping away in 1944 was charged with ruling responsibility for six years out of twelve after the end of World War II.

The 1957 election brought a drop in the number of Fine Gael's seats to forty. Fine Gael fell upon hard times during the 1960s as its only viable partner in a coalition against Fianna Fáil, Labour, decided to opt for an independent strategy and not run in tandem with Fine Gael. Shut out from the possibility of governing, Fine Gael appeared to be destined to spend its new strength in the frustration of opposition. Even though Fine Gael gained ten seats in the elections from 1951 to 1969 (from forty to fifty), the growth did not diminish the strength of Fianna Fáil but came at the expense of the minor parties and independent candidates.

Some Fine Gael members recognized that the image of the party was rather negative and conservative. In response to the economic growth generated by Fianna Fáil in the 1960s, Fine Gael responded with a program entitled "the just society." Accepted in 1965 by the party convention, the program was an attempt to present alternative policies of economic and social change to the voters. The program also precipitated a split between the more con- servative leadership, attuned to the party's traditional middle class and ag- ricultural support, and the younger, more liberal members who wished the party to present a positive alternative to Fianna Fáil.

In 1973 Fine Gael and Labour defeated Fianna Fáil and took power. The crucial elements in the victory of the coalition were the agreement on a common policy, the Fourteen Point Program, and the discipline of the voters in giving their second-preference votes to the partner party in the coalition.

The number of Fine Gael voters' giving their second-preference votes to Labour, and vice versa, was substantial and had the effect of increasing the number of seats of both parties, despite the fact that Fianna Fáil actually increased its percentage of the total vote.[13]

Fine Gael held power from 1973 until 1977 as the senior partner of a coalition government. The party had the political initiative and the power of the ministries. True to its history of ramshackle organization and conservative policies, the party did not take the opportunity to reorganize internally and retained the paternalistic autonomy of the TDs, a tendency toward authoritarianism, and cautious policies. Liam Cosgrave was not a dynamic leader and embodied a conservative style toward party and policy. While the coalition was governing, Fianna Fáil was girding for the next election with substantial changes in organization and style under Jack Lynch. Fine Gael let the opportunity to do the same slip away while in power, so when Cosgrave called for an election in 1977, his own party was less prepared to campaign than the opposition was.

Fine Gael again returned to opposition as Fianna Fáil won a landslide vote, increasing the number of that party's seats to eighty-four while Fine Gael dropped to forty-three and Labour lost two seats, which left that party with seventeen seats. Fianna Fáil had garnered over 50 percent of the total vote, and the damage to Fine Gael was considerable. Three ministers in the government lost their seats, and eighteen Fine Gael TDs were defeated.

The effect of the election on Fine Gael was dramatic. Liam Cosgrave resigned as leader, and after a brief flurry of candidates the party settled on Garrett FitzGerald, who had served as foreign minister in the 1973–1977 coalition government. FitzGerald had learned well from the example of Fianna Fáil and immediately began to restructure Fine Gael from top to bottom. Recognizing that Fianna Fáil had captured the young voters through recruitment and campaign promises, FitzGerald began to cultivate the younger voters in the electorate and to bring the younger TDs in Fine Gael into leadership positions. FitzGerald appointed a new national organizer, a press officer, and a youth officer. Examining the party through a poll he had commissioned, FitzGerald began the delicate task of trying to regain the party's traditional support from more conservative followers and at the same time, following his own somewhat more liberal inclinations, to build a new base of support among the young and the liberals. FitzGerald, in a symbolic gesture, even moved the Fine Gael headquarters in Dublin. FitzGerald's intellectual qualities, character, and leadership not only helped to prevent Fine Gael from sinking into a demoralized apathy but, in fact, molded the party into a more competitive, aggressive, and professional political opponent to Fianna Fáil.

The election of 1981 revealed the degree to which FitzGerald had succeeded. The weakness of Fianna Fáil and the strength of the reborn Fine Gael produced the largest victory for Fine Gael in its history up to that point. Fine Gael took support not only from Fianna Fáil, but also from Labour, and increased its number of seats from forty-three to sixty-five. Labour slipped to fifteen seats, and Fianna Fáil dropped to seventy-eight. FitzGerald formed a government with the support of Labour, giving that party four cabinet positions out of fifteen. Holding power only nine months, the FitzGerald government fell from power when it presented an austere budget in early 1982. The party lost only two seats in the election and was in a strong position when yet another election was called for November of 1982. Fine Gael reaped the largest number of seats in its history, seventy, only five fewer than Fianna Fáil. This outcome led to another Fine Gael–Labour coalition government under FitzGerald.

Support for Fine Gael has traditionally been hard to identify, and, like Fianna Fáil, its support has not been drawn from a single social base. Although seen as a middle-class party supported by bankers, professionals, and large farmers, Fine Gael has not drawn as much support from the middle class as Fianna Fáil has. Essentially, the support for Fine Gael, from the time the party was Cumann na nGaedheal, has come from people from all regions of Ireland and all classes who were not giving their support to Fianna Fáil, Labour, Farmers, or other parties. Over the years the base of Fine Gael's support did not solidify around the middle class and the larger farmers, but like Fianna Fáil, support is spread across all social classes with 20 percent of the middle class, 46 percent of the large farmers, and 26 percent of the small farmers expressing their preference for Fine Gael in 1969.[14] FitzGerald managed in 1981 to increase the heterogeneous support for Fine Gael by drawing on disaffected voters who had supported Fianna Fáil in 1977.

Labour

The Labour Party, the third of the major Irish parties, is unique in that it did not originate in the Sinn Féin movement, though that fact is a mixed blessing. Founded in 1912 as an adjunct of the Irish Congress of Trade Unions, the party was rather exclusive in limiting its membership to union members. In choosing to create a political arm, the unions had to confront what then was the crucial political question—home rule. Recognizing that worker solidarity was supposed to transcend local loyalties, the party leaders also recognized that Belfast industrial workers were bitterly opposed to home rule and intensely loyal to the Orange Order. The Labour Party took no stand on home rule in order to preserve the illusion of worker unity, North and South. Despite James Connolly's participation in the 1916 rising, the Labour Party was outside the enormous wave of support that was building behind Sinn Féin. Preservation of unity with the workers of Ulster was to be costly for the Labour Party as social and economic issues were not a sufficient bridge to hold the two groups of workers together in the face of the independence movement.

The 1918 election, which Sinn Féin won with widespread support, proved to be damaging to the Labour Party. Despite its growth in numbers and popular support Labour decided not to contest the 1918 election, a strategy designed to allow the nation to vote on its political future and to preserve labor solidarity in the face of Sinn Féin and Unionist combat. In fact, the workers in the two regions were polarized on the question of independence, and Labour did not gain or hold the allegiance of Ulster workers yet excluded the party from the election that was to set the pattern for Ireland in the years to come. The effect was to accomplish the worst of both worlds: a split in the workers and an abdication of any Labour voice in Sinn Féin.

When the Free State was established, Labour chose to accept its legitimacy and participate in the Dáil, and in 1927 Labour gained the largest number of seats it was ever to achieve, twenty-two. But after Fianna Fáil representatives entered the Dáil, Labour's number of seats dropped to thirteen in the second election of 1927. Fianna Fáil was to preempt the role the Labour Party had served as it became the opposition party and the party committed to social and economic reforms.[15] In 1936 the Labour Party called for the creation of a "workers republic" and for a nationalization of industry. This bold move eventually lost its impact as the Catholic hierarchy let it be known that such notions were at odds with the church's position, and the Labour Party later diluted its commitment to socialism. The 1938 election left Labour with nine seats, and the party was in a state of decay as profound as that of Fine Gael.

In 1948 Labour participated in the interparty government and again in 1954 acted in coalition with Fine Gael. During both terms Labour was the junior partner, and under Fine Gael leadership it could hardly press for extensive social and economic reforms. Participation in government had the effect of reviving the Labour Party, as it did Fine Gael, but making Sean Lemass the head of Fianna Fáil brought that party out of the doldrums and into power again.

The Labour Party had chafed under Fine Gael in the coalitions, and when Brendan Corish became head of the party in 1961, he opted to forgo electoral coalition with Fine Gael. Labour believed that the electoral trend of the future would be toward socialism, and at that point Labour would be prepared to become a majority party. The defect in this strategy was that electoral alignments are not quite that supple, and rejecting coalition meant virtually permanent rule by Fianna Fáil.

Labour's support grew in the elections from twelve seats in 1957 to sixteen in 1961 and twenty-two in 1965. Corish's strategy appeared to be working until the election of 1969 when Labour lost four seats. Fianna Fáil had achieved another extended period of unbroken rule, and the Labour Party did not seem to be as much of a wave of the future as it had anticipated.

The weakness of Fianna Fáil in the early 1970s, coupled with the lack of any startling Labour successes, prompted the latter party to reconsider coalition. Although not popular with the left wing of the party the pragmatists won the day, and talks were begun with Fine Gael in 1972 that culminated in a common program and electoral cooperation in the 1973 election. Labour gained one seat and entered the coalition government, which ruled from 1973 to 1977, and also the FitzGerald governments in 1981 and 1982.

The support for the Labour Party in Ireland is somewhat peculiar in that historically the party has not drawn its strength from urban workers, and until the 1960s rural agricultural workers provided the backbone of the Labour votes. Never all that well organized until the 1970s, the TDs from the rural areas often earned their support by cultivating their constituencies rather than by adhering to socialist doctrines. Some, in fact, opposed the more leftist tendencies of the Labour Party.

The natural base of support for Labour, the working class, in fact supports Fianna Fáil. More Labour supporters are from the working class than any other class, 28 percent, but more working-class voters support Fianna Fáil, 42 percent. Skilled workers and those affiliated with trade unions are more likely to support the Labour Party.

Since about 1965 Labour has been able to draw support from Dublin to a much greater extent and has become the most significant opponent of Fianna Fáil in that city. From 1961 to 1969 Labour increased its number of seats in Dublin from one to ten and its popular vote from 20,600 to 93,440. The total number of Labour seats has not increased, however, as the number of seats in the rural areas has declined correspondingly so that Labour seems perpetually able to gain only between twelve and twenty-two seats. The future does not look that encouraging for Labour as the party's percentage of the total vote slipped from 17 percent in 1969 to about 11 percent in 1977 and the organizational base of the party has eroded.

Smaller parties and independent candidates have had only a marginal impact on the pattern of Irish electoral support. Only in the 1920s, when elected Sinn Féin members were not taking their seats, and in the 1940s, when Clann na Publachta appeared to be on the rise as a real alternative to the major parties, have third parties made a difference. At no time did the first-preference votes for the three major parties fall below 70 percent (1948), and in the last five elections minor parties and independents have garnered only between 3 percent and 7 percent of the first-preference votes.

NOTES

1. This section draws heavily on the work of Basil Chubb in *The Government and Politics of Ireland* (London: Oxford University Press, 1974), pp. 43–61.

2. See Roger Hull, *The Irish Triangle* (Princeton: N.J.: Princeton University Press, 1975), pp. 91–121.

3. Basil Chubb, *A Source Book of Irish Government* (Dublin: Institute of Public Administration, 1964), p. 58.

4. Frank Pakenham (Earl of Longford) and Thomas P. O'Neill, *Eamon de Valera* (London: Hutchinson Publishing, Arrow Books, 1974), p. 296.

5. The constituencies must be redrawn every five years as a result of population growth in Ireland. The number of TDs in 1981 was 166.

6. The quota is the number of votes divided by the number of seats in the constituency, plus one.

7. Basil Chubb, "The Electoral System," in Howard Penniman, ed., *Ireland at the Polls, 1977* (Washington, D.C.: American Enterprise Institute, 1978), p. 27.

8. Basil Chubb, "Going About Persecuting Civil Servants: The Role of the Irish Parliamentary Representative," *Political Studies*, 57:2 (1963), pp. 272–286.

9. Brian Farrell, *Chairman or Chief? The Role of the Taoiseach in Irish Government* (Dublin: Gill and Macmillan, 1971), p. 85.

10. See R. Sinnott, "The Electorate," in Penniman, *Ireland at the Polls, 1977*, pp. 60–61.

11. John H. Whyte, "Ireland: Politics Without Social Bases," in Richard Rose, ed., *Electoral Behavior: A Comparative Handbook* (New York: Free Press, 1973), pp. 631–632.

12. Data for 1977 derived from Sinnott, "The Electorate," p. 64.

13. See Maurice Manning, "The Political Parties," in Penniman, *Ireland at the Polls, 1977*, pp. 80–81.

14. Whyte, "Ireland," pp. 631–632.

15. Fianna Fáil used the semistate bodies as the means to address social and economic concerns. Inhabiting a netherworld between private enterprise and government

ownership or regulation, the semistate bodies defy exact categorization. A government minister is responsible for these bodies, but most operate relatively free of direct supervision. Employees are not civil servants, although they are public servants, and compose approximately 5 percent of the labor force of Ireland. Their functions include promoting tourism, providing electricity, promoting industrial development, selling life insurance, producing steel, running the railroads, and regulating and promoting the use of peat as well as responding to numerous other needs.

7

Elections and Issues

THE ELECTIONS OF 1977, 1981, AND 1982

The most recent elections in Ireland reveal some of the changes that have occurred in the Irish political parties, the composition of the electorate, and the agenda of issues.

An *Irish Times* editorial, in discussing the coalition government in 1981, stated:

> All parties are to some extent sold out to the public relations men and the pollsters; all policies are at least retouched by these artists; what is right, what must be defended to the last ditch, what alone will serve the nation—all that has in so many ways given way to what the customer can be persuaded to take.[1]

Such laments have long been part of the postmortems on U.S. elections, but they are relatively new in Ireland. The first major effort at public relations professionalization occurred in the Fianna Fáil Party under Jack Lynch in preparation for the 1977 election. Lynch appointed Frank Dunlap to be a full-time press and information officer for the party to achieve a more sophisticated use of the press. Additional methods were drawn from U.S. electoral techniques. Notable was the effort not only to create a comprehensive program different from that of the coalition, but also to target certain issues to certain segments of the electorate. Fianna Fáil used three different advertising agencies; the principal one was to promote the general program, and the other two were to direct specific appeals to women and young people. As the campaign proceeded, Fianna Fáil's campaign committee adjusted its advertising to include segments of the electorate not encompassed at the outset. Adding to this effort were slick jingles, buttons, hats, Lynch's face on T-shirts, and a presidential-style election tour by Jack Lynch.

Fianna Fáil had commissioned polls of the electorate prior to the election to assess the support of the national coalition and the issues that were most pertinent to the voters. Following the direction the polls indicated, as well as subsequent "market research," the Fianna Fáil campaign committee was on the mark in identifying those issues and areas of support that could be turned to its party's favor. Although polling of the electorate had shown a diminution of support for the national coalition since 1976, Fine Gael leaders had dismissed this evidence; Fianna Fáil capitalized on it.

Organizationally Fianna Fáil had geared up as early as a year and a half before the election. Senior party members, headed by George Colley, formed a campaign committee, and the party had a new general secretary, Seamus Brennan, whose predecessor had served three decades in the position. Program development began drawing on the younger leadership levels in Fianna Fáil. When the election was called, Fianna Fáil had targeted its candidates, new and old, identified the critical constituencies, and prepared a slick advertising campaign and a forty-seven-page manifesto, which was carefully crafted to appeal to all sectors of the electorate. In contrast the coalition was ill-prepared for the campaign and was on the defensive from the outset, despite having the advantage of knowing when the election would be called and despite having reorganized electoral districts to favor coalition candidates (the Tullymander, so-called because the minister who created the districts was James Tully).

In 1981 the tables were turned. Fianna Fáil, in power for four years, had to call an election. Only eighteen months earlier the party had changed leaders as the same Lynch who had led the party to electoral triumph in 1977 appeared to Fianna Fáil's TDs to be a liability in 1980. In order to improve their chances for victory, Lynch was replaced by Charles Haughey. Haughey was not unopposed in this contest as the passing years and the arms trial a decade earlier had tarnished his earlier image as the natural heir to the Fianna Fáil throne.

On the other hand, Fine Gael had metamorphosed itself after 1977 into a rigorous contender under the leadership of Garrett FitzGerald. After the loss of the 1977 election Cosgrave stepped down as party leader, and FitzGerald wasted no time in undertaking the changes he wanted. A new party secretary, Peter Prendergast, was appointed as well as new officers for press relations, youth, and European affairs. FitzGerald commissioned a survey from the Market Research Bureau of Ireland to assess the crucial issues among the electorate and the reasons for the Fine Gael loss of 1977. This process was continued up through the election of 1981, and the polling led FitzGerald to seek out, as Fianna Fáil had done, the votes of youth, women, and the suburbs.

FitzGerald personally set out to revitalize the constituency organizations with a direct appeal to young people to join Fine Gael. A Young Fine Gael organization was created, which was relatively autonomous of the senior party organization. FitzGerald himself often proved to be the most important element in drawing the young people to Fine Gael. Fianna Fáil was seen, as one young woman put it, as "an unshakeable monolith of gombeenism (jobs-for-the-boys), provincialism, insular thinking, and mediocrity. It embodied the mentality that prevented Ireland from becoming a modern pluralist state."[2] FitzGerald was identified with the liberal wing of the party and had taken relatively bold positions in the past on Northern Ireland and on social issues such as divorce and contraception. FitzGerald not only attracted new young members but brought visible progressive figures into the party such as Nuala Finnell and Maurice Manning. The overall effect was to put new items on the Fine Gael agenda that were oriented to the younger, suburban, and female voters. FitzGerald presided over the selection of candidates for the 1981 election and placed some of his candidates on the ballot in certain constituencies. The party, much to the dismay of the conservative wing, was to shift leadership and momentum to the liberals and replace a loose and paternal organization with a modernized and integrated structure buttressed with young, enthusiastic campaign workers.

As with Fianna Fáil's campaign in 1977, the campaign mounted by Fine Gael in 1981 was characterized by public relations techniques, a focus on FitzGerald as a national leader, and a program geared to the various sectors of the electorate Fine Gael needed to reach. The largest victory ever for the party was a vindication of the leadership of FitzGerald and the professionalization of the party. This victory was not totally without cost, however, as Fine Gael's base of support has always been conservative and the changes alienated some of the old guard who preferred tradition to victory.

As we will see in discussing the issues, organization, leadership, and electoral competition, both Fianna Fáil and Fine Gael have rapidly modernized into pragmatic and professional machines. Both are "new wine in old bottles." While retaining their traditional labels and bases of support, both parties have moved far beyond the issues of 1922–1959. Protreaty or antitreaty and Blue Shirt or republican have slipped quickly into the past to be replaced by issues such as mortgage rates, taxes, the Common Agricultural Policy of the European Community, the amount of foreign debt, rates of employment, and provision of social services. Both parties differ only slightly on the Ulster question as both now have opted for the path of a negotiated transition in the status of Ulster in cooperation with London.

In the 1960s Fianna Fáil, under the leadership of Sean Lemass and later Lynch, adapted to the modernization of Ireland by pragmatically absorbing the new entrepreneurs and the middle class into the party while retaining the traditional rural republican elements. Since 1965 Fine Gael has slowly transformed itself from a conservative, agricultural party to a pragmatic, social-democratic party that has adapted both organizationally and ideologically to modern pressures. The number of Fine Gael members of the Dáil who could be described as liberal has risen from eight out of forty-six in 1965 to thirty-nine out of sixty-five in 1981.[3]

Coalition with Labour was necessary to form a government in the 1981 election, but Fine Gael may have acquired the base of organization, leadership, and support necessary to gain a ruling majority without Labour in the future. Were that situation to occur, the most significant change in Irish electoral politics would not only be the modernization of Fianna Fáil and Fine Gael but the fact that a new party system, composed of two equally competitive parties, could emerge from the transformation within the major parties.

The electorate in Ireland has undergone a dramatic shift both in composition and in attitudes since 1960. The economic regeneration of Ireland that swirled through the island in the 1960s was accompanied by a sharp drop in the rate of emigration. The economic changes and the relative prosperity were the incubator of material and consumer demands. The advent of television brought images of the wider, modern, and secular world of Europe and the United States, and the decrease in the rate of emigration meant that young people received the fullest impact of those images. Moreover, a traditionally rural Ireland has become an urban Ireland, with one in three people in the Republic living in greater Dublin.

Dame Street in the business district of Dublin. (Courtesy, Irish Tourist Board)

Thus economic changes, increasing urbanization and suburbanization, and a young electorate (48 percent of the population is under twenty-five) have brought a different agenda of issues into the political arena. The younger voters are not particularly radical as they supported the major parties in 1977, 1981, and 1982, but they are asking for a different legislative response in areas related to the family (e.g., contraception and illegitimacy) and the economy (e.g., employment and home ownership).

All Irish voters have been influenced by the economic and social transformation. Despite the persistence of the problems of partition and the constant violence and agitation in Northern Ireland, the Irish voters have consistently judged their governments by their economic promises and their economic performance. The 1977 election clearly was contested on economic issues. In April of 1977 voters were asked to assess the performance of the national coalition in several areas. Three could be considered social—health, pensions, and security; three could be considered economic—unemployment, prices, and new jobs for the young people; and, finally, there was Northern Ireland. Satisfaction with social issues was expressed by more than one-half the respondents: In regard to health, 54 percent approved; pensions, 53 percent; and security, 47 percent. Moreover, the respondents were not convinced that Fianna Fáil could do a better job. The government's performance in regard to Northern Ireland was less enthusiastically endorsed, 33 percent approved.

But the bottom fell out when the public evaluated the government's performance on economic issues. Sixty-one percent, 76 percent, and 71 percent believed that the government was doing badly in regard to unemployment, prices, and new jobs, respectively—and that Fianna Fáil was capable of doing better.[4] Prior to the campaign three-quarters of the voters identified prices, inflation, and employment as the most important issues; only one-quarter mentioned social services and one-fifth, Northern Ireland.

Fianna Fáil was not only aware of these sentiments but was tailoring a program that would attract the voters on these issues. Its manifesto included the abolition of domestic rates (local property taxes) and a reduction in taxes of £160 million ($240 million). Policies aimed specifically at younger voters included the abolition of taxes on small cars and motorcycles and a grant of £1,000 ($1,500) to people purchasing their first home. Appealing to the unemployed as well as to young people entering the job market, Fianna Fáil promised the creation of 20,000 new jobs in one year, and more thereafter, as its prime goal.

The debate during the campaign hinged on the coalition's assertions that the economy was on the rise and that its management was sound. Although both parties were unclear as to the costs of and how to pay for their new programs, the voters were clear on their preference for Fianna Fáil. Government efforts to offer enticements similar to those of Fianna Fáil (e.g., reducing domestic rates) and to show that the costs of the Fianna Fáil programs were enormous (e.g., Garrett FitzGerald argued that Fianna Fáil had underestimated the cost of £119 million) fell on deaf ears.

Historically a powerful issue, Northern Ireland did not sharply separate the two parties, as Brian Farrell and Maurice Manning note:

> Despite the pressure of Northern troubles on the domestic politics of the Republic since the late 1960s, the complex of potential issues clustering around relations with Northern Ireland, national security against subversive groups, and the political and constitutional aspects of law and order were not central to the 1977 election.[5]

The absence of this issue in 1977 was not idiosyncratic. In 1981, when the hunger strikes carried out by IRA prisoners in the H Block of the Maze Prison had supercharged attitudes on Northern Ireland, the electorate was still primarily moved by economic issues.

Fianna Fáil, although having swept the 1977 election, was already suffering reverses by 1979. In the June elections for the European Parliament the Fianna Fáil vote dropped 15 percent, and in two local by-elections in the autumn the party's vote dropped 22 percent and 12 percent. The perception on the part of the TDs was that Lynch's leadership was indecisive and ineffectual and that were he to continue as leader, the party would suffer a disaster in the next election. Charles Haughey was elected over the establishment figure, George Colley, to provide the spark that was needed to make the party competitive. Haughey chose to place Northern Ireland high on his list of priorities, despite the fact that it was electorally an issue of low concern and would require the nearly impossible task of accomplishing a settlement to attract a large number of votes. The economy, however, was deteriorating rapidly, not only from 1977 to 1978, but also during the eighteen months that Haughey was prime minister. The reason was simple: The Fianna Fáil manifesto had been implemented after the 1977 election and had cost the government severely. Imports, especially of oil, and generous wage agreements had pushed inflation to 20 percent, and the government was borrowing heavily to maintain services. Although the number of jobs had increased by 1979, growth had slowed, and Ireland was in a recession.

Opinion polls taken by the *Irish Times* indicated that the degree of satisfaction with the government's performance was decaying rapidly. In March of 1980 the proportion of people dissatisfied was 49 percent with 43 percent of those surveyed satisfied. Approximately a year later the dissatisfied percentage was 58, and the satisfied was 33. The increasing negativity was focused on economic issues. In fact a greater number of the people surveyed, 36 percent, felt that the Fianna Fáil government could better handle the Northern Ireland issue than an alternative government could, 33 percent. However, with respect to economic affairs, unemployment, and inflation, the Irish voters felt that these problems could be handled better by an alternative to the Haughey government by substantial margins (economic affairs, 41 percent to 29 percent; unemployment, 43 percent to 29 percent; and inflation, 43 percent to 27 percent).[6] Surveys have shown repeatedly that the economic cluster of inflation and employment is the most important issue area for about three-quarters of the Irish voters. Thus the Fianna Fáil government was in the same position the national coalition had been in 1977. Voters expressed approval of certain dimensions of the government's performance, but on the crucial issues of economic management, the government lacked the confidence of the public.

As in 1977 the voters perceived differences in leadership to be significant. Liam Cosgrave in 1977 could not match Lynch's ability to create a rapport with the public. In 1981 Haughey, more deft than the diffident Cosgrave, was nonetheless seen as a less effective leader than FitzGerald. FitzGerald was rated substantially ahead of Haughey as a party leader and was also the voters' choice for prime minister.[7]

Haughey, in the brittle atmosphere of the hunger strikes, chose to make Northern Ireland a campaign issue, an electoral tactic not marked by brilliance in the face of evidence that indicated that the public was far more concerned with jobs. The economy, however, soon became the critical issue of the campaign, and the Irish voters saw no contradiction in now turning away from a government that had incurred a massive debt providing those benefits the electorate had opted for in the 1977 election. The government was forced, as Cosgrave had been in 1977, to argue that its performance had been good and that the current problems were just temporary. FitzGerald and Fine Gael candidates hammered away at the issues of inflation, public debt, and employment. Fine Gael also developed programs that were designed to appeal to the sectors of the electorate that were needed for election. The appeal to women was substantial as a weekly stipend of £9.60 ($14.00) was offered to housewives and changes in the divorce laws were promised.

The results were to reveal, as in 1977, that the modernization of the Irish economy, the composition of the Irish electorate, and the professionalization of the major political parties have woven together to change the face of Irish elections. The demands placed upon the parties may be almost impossible to meet as members of each sector of the electorate wants benefits distributed to them, such as lower mortgage rates, reduced taxes (or no taxes in the case of farmers), higher pensions, more housing, and job creation. Conversely the electorate also wants to curb inflation and lower taxes. One pressure is to spend, as the cost of promising jobs and social services is onerous, and the other pressure is to conserve to combat inflation and lower taxes.

FitzGerald held power through a coalition with Labour and the support of a few independents. With a slender majority, FitzGerald began governing as though he had a large and secure margin. He brought new faces into his cabinet and attempted new initiatives on Northern Ireland in meetings in November and December of 1981 with Prime Minister Margaret Thatcher. However, the critical question of Ireland's debt was to be the downfall of this brief government. FitzGerald proposed a tough austerity budget for 1982, which came under sharp criticism because of the new taxes it introduced. Although FitzGerald was bold enough to attempt to curb the mounting Irish deficits, the independent supporters of the government were not, and in February 1982 new elections were held. The results were remarkably similar to those of the prior election as Fianna Fáil gained only three seats and Fine Gael lost only two. Charles Haughey bargained for support from the independents and from Sinn Féin, the workers' party, which held three seats. The result was a Fianna Fáil government under Haughey in 1982. Haughey's administration was plagued by a worsening of the economic problems of inflation, unemployment, and foreign debt. In addition scandals involving cabinet members and government wiretapping raised the question of integrity in the administration. In November Haughey's government fell after eight months. The issues were integrity and Haughey's leadership. Fianna Fáil stressed the need for stability in government as this was the third general election in eighteen months. The electorate chose FitzGerald, however, and a Fine Gael–Labour coalition with a sufficient majority to govern for several years came to power.

Barring a new, miraculous economic boom, made more unlikely by the depressed state of the Western economies and Ireland's dependence on imported energy, no government can satisfy the spectrum of political demands. The parties have, at the same time, modernized their abilities to identify what the voters desire and to create and sell programs tailored to those desires. The result may be electoral success, followed by failure to keep contradictory and expensive promises, followed by electoral failure in a continuous cycle of trading economic promises for electoral triumph.

PRESSURE GROUPS

The major parties have learned that their appeal has to be segmented to the differentiated electorate, which has been brought about by modernization. The explicit, organized voices of those segments are the array of Irish interests groups.

Numbering in the thousands, large and small, the interest groups considered here represent important social sectors and/or have emerged since

Dr. Garrett FitzGerald, the prime minister of the Republic of Ireland. (Courtesy, Embassy of Ireland)

1960. The functions of these groups, as with pressure groups anywhere, are to recruit and organize members, promote their interests, and most important, persuade the government to listen to their advice in implementing policy or to adopt new policies that bring advantages to the group. All groups tend to rationalize their specific interests in terms of benefits to the common good. In most cases this claim is at best a partial truth, which in fact represents an attempt on the part of one segment of society to enlarge its slice of the pie. Crucial to the success of all interest groups are public legitimacy—a powerful asset for the church, for example—size, resources, and organization.

Of the major pressure groups in Ireland the church is the most visible, and it is considered by some people to be the most powerful. Identifying the power of the church per se, however, is difficult in a country that is 94 percent Catholic and extraordinarily devout. To separate when the church has promoted or prevented a policy, or when the people have done so, is not always easy. Examples abound of political figures' simply ignoring the official pronouncements of the church up to the point of excommunication, including, for example, as devout a Catholic as de Valera. On the other hand, Brendan Corish, former leader of the Labour Party, stated in the Dáil: "I am an Irishman second; I am a Catholic first. . . . If the Hierarchy gives me any direction with regard to Catholic social teaching or Catholic moral teaching, I accept without qualification in all respects the teaching of the Hierarchy and the Church to which I belong."[8]

Virtually all leaders in the major parties, civil service, and pressure groups are Catholic, and thus ascertaining the difference between the personal convictions of those leaders and "pressure" from the church in supporting a particular policy is not at all easy. Moreover, the position of a single cleric, bishop, or cardinal is not always the position of the church. Individual voices, such as that of Cornelius Lucey, the bishop of Cork, who has spoken out on virtually all public issues, may not represent the collective thinking of the Irish Catholic church. Clearly, in the past, the conservative voice of the hierarchy did not always parallel the political convictions of the local clergy, committed as they were to the Irish nationalist movement. In the contemporary setting the younger, post–Vatican II clergy are not always of the same mind as the hierarchy on matters of birth control and education.

As recently as 1970, Morley Ayearst commented on the influence of the Church: "It is obvious that no Irish political party can afford to advocate policies that are contrary to the Church's view concerning education, the family or moral questions generally. Nor can a politician who hopes for a successful political career, especially within one of the two main parties, afford to flout Catholic opinion in such matters."[9] It is testament of the rapid change in Ireland that since about 1975 that which Ayearst declared so unlikely has in fact transpired. At the 1978 ard fheis ("party convention") of Fine Gael a resolution was passed to submit to a referendum the question of removing the constitutional prohibition on divorce. Contraception, long a taboo subject in Irish politics, was legalized by a bill introduced by the Haughey government in 1979. Although opposed by Fine Gael, the opposition, in fact, was based upon the fact that the bill did not allow all adults who wanted contraceptive devices to have access to them as they were to be dispensed through a doctor's prescription. Public opinion polls have shown a steady increase in support of a law that would allow divorce, reaching over 65 percent in 1977. Without question, the church would oppose such legislation with all of its considerable resources, but clearly the political parties today can afford to advocate policies that are contrary to church doctrine, and today Catholic opinion is no longer to be simply equated with unquestioning adherence to church doctrine.

The church has been successful in the past in directly and indirectly shaping public policy in Ireland because the Irish people and the church were symbiotically united and the authoritarian sway of the church was matched by a complementary deference on the part of the people. The slow erosion of that deference has placed at least some of the people in the Republic outside of, and in some cases in heated opposition to, the writ of the church. The reasons—Vatican II, travel, television, pop culture, urbanization, and relative affluence—flow from the modernization process, and the effect has been to diminish the impact of the church as a pressure group.

Farmers in a rural country in which agriculture is an important industry would be expected to speak with a strong voice. In fact, the farmers in Ireland have never developed the kind of pressure group, or groups, seen in Europe in the last century. That lack does not mean that the farmers are without influence; on the contrary, the farmers are quite powerful. However, the way property was acquired in the late nineteenth and early twentieth centuries produced a country of small proprietors who were socially and economically conservative and parochially oriented. Largely broken down into almost 160 specialized organizations—concerned with, for example, sugar beets, beef exports, cattle breeding, and milk production—the farmers have never been able to support a political party of any significance.

The largest single agricultural organization is the National Farmers Association (NFA), which was created in 1955 and represents about 60 percent of all farmers. The national executive of this group is charged with the responsibility of monitoring agricultural developments at home and abroad in order to enhance the future of Irish agriculture and livestock. In close contact with the minister for agriculture, the NFA attempts to present its point of view on agricultural policy, and the organization has a committee that reviews proposed bills before the Dáil that concern agriculture. The principal interest of farmers in recent years has been the effort to protect their incomes when the market declines. For the most part they have been successful in the tax category, although less so in recent years as the coalition government imposed an income tax and a wealth tax. The farmers' resistance to such taxes, and discussion of additional levies, took the form of protest marches, road blocking, and demonstrations in the late 1960s.

The greatest impact on the farmers was Ireland's entry into the European Economic Community, which not only sharply increased their incomes but also forced the creation of organizational skills needed to operate, not only in Dublin, but also in Brussels. Tim Pat Coogan notes the sophistication of Irish farmers today: "The Irish Farm Association, with a high powered office in Brussels, a top class secretariat of young economics graduates, and a range of business activities related to farming would make an old-time, fork-in-hand, muck-spreading farmer blink in amazement."[10]

The farmers have shifted their efforts toward protecting their incomes, which dropped severely in the mid-seventies and 1980. The head of the NFA since 1966, T. J. Maher, ran for the European Parliament and won a resounding victory. Supporters who were disillusioned by Fianna Fáil and Fine Gael even hinted at the creation of a new farmers' party. Although nothing came of that idea, its mention does indicate the degree to which the farmers are not in such a favorable economic position and are becoming increasingly militant on the issues of taxes and income.

Labor shares with farmers the propensity to proliferate as there are about 100 small unions. Half of the Irish trade unions have 1,000 or fewer members, and only a few have membership over 15,000, the largest being the Irish Transport and General Workers Union with approximately 150,000 members. About 50 percent of the unions are members of the Irish Congress of Trade Unions (ICTU), which speaks for the union members in the same manner that the NFA speaks for the farmers. The ICTU has become the voice of the working class in a way that the Labour Party is not. In practice the ICTU is not the clarion voice of a united labor movement but a loose association of autonomous unions. Union membership has been growing since 1961, both in absolute terms and as a proportion of all employed workers.

Labor's array of concerns is wide, and its ample agenda obviously deals with such issues as rates of employment, employee disputes, insurance benefits, unemployment compensation, representation of workers, industrial relations, holidays, and worker safety.

In addition to the church, labor, and agriculture, a host of groups with varying degrees of power speak for their adherents in the traditional sectors of Irish politics. Industrial and commercial interests are represented by over 200 associations, most of which are relatively weak and lacking in resources. In the period of economic growth after 1960, however, a group of sophisticated entrepreneurs schooled in the tumult of rapid economic change emerged. Although not an interest group in the classic sense, its influence is both important and increasing. Figures such as "Tony" O'Reilly, Dermott Ryan, Paddy Hughes, and Nicholas Leonard have brought the skills of mergers, takeovers, and international financial craftsmanship to a financial environment that was as sleepy as the Irish countryside. Whether in mines, newspapers, hotels, or banking, their impact has been praised, criticized, and condemned, but there is little doubt that such men and the interests they control are powerful in a way that is different from the influence of the traditional wealthy families in Ireland. Professional associations for doctors, teachers, architects, and engineers, among others, also vie for a say in the policies that affect their members' livelihood.

In recent years the modernization of Irish politics and the Irish economy have brought to the fore a spate of new interest groups that reflect the changing agenda of issues in Irish life. The building of a nuclear power plant at Carnsore Point in Ireland brought antinuclear power groups onto the political stage, and pollution from chemical plants in Mayo, a massive oil spill in Bantry Bay in 1979, and the destruction of lakes and streams by agricultural pollutants have galvanized environmentalists into exerting political pressure to preserve Ireland's ecology.

Finally, women have been increasing both their political organization and their political impact. In 1970 a Commission on the Status of Women was created in what would have to be considered an inhospitable environment— a conservative society with a powerful church and a long tradition of women as child rearers. In the decade since the establishment of the commission, the women's movement in Ireland succeeded in making women aware of the inequities they suffer and in bringing women's issues to the foreground in the media and in the political fray. As in other movements that are not oriented toward a function but rather toward a social sector, the women's movement is hardly unanimous in perspective. However, positions that challenge the traditional roles of women in Irish society and in Catholic doctrine are increasingly prevalent. A conference in 1980, sponsored by the liberal Council for the Status of Women, passed resolutions calling for, among other things, freely available contraceptives; a recognition of divorce; increased promotion of women in the media, government, and industry; elimination of discrimination against rural women; and the introduction of women's studies into the schools.[11] In February of 1981 the publishers of *Magill,* a current-affairs monthly, began publication of *Status,* a current affairs magazine for women. *Status* failed after a few months, but it was a reflection of the changes in Ireland that a magazine for women would be attempted at all.

CONCLUSION

Irish political culture, Irish government, and Irish politics have all undergone substantial change in the twentieth century. The broad pattern is still predominantly authoritarian, but it is leavened by increasing demands for a more pluralistic pattern in the realms of individual freedom and public policymaking.

The authoritarian pattern is described by Alan Ward:

> A society with an authoritarian political culture will be hierarchically ordered with an emphasis on strong leadership and centralized decision-making. It will not encourage broad participation in decision-making. There will be a rigid system of social controls, sanctioned and enforced by the state and other agencies such as the Church, to restrict personal freedoms. Innovation and change will be repressed to protect public safety or the moral standards of the community, although often because change also threatens the prevailing social order and those who control it.[12]

Ireland's political values, structures, and processes have historically displayed such patterns. Whether because of centuries of subservience or an authoritarian church, the individual in the political system feels relatively powerless in effecting change from above. Numerous commentators have noted that the Irish individual approaches the state indirectly through personal contact with a member of the Dáil, and in fact, this role has emerged not only as the principal task of a TD but as one of the crucial determinants of continued election.[13]

The Seneád, the Dáil, the cabinet, and the prime minister are ascending steps in the concentration of power. This concentration creates a hierarchical system, which, coupled as it is with the control of the bureaucracy and local government, does not encourage widespread participation in the decision-making process, even by senators and deputies.

The political values embodied in the 1937 constitution reflect the tension between the freedom of the individual and the authority of the state. The liberal principles of representative government and civil liberties were blended with Catholic moral and social teaching to cast the state in a paternal role. Constraints within the constitution, and Dáil legislation, on such personal matters as divorce, contraception, and censorship reflect the assumption that the individual must be both morally guided and protected. Alan Ward concludes that Ireland is not a particularly comfortable place for a person who values individuality and participation and who shrinks from paternalism, but there is little evidence that the Irish would have it any other way.[14]

In recent years, however, the people of Ireland have been displaying less deference than has been characteristic in the past. Demonstrations by farmers and students, increased demands for changes in the role of women, challenges to the moral restrictions enshrined in the law on such matters as divorce, and challenges to the heretofore virtually ironclad reverence for the church have revealed the brittleness of the traditional political culture of Ireland. Although hardly as socially and politically fluid as other European states (Dublin is certainly no Amsterdam), the impetus of modernization in the political values of the young people of Ireland has pressured the political parties to shift the agenda of issues and the speed with which they are addressed. Pluralism is hard to reverse once it is introduced into the political life of a nation, and Ireland will not escape the stresses that the resulting value conflicts engender.

NOTES

1. "Two into One," *Irish Times*, June 29, 1981, p. 11.
2. Pat Brennan, "The New Face of Fine Gael," *Magill* (July 1981), p. 18.
3. Ibid.
4. R. Sinnott, "The Electorate," in Howard Penniman, ed., *Ireland at the Polls, 1977* (Washington, D.C.: American Enterprise Institute, 1978), pp. 56–57.
5. Brian Farrell and Maurice Manning, "The Election," in Penniman, *Ireland at the Polls, 1977*, p. 144.
6. Percentages from data in Vincent Browne, "Has Fianna Fáil Got a Prayer?" *Magill* (March 1981), pp. 22–23.
7. Ibid., p. 23.
8. Quoted in Basil Chubb, *The Government and Politics of Ireland* (London: Oxford University Press, 1974), p. 103.
9. Morley Ayearst, *The Republic of Ireland* (New York: New York University Press, 1970), pp. 222–223.
10. Tim Pat Coogan, *The Irish: A Personal View* (London: Phaidon Press, 1975), p. 160.
11. Pat Brennan, "National Woman's Forum Report," *Magill* (December 1980), pp. 4–6.
12. Alan J. Ward, "Politics and the Individual in Ireland" (Paper presented to

the American Committee for Irish Studies, James Madison University, Harrisonburg, Virginia, April 1979), p. 2. The conclusion section of this chapter draws heavily on Professor Ward's analysis.

13. See R. K. Carty, *Party and the Parish Pump* (Waterloo, Canada: Wilfred Laurier University Press, 1981), pp. 109–139.

14. Ward, "Politics and the Individual," p. 12.

8

Northern Ireland: The Rise and Fall of Stormont

In 1981 Bobby Sands, a member of the Irish Republican Army, died of a hunger strike in the Maze Prison near Belfast, and the streets exploded in violence. Sands's hunger strike and death wove together a number of the most heroic and tragic strands of Irish history and contemporary Northern Ireland. The tactic of the hunger strike evoked memories of the death of Terence MacSwiney in 1920 as the result of a hunger strike in a British prison. Shortly before his death Sands had been elected to the British Parliament, whose rule over Northern Ireland he rejected; Sinn Féin had used the same tactics in 1918 to create the first Dáil Éireann. Sands had been jailed for possession of firearms and involvement in the blowing up of a warehouse; the IRA had taken the path of the gun against British rule from 1918 to 1921. During Sands's hunger strike violent confrontations had occurred in the streets of Belfast, and on Easter Sunday they resulted in the death of two youths who were crushed by a British army truck. Their funerals were two more in a long string of funerals in Belfast and Derry, not only from the violence since 1968 but from trouble in the 1920s and 1930s. The British were adamant in refusing to make concessions to Sands's demands for better treatment in prison, reflecting the "not-an-inch" position that the Ulster Unionists had adopted toward Catholic demands for half a century. International opinion favored a concession, but the British prime minister felt that such a move would cause a backlash from the Protestant community, a pressure not unfamiliar to Lloyd George in 1921.

Sands's death mirrored the dimensions of one of Ireland's and Britain's historically most intractable political problems—the relationship of the two communities in Northern Ireland and the problem of governing that province in light of that relationship. Assessment of this political tangle in Ulster evokes powerful partisan commitment. The history of Northern Ireland by Catholic Nationalists is seen as the theft of a province of Ireland in 1921 by British imperialists. In the Unionist view the history of Northern Ireland is one of loyal citizens of the United Kingdom resisting being coerced into a nation with which they do not share religious or political convictions. The struggle has been to control Catholic irredentists in Ulster who violently resist the democratically expressed will of the majority of the citizens. Threading a narrative through this political and ethnic minefield is difficult; this chapter

117

and the next rely on some of the principal non-Marxist interpretations of Northern Ireland.[1]

The history of Northern Ireland, while never completely severed from that of the Republic, began to veer in a separate direction in 1920 with partition under the Better Government of Ireland Act, and the two parts of the island became even more isolated after the settlement of the boundary in 1925. Both parts of the country became preoccupied with problems that had a certain similarity: establishing a new government, maintaining civil order, and coping with economic setbacks.

THE CREATION OF NORTHERN IRELAND

The conditions that were institutionalized politically in Ulster in 1920 had had a long history. There had perhaps been an even greater sense of antagonism in Ulster between Protestant and Catholic in the seventeenth and eighteenth centuries due to the particularly comprehensive nature of the plantations after 1607 and the fact that the planters were alien in culture and religion. A common bond emerged between Presbyterian and Catholic in the late 1700s as both suffered under the penal laws, the former to a lesser and the latter to a greater degree. Although not negligible, that bond was certainly only one part of the Protestant-Catholic relationship. The symbolic union of the two faiths in the Society of United Irishmen occurred at the same time as the emergence of the Orange Order and persistent violent clashes between Catholic and Protestant secret societies. The nineteenth century saw an increasing separation of Ulster from the rest of Ireland. The Industrial Revolution occurred only in that province, and added to religious and ethnic differences were those of prosperity and an urban, industrial way of life.

Presbyterian liberalism at the end of the century declined and was attacked by the Ian Paisley of the nineteenth century, Henry Cooke. Cooke associated his conservative brand of religious evangelism with the political and ethnic views of the Orange Order. Throughout the century antagonism between Catholic and Protestant boiled over into rioting between the two communities. On occasion this mutual dislike became extremely bitter and caused numerous deaths in 1834, 1864, 1886, and 1893. Thus, at the same time that Ulster was drawing away from the rest of Ireland, antagonism between the two communities within Ulster was increasing as well.

Home rule was the forge on which Protestant Ulster was formed. The alliance of Ulster Protestants with British Conservatives emerged from this dispute as did the increased reputation and power of the Orange Order and the Ulster Unionist Council (later to become the Unionist Party). In the period 1912–1914, when Asquith put a home rule bill through the British Parliament, Ulster intransigence rose to a crescendo and ignited the formation of the Ulster Volunteers, the near mutiny of British army officers, near treasonous statements by Conservative politicians, and the threat of civil war. Several reasons lay behind the negative posture of the Unionists. The Conservative politicians in London exploited and inflamed their traditional antipathy to Catholics so as to buttress their position against any risk of dissolution of the empire. That the traditional antipathy existed, there is no doubt. The hostility built up between Protestant and Catholic had grown since the Reformation, and the Unionists coupled this hostility with anti-Catholic cultural superiority. As they would be a minority in a home rule assembly, the Protestants could not accept being governed by people they considered their cultural, religious, and ethnic inferiors. Finally, economic interests were at issue in that industrial Ulster had a powerful stake in not threatening its advantageous position within the British free trade area.

In an attempt to seek a way out of the impasse of Ulster ardor for union and Sinn Féin warfare for independence, Lloyd George sponsored the 1920 act, which called for separate parliaments for the six counties of Ulster and the other twenty-six counties of Ireland. The Ulster Unionists accepted their separate Parliament only reluctantly. They did not ask for devolution, let alone demand it, as they preferred that all of Ireland remain united with Britain. The remaining provisions of the 1920 bill were aborted as Sinn Féin transformed the southern Parliament into the second Dáil Éireann and the Council of Ireland, which was supposed to have representatives from both sections, never met. The 1921 treaty contained a provision that Ulster could merge with the Free State or, if it chose, opt out. Ulster opted out immediately.

In the 1914 home rule crisis the spokesman for Ulster unionism, Sir Edward Carson, had demanded that all of Ulster be retained in the Union and that home rule apply only to the other twenty-three provinces of Ireland. At that time the population of the province of Ulster consisted of only slightly more Protestants than Catholics, and five of the nine counties had Catholic majorities. When the boundary was determined for Ulster in 1920, the province was collapsed to only six counties—Down, Armagh, Derry, Tyrone, Antrim, and Fermanagh—in which there were 820,000 Protestants and 430,000 Catholics. The design was clearly to maintain a Protestant majority.[2]

That the Catholic nationalists would immediately dispense with their feelings of religious and cultural identity, eliminate their political opposition, and embrace with open arms a statelet designed to preserve what they had died trying to destroy was so improbable as to defy reason. The 1920 act provoked brutal sectarian rioting in Belfast, and over 500 people had been killed by 1922. The Catholic nationalists, still strongly identified with Sinn Féin, saw the government of Ulster as not yet permanent while the guerrilla war with the British continued. When the treaty of 1921 was signed and partition accepted by Sinn Féin, the nationalists in Ulster were left only with the promises of Michael Collins that the treaty would be a stepping-stone to an all-Ireland republic. The antitreaty forces promised only more fighting and were not supported by the Irish people in the other twenty-six counties. Without even the balm of living in a free state, the Catholic nationalists in Northern Ireland were left holding the bag of Irish nationalism, and, what was worse, they were to be ruled by a government controlled by their local Protestant opponents, not London.

The Stormont government (named after its building outside of Belfast) consisted of a House of Commons with fifty-two members and a weak Senate elected by the House. It was cabinet government, as in Britain, with executive power in the hands of the prime minister, the leader of the majority party.

The monarch was represented by a lord lieutenant. Although the British government circumscribed the powers of the Stormont government—retaining control over foreign affairs, the post office, taxation, customs, and foreign trade—it gave substantial local authority to the Ulster Parliament, which tended to absorb the functions of local government as well. Stormont had responsibility for local order and the court system; its ministries were finance, home affairs, health and social service, education, agriculture, commerce, and development—all a bit elaborate for a province of 1,250,000 people. James Callahan, a former British prime minister, commented: "Here they are with all the panoply of government—even a Prime Minister—and a population no bigger than a few London boroughs. They don't need a Prime Minister. They need a good Mayor of Lewisham."[3] The Stormont government was forbidden to pass laws aimed at religious discrimination or laws contrary to those of Westminster. The effective power of the Northern Ireland government, however, was increased by the reluctance of the British government to involve itself in the affairs of Ulster for the next fifty years.

The nationalists, in the tradition of Sinn Féin, ran for seats in the Stormont Parliament and then refused to take them when elected. Thus, over the next half century, a social structure emerged that was based upon the Catholics' being members of an underclass and Protestants', a dominant class. Each segment of the society had its institutions to support its traditions and prejudices: for the Protestants their churches, the Unionist Party, and the Orange Order; for the Catholics the church and the Nationalist Party. Each community developed separate institutions to preserve its beliefs, which had the result of reinforcing the negative stereotype of each. Not every Catholic nor every Protestant fit into the established pattern, but the vast bulk of each of the respective ethnic communities did.

The founding of the Ulster government was bathed in blood, and the ritual response of the Protestant Unionist Party was to label all the Catholics as nationalist supporters of the Free State of Ireland, a judgment that was substantially correct. Thus the initial governing premise of the Unionists was that the Catholics were not only papists, and thus inferior, but also traitors to the Stormont regime. As the years went by tensions cooled, and some Catholics came to an accommodation with the fact that Ulster was self-governing. By that time, however, the Catholics found that they were excluded from positions of power. The Unionists, for psychological as well as for political reasons, continued to consider *all* Catholics traitors. Sir Basil Brooke, the minister of agriculture in Ulster in 1934 commented, "I recommend those people who are loyalists not to employ Roman Catholics, ninety-nine percent of whom are disloyal."[4] As this statement was made in the 1930s, the certitude (to say nothing of the statistics) of the comment reflects pure prejudice rather than common sense. For fifty years such attitudes created a pattern of discrimination and separation. The two groups perpetuated and reinforced the disparaging portraits that they had of each other.

DISCRIMINATION AND SEPARATION

Governmental discrimination fell into several categories—voting, employment, housing, regional development, and law enforcement. In the realm of voting (after 1920) Ulster retained property qualifications for local government voting and additional votes for businessmen. The effect, of course, was to discriminate against the poor or nonproperty owner. Since, historically, the Catholics had more poor, the exclusion fell most heavily on them. When property qualifications were coupled with the pattern of gerrymandering districts to the advantage of the Unionists, the effect was to dilute the vote of the Catholics. The most oft-cited example is the city of Derry, in which a majority of the population, 60 percent, was Catholic. Property qualifications allowed only 40 percent of the Catholics to vote but 50 percent of the Protestants. The three districts were aligned so as to allow slender Protestant majorities in two to elect twelve members to the city council while a massive Catholic majority in the third elected eight. The net effect was that 60 percent of the voters elected 40 percent of the members. Catholics were not prevalent in government on the local or Stormont levels. Not surprisingly, a great number of Catholics rejected the idea of serving the Stormont regime, but even given that reticence, Catholics held a disproportionately low number of the positions: in the Royal Ulster Constabulary, 10–12 percent; in the judicial system, 8 percent; in the higher-level civil service, 5 percent; and in local government, Derry 15 percent, Belfast 5 percent.[5]

In the allocation of public housing the local governments used the location and the tenants as a way to reinforce control of an area. The practice varied from place to place, but the cumulative effect was both a form of political manipulation and a denial of housing to Catholics.

The Catholic and Protestant populations in Ulster were mixed together in a patchwork-quilt fashion. Within the cities the sections were also mixed, but in the province as a whole more Catholics lived in the western section, separated from the eastern part by the Bann River. The Stormont government did little to prevent the decay of that region, or to rebuild it when the population began to decline. Industrial development, new towns, and transportation were all focused in the east. Locating a new university of Coleraine, in the northeast, was a rejection of Derry's claim from the west, despite the fact that Derry was four times the size of Coleraine.

Perhaps the most frustrating form of discrimination for the Catholics was in the area of law enforcement. In 1922, under conditions of intense sectarian conflict, the Stormont government passed the Special Powers Act. Renewed regularly it was made permanent in 1933. The act empowered the home secretary to put forth a wide array of regulations, including curfews, searches without warrant, the banning of organizations as illegal, legal forcible entry, and arrest and detention of individuals on mere suspicion. In 1951 the act was augmented to include the prohibition of offensive flags and emblems and public meetings. The effect of the act was to create somewhat elastic powers to curtail threats to civil disorder. Catholics were opposed to the act, not only because it was legally questionable in its extraordinary grant of authority, but also because it was used almost invariably only against the Catholics. The Catholic political associations were banned but not the Protestant ones. The IRA was, of course, banned, but Protestant paramilitary organizations weren't forbidden until the 1960s. The internment provisions were used exclusively against Catholics.

Adding fuel to the fire was the Royal Ulster Constabulary (RUC). Almost completely Protestant in composition, this police force persistently directed its threats and coercive acts toward the Catholic community. The RUC was rarely used against Protestant mobs or during Protestant demonstrations, but the Catholics felt the brunt of it for fifty years. A third element in the area of law enforcement was the auxiliary forces called the B Specials. The B Special auxiliaries were completely Protestant, poorly trained, heavily armed, overtly anti-Catholic, and responsible for a number of deaths in clashes with Catholics over the years. The combination of the Special Powers Act, the RUC, and B Special violence convinced the Catholics that the law in Northern Ireland was an instrument of harassment, not a guarantee of equal treatment.

Nongovernmental discrimination occurred in the economic sphere. The Ulster Unionist Party was antilabor, devoid of a social or economic policy worthy of the name, and committed only to the preservation of the Union with Britain. When established, the government of Northern Ireland was to turn its revenues over to London, but by 1938 London was the financial guarantor of a debt-ridden Northern Ireland. Unemployment in the 1920s began to rise as the linen and shipbuilding markets diminished. By the late 1920s the rate had reached approximately 20 percent, and the Depression drove the rate to over 25 percent for a decade. No ships were built in Belfast in 1933 for the first time in a century, and 90 percent of the workers in that industry were unemployed. The steady downward spiral in the economy meant that the competition for jobs was fierce, and the resulting animosities augmented both discrimination and separation. Catholics blamed the government for both their unemployment and their exclusion from the work that did exist. Protestant employers hired Protestants under the impetus of their traditional enmity against Catholics and the prodding of organizations such as the Ulster Protestant League. In 1935 violent clashes occurred, which left 12 dead and 600 wounded, as economic deprivation and sectarian hatred blended.

World War II brought prosperity to Northern Ireland, but although economic growth was sustained to some degree, the pattern of discrimination in employment continued. Unemployment was higher in the area west of the Bann and in Catholic areas of all cities in Ulster. Extreme cases are necessarily only illustrative of the problem, but they are revealing. The Harland and Wolf Shipyard in 1971 employed 9,000 manual workers, of whom 500 were Catholic; Mackies Engineering employed 8,500 workers, and of them 120 were Catholic. From 1920 until 1972, when it was suspended by London, the Stormont government either overtly discriminated against Catholics or encouraged such oppression.

Coupled with, and encouraged by, discrimination was the separation of the two ethnic communities. Separation, however, was voluntary as each group sought to preserve its heritage and identity. The principal conservators of the separate traditions were the schools and the churches, which socialized the children into separate value systems.

In a rare display of unanimity all the churches in Ulster opposed a bill put forth in 1923 which called for mixing the children in the public schools and hiring teachers without regard to religion. The Catholic church had fought this battle before, from 1831 to 1883, with regard to the British system of education in Ireland, which the church had slowly transformed into a denominational one. Clearly, in Protestant-dominated Ulster, the Catholics would resist nondenominational schools, even at the cost of losing state support, and the Protestant churches and the Orange Order also challenged the "godless" schools. By 1925 the law had been undermined, and by 1930 education was again denominational. The state supported Protestant education financially but did not provide any money for Catholic education until 1930. After 1930 the government subsidized Catholic education at 50 percent of cost; that figure was raised to 65 percent in 1947 and later to 80 percent. This differential could be seen as discrimination rather than separation, but, in fact, the Catholic church preferred "going it alone," as financial independence preserved its control over the schools.

The resulting differences are obvious, not only in the realm of religious education, but in the children's views of their culture and identity. Catholics learn Irish history and absorb a view of the world of religion, politics, and social life that is rooted in nationalist images. Protestants learn British history and a unionist view of the world.[6] Clearly the education system was designed to reinforce identity with each community, not to transcend it. In an utterly divided sectarian atmosphere such a way of thinking was no surprise, but it also contributed little to empathy between the communities then, nor does it today.

Church affiliation in Northern Ireland is extremely tenacious. Roughly one-third of the people are Catholics and one-third Presbyterians—the rest are Anglicans and Methodists—and both major religions make strong claims on the life of a person. In the period from 1920 to 1972 the Catholic church in the Free State/Republic gave no indication to Protestants in the North that the church influence that had been present in the nationalist movement was diminishing in the southern government. The Catholic aspects of the 1937 constitution hardened the Presbyterians' exaggerated claim that Éire was a theocratic state. Those preachers who had a vested interest in the sectarian division in Ulster could use the Catholicity of the Republic to pull their flocks ever closer to Protestant fundamentalism and separation from the Catholics in their own province. Catholic doctrines—such as those on divorce, inter-marriage, abortion, birth control, and the papacy—were seen by the Protestants as proof that Catholics submissively conformed to the dictates of an authoritarian church.

Church and school reinforced a pattern of separate social life and values. Church-related social organizations drew the people of each ethnic community together for song, dance, and companionship—Orange halls for Protestants and church halls for Catholics. Sports were another cause of division, especially after the creation of the Gaelic Athletic Association. For Catholics the principal sports were hurling and Gaelic football; for Protestants, rugby and cricket. The professional associations, or special-interest organizations like art or film, were nonsectarian in a gingerly way, especially in the later years. The closer such groups got to the working class, however, the more they were divided into Catholic or Protestant organizations.

Symbols reinforced the division. The Orange parades on July 12 of each year to celebrate the victory of King "Billy" at the Battle of the Boyne in 1690 were an extraordinary display of pomp that alienated the Catholics.

Conversely, playing "The Soldiers Song," the Republic's anthem, flying the tricolor, and celebrating the Easter Rising all grated on the Protestant community. More than once such observances led to severe sectarian violence in Belfast and Derry.

Less formal differences have become magnified over the years into sectarian separation. The Ulster Protestants are laconic in speech, the Catholics are more effusive; Catholics use Sunday for recreation, most Protestants do not. Catholics have higher rates of unemployment, which is transferred by the Protestants into a stereotype of lazy irresponsibility. Catholics react to Protestant taciturnity and reserve with a stereotype of selfish, cold inhumanity.

Perpetuation of both discrimination and separation was assured as children absorbed their community's values and hatreds. Violence was regular enough in each generation so that the sectarian hatreds were annealed by lootings, bloodshed, burning houses, and police searches, which ensured that there would be little or no diminution of the rift. Robert Coles asked a ten-year-old in 1980 in Belfast about his future. The youngster replied, "The IRA; I'll not be a stooge or a slave."[7]

For the entire fifty-two-year span of the Stormont regime Northern Ireland was governed by one party, the Unionist Party. Leadership was stable—James Craig, the first prime minister, ruled for twenty years—and the Unionist political program was simple, to maintain the Union with Britain. Unionist organization was powerful, interlocked as it was with the Orange Order, which in turn interlocked with the Ulster Protestant churches of all social levels. The political opposition ran the gamut from nonexistent to minuscule. Labor could not transcend the sectarian split in the working class in Ulster and so could never mobilize nonsectarian voting on the economic issues. Thus voters remained in the Unionist or Nationalist parties. Sinn Féin sporadically contested elections, but elected candidates would not take their seats. Sinn Féin, however, was transformed into the IRA in Ulster and took on the role of community defense. The Nationalist Party, representing the Catholic community, could never hold enough seats to make any political difference and was relegated to the marginal work of ameliorating problems for the Catholic community.

The British government after World War II forced a reluctant Unionist Party to accept the program of social welfare that was being enacted in London. Payments for unemployment, illness, orphanhood, retirement, health care, housing, and a host of other programs flowed into Ulster from London. One effect was an improvement in the standard of living of Catholics. Another effect was a reinforcement of the difference between the two regions of Ireland. Political differences were now multiplied by significant differences in state-supported welfare programs. By 1955 the change was demonstrable, and a backward Ulster had gone through a social transformation. The change in Northern Ireland had some effect on the Unionist Party as it developed a liberal wing—liberal, that is, in Unionist terms. The possibility of a Catholic being a Unionist candidate was even raised; the Orange Order, however, quickly put a stop to that notion.

Educational opportunity increased when Catholics took advantage of 1945 and 1947 acts that provided for free secondary schooling and went on to gain university educations. Catholics moved into the middle class in growing numbers as the professions of teaching, medicine, and law were opened to them. Many of these Catholics were less interested in Irish unification than in obtaining first-class citizenship in Northern Ireland.

From 1956 to 1961 the IRA carried on a campaign to drive the British out of Ulster by force. Sporadic and poorly organized, the effort took nineteen lives, and the campaign produced no wellspring of support in either the Republic or Ulster. De Valera took stern measures in the Republic, and the Stormont government did the same, so the whole effort petered out. As a result the IRA in Northern Ireland shifted its attention to social and economic matters and metamorphosed into a semi-Marxist pressure group.

In the Republic the rise of Sean Lemass represented a new stage in Fianna Fáil's traditional leadership and policies. In Ulster the choice of Terence O'Neill as prime minister in 1963 represented the victory of the liberal wing of the Unionist Party. To the ultraloyalists O'Neill's actions were shocking, to liberals they were pathbreaking, to people used to politics outside of Northern Ireland they were quite ordinary and would scarcely warrant such a fuss. O'Neill, for example, visited a Catholic school in 1965 and exchanged visits with Sean Lemass the same year, thus initiating official-level contacts between the two regions.

Tensions in Northern Ireland had cooled, the IRA campaign had been a failure, and talks between the two governments were proceeding tentatively on economic matters. To all appearances every indication was that Ireland was entering a new stage in intergovernmental and intercommunal relationships, but less attention was directed at the more negative developments that were occurring during the same period. It was true that Ireland was entering a new stage, but that stage was to be one of the most bitter and bloody in the long history of antagonism between Catholics and Protestants. The Reverend Ian Paisley, a Presbyterian fundamentalist minister and a demagogue, was attacking the Unionist Party from the right and denouncing the drift toward liberalism by the O'Neill wing. In the mid-sixties Paisley broke away from the Unionists to form the Protestant Unionist Party (later to become the Democratic Unionist Party) in order to organize the more extreme loyalists. Paisley directed his attack not only at the Unionists but at all attempts to establish a religious dialogue with Catholics. Paisley's demagogic appeal to the working-class Protestant and his militant tactics earned his party seats in Stormont and in Parliament. In 1966 a Protestant paramilitary force was created, and it took the name of the old Ulster Volunteer Force of 1913. This group announced that it would execute IRA men, and it did kill two Catholic men. That same year the organization was outlawed by the Special Powers Act, but it did not disappear. The year 1968 brought the political activity of the Northern Ireland Civil Rights Association, and what Conor Cruise O'Brien had called "the frozen violence" in Ulster promptly melted.

YEARS OF VIOLENCE, 1968–1972

The Unionist Party became completely disoriented by a change in Catholic political demands and methods. The Northern Ireland Civil Rights Association (NICRA), formed in 1967, did not set out to destroy the Stormont government, drive the British from Northern Ireland, or unify with the Republic. The group was composed of both Catholics and Protestants, and their objective was to reform the political system by ending discrimination in hiring and housing, eliminating the B Specials, ending the Special Powers Act, redistributing electoral boundaries, and expunging electoral restrictions. The methods they adopted were those of the U.S. civil rights movement—nonviolent demonstrations and marches. But the spark that lit the tinder was a demonstration in Derry in October of 1968. The demonstration had been banned by government officials because they feared violent confrontation with Protestants. Violence did occur, but it was between the RUC and the demonstrators; the police attacked the crowd, and eighty-eight police and demonstrators were injured. Feelings were aroused among the civil rights people, especially the more radical student movement (called People's Democracy) at Queen's University. Of lasting importance was the television exposure to the wider world of the Republic of Ireland and Britain of the "normal" procedures of the Ulster government and police. The glare of the camera brought international pressure on London to institute reforms, which then brought pressure on Belfast.

Unionist politicians could never quite comprehend why the world viewed the Stormont government as a backward group of oppressive bigots. Conservative Unionists were incapable of differentiating between the civil rights activities and the Catholic nationalist irredentist politics of fifty years earlier and treated the former as if they were the latter. O'Neill knew the difference, but he was caught in a trap between the loyalist Unionists and the British government, which was urging reforms along the lines demanded by the civil rights movement. In a 1968 speech O'Neill said Ulster stood at the crossroads between perpetual violence and an attempt to provide justice. O'Neill's personal commitment to reform was sincere, and he pressed the reforms on an increasingly recalcitrant Unionist Party. The reforms included replacing the local government in Derry with a Development Commission, appointing commissioners to investigate governmental discrimination, and rearranging housing allocation procedures into a more equitable system. Promised, but not implemented, were changes in the election laws and limitations on the Special Powers Act. O'Neill also dismissed William Craig, a conservative Unionist whose response to the civil rights agitation was simply to yell, "No surrender," and crush it, from his position as minister for home affairs.

The reforms had several effects, the first of which was to harden the position of the conservative Unionists against both O'Neill, who they believed was selling out, and the Catholics, who needed to be controlled (the civil rights movement, from their perspective, was simply Catholics up to their old tricks). The reforms split the civil rights movement into moderates, who, responding to O'Neill's plea, wished to wait and see if the government would undertake additional reforms, versus People's Democracy, which wished to continue pressure on the government until complete reform was forthcoming. The next march from Belfast to Derry was the work of the People's Democracy because Protestants and moderates were slipping away from the NICRA. At Burntollet Bridge in January of 1969 the marchers were viciously attacked by both Protestant mobs and the police. The antiwar demonstrators in the United States used to chant, "The whole world is watching," when police would break up demonstrations. Burntollet was watched with revulsion by British, U.S., and European television viewers as marchers were beaten with clubs and pipes. The Catholic community in Derry was attacked by the police as well. Tension was high in the following months, and there were additional clashes in Newry, Strabane, Derry, and Belfast.

In February of 1969 an election was held for the Stormont Parliament, and the results revealed the polarity of the different political groups. O'Neill was embarrassed by the strength of the hard-line Unionists, who were prompted by Craig and Paisley. The Nationalist Party virtually disappeared and was replaced by the Catholic civil rights activists led by John Hume and Austin Currie. The Unionists were fragmented, and the liberal Unionists certainly gained no mandate from the people. Under pressure from London and demands from his right-wing colleagues, and beset by the violent demonstrations and marches, O'Neill stepped down in April, and Major James D. Chichester-Clark became prime minister. In April an election was held in mid-Ulster for a parliamentary seat, and Bernadette Devlin, a young leader of People's Democracy, won. The result not only indicated Catholic sentiment, but it meant that in July a member of Parliament could be seen hurling paving stones at the police during riots provoked by the Orange Parade.

The Apprentice Boys' March in Derry is held each August 12 by Protestants to celebrate the siege of Londonderry in the spring of 1689 when the city held out against the forces of James II. Two hundred and eighty years later the city was to be the site of another form of siege. The parade in 1969 brought predictable confrontation, only it escalated into a virtual civil insurrection. The RUC tried to enter the Catholic district, the Bogside, and was driven out. The district was sealed off by the residents who denied entry to the police, which resulted in the forming of "no go" areas. The B Specials were called in, and restraint disappeared on all sides. Violence rose all over Ulster. In Belfast rioting and confrontation between Protestant and Catholic mobs broke out on August 14 as the violence continued in Derry. Police fire killed a nine-year-old, and five men died. Over 100 homes were burned out as Protestants attacked Catholic areas.

The Stormont government could not keep order, and British troops entered Derry on August 14 and Belfast one day later. Violence continued, but it subsided substantially. On August 13 the prime minister of the Republic, Jack Lynch, made a speech on television that did no more than cement the traditional attitudes of the two communities. He stated, "The Irish Government can no longer stand idly by and see innocent people injured and perhaps worse." Lynch went on to raise the specter that haunts the Protestant community: "Recognizing, however, that reunification of the national territory can provide the only permanent solution of the problem."[8] The first statement was taken by the Catholics to mean that the Republic would actually do something to respond to their plight (other than request UN troops) and that the traditional objective of a united Ireland was again a possibility.[9] The Protestants took little comfort as they had become convinced that a united Ireland, not civil rights, was the fundamental objective of the Catholics.

Initially the Catholics were buoyed by the arrival of the British troops as they represented security from both the Protestants and the police. "No go" areas such as "Free Derry" remained, however. The Chichester-Clark government was no more effective than O'Neill's had been at containing extreme Unionist sentiment or the violence. A number of significant reforms were enacted under British pressure, such as elimination of the B Specials, disarming the RUC, reforming local election laws, passing an Incitement to Hatred Bill, and creating a Central Housing Authority. By now, however, reform was seen by the Unionists as a concession to the rebels and by Catholics as mere window dressing in the face of RUC and B Special violence.

In the Catholic neighborhoods of Derry and Belfast in 1969 the statement, "IRA—I Ran Away," was written on the walls. Such comments were an embarrassment to that organization, which until the mid-1960s had seen its role to be protection of the Catholic community. The failure of the 1956–1962 campaign, however, had transformed the IRA. Economics and social issues, from a socialist point of view, were now the mainsprings of IRA political activism. In early 1970, under the press of events, the IRA split into two segments. The Northern Ireland IRA developed its own command, and at the same time, the new Provisional IRA broke away from the old Official IRA. The Provisionals (Provos) sought to provide protection to the Catholic community by using guns and working toward the restoration of a united Ireland. The Provos drew support from traditional Irish nationalists, especially in the United States, and after the split sometimes only an uneasy truce existed between the two IRA organizations.[10]

In June of 1970 the Conservatives came to power in London, and a combination of circumstances caused the situation in Northern Ireland to deteriorate rapidly. Although the Unionists were more politically in tune with the Conservative Party in London, the Conservatives knew little or nothing about Ulster. Ted Heath, the prime minister, appointed Reginald Maudling home secretary with responsibility for Ulster. Maudling's efforts were decidedly less than spectacular. The tail of Stormont wagged the dog of London during this period, and the use of the army and of repressive measures was approved by Maudling as he was relying on the perceptions and inclinations of the Unionists. The army began using CS gas, which, though not lethal, is debilitating and indiscriminate. In June 1970 the Catholics were not defended by the army during attacks by Protestant mobs in Belfast; in July the army imposed a curfew and carried out searches for weapons in the Catholic districts. The cumulative impact was to break the original bond between the Catholics and the army; the army was now seen as another arm of the Stormont government, imposing its will by force on the Catholics. The RUC, the Ulster Defense Regiment (a part-time security force), and the army were all at the service of Chichester-Clark, who by now was on a complete law-and-order path.

The "marching season" of July and August 1970 brought bitter and bloody clashes in Belfast and Derry. The anti-Unionist groups welded together in August to form the Social Democratic and Labour Party (SDLP). The title reflects the variety of political forces brought to the new party. The first leader, Gerry Fitt, hewed to a republican-labor standard, and John Hume, presently the head of the SDLP, came from the civil rights movement; other members were from the Nationalist Party and the Northern Ireland Labour Party. The

SDLP's program was socialist, nonsectarian, and advocated the reunification of Ireland through peaceful, democratic processes. However, the reunification position canceled the nonsectarian posture so the bulk of the party's supporters were Catholic.

Early 1971 brought fresh rounds of violence, and the first British soldier was killed by the IRA in February. Chichester-Clark's response was to demand more troops. In March Chichester-Clark was replaced by Brian Faulkner as prime minister, and the right wing of the Unionists agitated for an increasing crackdown on the violence. Faulkner took a two-pronged approach: He continued to implement reforms, but he also pressed for an increase in law and order. The situation was no better throughout the summer of 1971, however, and the shooting of two men in Derry by the British army prompted the SDLP to withdraw from Stormont. Their act was ineffectual, but it did indicate, along with the persistent violence, that the Stormont regime could do nothing more than satisfy an increasingly truculent Unionist right wing.

The Provisional IRA had undertaken a bombing campaign throughout the summer, which added to Unionist fury. The result was internment, which was introduced on August 9, 1971. Approximately 350 people were arrested at the outset and put in detention centers. The Catholic community was quickly radicalized as the policy of internment was directed solely at the IRA. The manner in which internment was carried out did not help either, as people were beaten, homes were searched, and innocent people were interned. The flow of young people to the IRA from 1969 to 1971 meant that the people who were interned were often old men or had been inactive IRA members for many years. Internees were overwhelmingly Catholic, and, moreover, they were treated harshly, virtually up to the point of torture. Thus the current leaders were not interned, and the movement surged with the addition of new members who were totally alienated from the London and Belfast governments.

Internment had the antipodal effect of its intent. IRA violence escalated rapidly, and the number of deaths in the next four months was almost six times as high as in the previous seven months. The Catholic community withheld rents, and Catholics withdrew from public office and local government. In October the SDLP set up an alternative assembly, which indicated the degree to which the two communities were distant and hostile.

The Catholics had been, in effect, driven into the hands of the IRA. The government lost all ability to govern in the Catholic ghettos, which were "no go" areas and devoid of social or economic ties with the larger community. Violence made life dangerous, and normal patterns of living disappeared and were replaced by a form of anarchy with troops in the streets, fires at night, homes burned out by the hundreds, bombs exploding in businesses, and snipers shooting at soldiers. Presiding over this chaos were Brian Faulkner and the Unionists, but Paisley and his followers formed the Democratic Unionist Party because Faulkner was not being harsh enough for their taste. Thus Faulkner stood, caught between the Unionists, who saw reform as the destruction of their statelet and were willing to shoot Catholics to preserve the Stormont rule, and the Catholics, who had long since abandoned civil rights and were now fighting for survival under the heel of the police and British troops. A move in any direction by Faulkner brought either cries of "sellout" or a new wave of bombings.

Paratroopers shot thirteen men dead and wounded more when they encountered an unauthorized civil rights march in Derry in January of 1972. It would be hard to conceive of a way to drive the Catholics to further fury and alienation, but Bloody Sunday, as the event was called, accomplished that end, and in the Republic of Ireland the British Embassy was burned to the ground a few days later. The specifics concerning the provocation of the paratroopers lost meaning in the bloody encounters that followed. William Craig drew the conservative, or traditional, Unionists together in a new organization entitled the Vanguard movement. Vanguard symbolized the degree of polarization in Ulster as Craig drew strong working-class support for an extremely militant line on the preservation of Stormont. Protestant paramilitary organizations such as the Ulster Defense Association were linked to the Vanguard movement; in fact, the Protestants feared a united Ireland more than they loved the Stormont government. The society they had preserved for fifty years was shattered into pieces, but if they could not have the restoration of their ascendancy, they could still preserve the political separation from the Republic, which was the very raison d'être of Ulster. Thus the Protestant threat of violence to preserve Stormont was less than the threat (and use) of violence against the Catholic community, because it was with the Catholics that the ultimate threat to Ulster resided.

In March 1971 the Heath government finally prorogued the Northern Ireland Parliament "temporarily," and the Unionist Party no longer had a political structure in which to maintain its domination. The objective of the Heath government in appointing William Whitelaw as secretary of state for Northern Ireland was to find a new foundation for governing the province as the Stormont regime demonstrably could not do so.

The collapse of the Stormont government was not the destruction of a stable civic order based upon popular support. On the contrary, the regime was capable of little more than perpetuating itself. Economic growth and employment came as a result of World War II, and as soon as the war ended the economic situation began to decay to levels only slightly above the prewar years. Social welfare and social services were pressed on Stormont by London, paid for by London (because the tax base of the province could not support such programs), and monitored by London. In matters of local authority and law enforcement the record was one of anti-Catholic discrimination and heavy-handed brutality. The regime did only one thing well: It preserved the colonial relic of the nineteenth-century Protestant ascendancy through the instruments of the Unionist Party and the Orange Order, which were based on opposition to a united Ireland. The regime had little will or incentive to transform or create. Unionist politics was a politics of preserving the abusive use of power under the guise of majority rule, in a provincial backwater supported by British taxpayers.[11] Few tears were shed by Ulster Catholics, citizens of the Republic, citizens of Britain, or even some Ulster Protestants when Stormont collapsed after half a century of being "a Protestant Parliament and a Protestant State."[12]

NOTES

1. See John H. Whyte, "Interpretations of the Northern Ireland Problem; An Appraisal," *Economic and Social Review* 9 (July 1978), pp. 257–282.

2. The collapsed boundary is a reflection of the fundamental contradiction accepted by Parliament in 1920. As Lawrence McCaffrey points out of the British Parliament in 1914: "They concluded that it would be unjust and unfair to place a twenty-five percent Protestant minority in a state controlled by a seventy-five percent Catholic majority. So in 1920 they placed a thirty-three percent Catholic minority under the domination of a sixty-six percent Protestant majority" (*Ireland: From Colony to Nation State* [Englewood Cliffs, N.J.: Prentice-Hall, 1979], p. 174).

3. Quoted in Thomas J. O'Hanlon, *The Irish: Portrait of a People* (London: André Deutsch, 1976), p. 244. Callahan, however, when he was British home secretary in the late 1960s, found the problems of Ulster far more difficult than those of the mayor of Lewisham.

4. John Darby, *Conflict in Northern Ireland* (Dublin: Gill and Macmillan, 1976), p. 85.

5. Ibid., pp. 48–79. Figures are adapted from the data presented by Darby.

6. Ibid. Darby cites the results of a study done by Alan Robinson in 1969 in which students in Derry were asked to name the capital of the country in which they lived. Over half the Catholics answered Dublin, over two-thirds of the Protestants answered Belfast. Ironically enough, both groups were wrong—such is sectarian education in Northern Ireland.

7. Robert Coles, "Ulster's Children," *Atlantic* (December 1980), p. 35.

8. Quoted in Conor Cruise O'Brien, *States of Ireland* (New York: Vintage Books, 1973), p. 179.

9. Lynch's suggestion of UN troops had surface plausibility, but the United Kingdom's being a permanent member of the Security Council (with a veto) and the British argument that the problem was one of domestic order meant that the United Nations could take no action.

10. Both segments used the name Sinn Féin for the public political wings of their organizations. This situation led to some confusion, and for some time the street on which a headquarters was located in Dublin became the identifying symbol: Officials, Gardiner Place Sinn Féin; Provisionals, Kevin Street Sinn Féin.

11. A heavy burden of responsibility for this state of affairs belongs to the British Parliament. It essentially ignored Ulster for fifty years and then was shocked in 1968 and 1969 to find an aggregation of bigots denying basic rights to British citizens through the use of violent means. The British government had little interest in or effort to put into Northern Ireland, and no cabinet-level officials or civil servants devoted full-time effort to the province until 1972.

12. James Craig, the first prime minister of Ulster, said this of the Stormont government in 1934 (quoted in Darby, *Conflict in Northern Ireland*, p. 84).

9

Northern Ireland:
The Search for Peace and Order

The violence in Ulster not only continued but escalated. On July 21, 1972, Bloody Friday, the IRA set off over twenty bombs, which resulted in the death of 9 and the injury of 130 people. The Ulster Defense Association began to respond to IRA violence with "no go" areas in Protestant neighborhoods. The British army removed the barricades, but its position was becoming increasingly dangerous as hostility was coming not only from the Catholics but from the Protestant militants as well. The crucial barricades were those of the Catholic areas in Derry and Belfast, as they had been in a state of isolation from law enforcement since 1969. In July the British army went in and removed those barriers and began to exert a tenuous form of control. It was not, obviously, a matter of uniformed policemen walking around and chatting with the locals; on the contrary, the army patrolled in armored vehicles amid unsheathed hostility on the part of the inhabitants.

The events since 1969 had split Unionists into several shards, the first being an extreme dissident wing, Paisley's Democratic Unionist Party. Craig now transformed his Vanguard movement of militants into the Vanguard Unionist Progressive Party, with the Ulster Defense Association and Loyalist Association of Workers as the paramilitary wing and the working-class base, respectively. The remaining Unionists followed Brian Faulkner and represented a moderate view in relation to the Paisleyites.

The Catholics, contrary to the Unionist pattern, had coalesced into the Social Democratic and Labour Party, thus eliminating the variety of representation that had existed in the Catholic community since 1920. The SDLP had lurking behind it the Official and Provisional IRAs, but the party took the position that Ulster could find a way to be governed without violence. The only other party of any weight was the Alliance Party. That party had grown out of the New Ulster movement, which had been founded in 1969 as a liberal-centrist pressure group. In 1971 it became a political party. The supporters of Alliance could not accept the extremists of the Unionist Party nor the radicals of the civil rights movement and stood for nonsectarianism, a constitutional settlement of Ulster's problems, and a concern for justice for all citizens. The sectarian gorge was so wide, however, that Alliance could garner only a small number of seats for its centrist position.

THE SUNNINGDALE EXPERIMENT

In March 1973 the British government put forth a white paper entitled *Northern Ireland: Constitutional Proposals*.[1] The central feature of the proposals was power sharing. Ulster was to have an Assembly of eighty representatives elected by a system of proportional representation. Firm guarantees of Catholic civil rights were to be accompanied by guaranteed seats on the Executive Committee in proportion to the number of Catholics in the Assembly. Powers of the Assembly were to be more circumscribed than those of the Stormont government had been. The British Parliament passed the Northern Ireland Assembly Act, and elections were held in June of 1973. The results indicated that the Faulkner Unionists still had somewhat of a grip on the party as they won twenty-three seats. SDLP won nineteen, Alliance had nine, and the conservative Unionists together had twenty-seven votes spread among the Democratic Unionist Party (DUP), Vanguard, and other hard-line Unionists. The majority of the people elected (about fifty-one) were committed to making the new government work. In the following months a power-sharing Executive Committee was formed, composed of one Alliance member, four SDLP members, and six Faulkner Unionists.

As so often happens in Ulster, when a bridge is built in the center, the extremes begin to torpedo it because their objectives are not served by moderation. The IRA denounced the whole idea of power sharing as a continuation of British rule, and to its members elimination of British rule was the real solution, not puppet assemblies. The Craig and Paisley forces denounced the plan as a step toward a united Ireland (because of the Council of Ireland proposal discussed below) and as a sellout of majority, i.e., Protestant, rule. In regard to the power-sharing Executive Committee, the blow would come from the extreme Unionists in the following year.

In December of 1973 a meeting was held in Sunningdale, England, to discuss a Council of Ireland, which had been proposed in the white paper. The power-sharing Executive of Northern Ireland and cabinet members from Dublin and London hammered out a plan for an elected Consultative Assembly and a ministry of fourteen members, half from Belfast, half from Dublin.

In many ways what was important about the Sunningdale meeting was not the new Council of Ireland proposal but the policy changes, assumptions, and directions of the governments involved. For London the very proposal of a Council of Ireland in the 1973 white paper was a major departure from the traditional posture that Ulster was exclusively British; it was no less than a formal recognition of what the SDLP called "the Irish dimension." In the Ireland Act of 1949 the British had committed themselves to no change in the status of Northern Ireland without the consent of a majority of the people, and the degree to which London's attitude had changed was a reflection of British public opinion against the Unionists and a recognition that Northern Ireland was never going to have peace unless it acknowledged its geographical, historical, and cultural ties to the Republic.

The Dublin officials went to Sunningdale optimistic that with a policy of power sharing, their coreligionists in the North could bring some peace and stability to the province. In time, then, the two governments could move slowly to expand the all-Ireland aspects, which would ultimately lead to a united Ireland. Liam Cosgrave, the prime minister of the Republic, promised to recognize Northern Ireland as a British territory as long as the citizens of Ulster chose to remain so. For the Republic this concession was both a repudiation of the constitutional claim as well as a step away from rhetorical claims on the North and a step toward dealing with the reality of 1 million Protestants who did not want to be unloaded onto the Republic by London or bombed into it by the IRA.

The Republic of Ireland's response to the Northern problem displayed a lot of ambivalence. The traditions of Fianna Fáil, and the deep-seated feelings of the people, pushed the Republic toward powerful condemnations of the Stormont regime and sympathy and support for the Catholics in Ulster. The arms trial and the fact that southern Ireland was a refuge for IRA men influenced this attitude. On the other hand, when bombs went off in Dublin in 1972, 1974, and 1975 and the British ambassador was assassinated in 1976, Dublin responded with antiterrorist legislation, an Emergency Powers Bill, and a declaration of a state of national emergency. IRA men were tried without juries, and interned, and civil liberties took a back seat to preventing the violence of Ulster from sweeping into the Republic. The early 1970s saw a debate in Ireland on the nature of the constitution and the Catholic nature of the state because Ulster Protestants often declared that the Republic was run by the church. In response to liberal pressure, the special position of the Catholic church was deleted from the Republic's constitution in 1972 by a national referendum. Overall, however, the impact of the Northern Ireland crisis on the Republic was less than one might have expected. Businessmen worried about investments, the Tourist Board worried about declining rates of tourism, and large numbers of ordinary people talked of Ulster as an alien place from which they feared violence but toward which they felt no sense of passionate nationalism.

In an atmosphere charged with hope, the power-sharing Executive assumed its duties in early 1974. The Assembly contained, in opposition to the power-sharing parties, a group of more extreme Unionists who did not want the Assembly to exist, let alone function, and those members withdrew in January. The Executive struggled along despite the handicap of the extreme wings of each sectarian community engaging in persistent violence. Power sharing and the Council of Ireland were too much for some members of Faulkner's Unionist Party to bear, and they abandoned Faulkner to form with other extreme Unionists the United Ulster Unionist Council (UUUC). Thus the power-sharing Executive now contained only a sliver of the original Unionist Party members, and what fragile consensus it had ever had was gone.

The end of the power-sharing Executive came in May 1974 when the Ulster Workers Council called a general strike in Belfast to protest the Council of Ireland and demanded that the council be eliminated. The Ulster Workers Council was tied to the more extreme wings of the Protestant organizations and received support from the extreme Unionists and paramilitaries. The strike began to take its toll, and the Unionists in the Executive were under a great deal of pressure. The SDLP, in a move that was totally self-defeating, agreed to the postponement of the Council of Ireland for four years. The extremists then demanded the resignation of the Executive members and new elections. Polls at the time in Ulster indicated that only 40 percent of the people supported the Council of Ireland but that 70 percent supported power sharing. The pressure proved too great, however, and Faulkner resigned. In two weeks the strike destroyed the power-sharing Executive. Once again the extremists, in this case the Protestants, had caused the center to crumble. Harold Wilson, the British prime minister, bore a great deal of the responsibility for the failure. Although the power-sharing Executive was too slender a reed to support the hopes that were built upon it, or to surmount the opposition against it, Wilson made the struggle impossible. Bringing in a few troops far too late to be effective, Wilson belied his assurances that he would preserve the government and the Executive. The new government in Northern Ireland was suspended after five months.

The efforts to create a new government had done little to diminish the violence, which poured forth in a steady stream. The extreme ends of the two communities had hardened their respective and irreconcilable positions and proceeded to shoot, burn, and bomb to achieve them. The Provisional IRA on the one hand and the UDA on the other engaged in a minuet of sectarian assassinations followed by reprisals, followed by revenge, followed by funerals, followed by people whose lives were being ravaged by tragedy. By the autumn of 1974 over 1,000 people had died in the violence, and 2,400 had been injured. The province had nearly 20,000 British troops stationed in it, and the bombings spread to Dublin where in May 1974, 23 people died and hundreds were wounded.

Once again London attempted to create a government in Ulster. In 1974 a British white paper called for elections to a Constituent Assembly, which would then form a government. The government, however, had to include power sharing and an "Irish dimension," and had to be acceptable to the British Parliament. The elections to Westminster in the fall of 1974 gave an indication of things to come as the UUUC took ten of twelve seats. The election to the Constituent Assembly displayed the same commitment to loyalist Unionists as they took forty seats, whereas Faulkner Unionists won twelve seats, Alliance took eight seats, and the SDLP won seventeen seats.

In the summer and fall of 1975 the Assembly met in an atmosphere of tension that was not conducive to compromise. The UUUC splintered as Craig was willing to come closer to power sharing than Paisley, but in the end the loyalists pulled together and proposed to London a government that rejected power sharing and the Irish dimension. Based as it was on majority rule, the scheme was designed to restore the domination of the loyalist Protestants. London rejected the plan, and the Assembly ended with Paisley spewing sulfurous invective at his opponents. The British diverted their efforts thereafter to talking with the various parties in Ulster. Officially committed to a devolved government, successive secretaries for Northern Ireland avoided efforts such as a power-sharing Executive and the Constituent Assembly until 1982 when

London proposed the election of another Assembly. In October elections were held, and they revealed again the polarity of the positions in the politics of Northern Ireland. Sinn Féin, representing the IRA, won five seats, and at the other end Paisley's DUP won twenty-one. Thus 32 percent of the vote went to the extremes. If we add the percentage given to the Official Unionists (the party that emerged out of the ruins of the old Unionist Party), 64 percent of the electorate would have to be characterized as extremely rigid. There is little common ground on the questions of local rule and the relationship with the Republic among the voters in Ulster.

THE WOMEN'S PEACE MOVEMENT

In 1976 the stage shifted from the corridors of Whitehall and Stormont to the streets of Belfast. Mauread Corrigan and Betty Williams, residents of Belfast, were revulsed by the continuing violence, especially when three youths were killed by a runaway vehicle driven by an IRA man. They contacted other women who lived in fear and began a series of small, silent marches and vigils to protest the violence around them. To the shock of the militant groups, who assumed they had the complete support of their respective communities, the movement mushroomed rapidly into a series of marches every weekend. The numbers were extraordinary, running from 5,000 to 20,000. What was more surprising is that the participants were nonsectarian and tapped a wellspring in both communities against the mayhem. Known as the Women's Peace movement, it also had behind the scenes a former journalist, Ciaran McKeown, who developed the movement's program while the two women drew public attention to the frustration in Ulster.

Clergy of several faiths marched together, thousands of people signed petitions, and activists flowed to the movement. The media in Ireland and Britain focused on the marches, and later the media of Europe and the United States did also. Money poured in from around the world. A massive march in London in November of 1976 riveted attention on the peace movement, and the militant groups were on the defensive. In the fall of 1976 the two women won the Norwegian Peoples Peace Prize and then the Nobel Peace Prize in February of 1977.

McKeown wrote a manifesto for the movement that stressed its pacifist and grass-roots orientation. He called for a movement that would be community based and oriented toward solving problems, such as needed playgrounds and health clinics, in an approach that would be relatively free of traditional doctrinal positions. The nonsectarian aspect was emphasized in the focus on common problems across the two ethnic communities at the local level instead of the constitutional status of Northern Ireland.

At its peak of success through 1977 and 1978 the movement did more to bridge the sectarian divide than had been done for a long time. Small groups of women from both communities would meet for tea and discuss common fears and suffering. Organizations sprang up in the towns, newsletters were printed, and local activities were initiated. These accomplishments were limited but not negligible. Williams and Corrigan kept the Ulster problem highly visible as they traveled extensively raising funds.

In the period from 1978 to 1980 the movement began to decay. The leading figures began to have differences of opinion, and the two women were sharply criticized for keeping the Nobel Prize money and not donating it to the movement. Betty Williams quit in 1980, and the movement finally ended up as a modest community-action group still operating in Belfast.

The Women's Peace movement confronted some deeply held bitterness and some hard men. The Protestant and Catholic communities' collective memories could not be swept away in the burst of emotional frustration, nor were the men of the UVF and the IRA simply going to drop their guns and join a peace march. The movement's attempt to be nonpolitical was a difficult if not impossible task. Initiated by emotional energy, the movement mobilized that emotion into a visible and constructive force. Such an effort requires money, time, and expertise, and thus organization becomes necessary. The group then was confronted with choices that in the highly charged atmosphere of Ulster became divisive. John Hume noted in 1977 that after the emotions of the peace movement wore away, the political divisions of Northern Ireland would remain.[2] At best the Women's Peace movement could only shape the climate for a settlement of the issues; it could not provide a settlement. But the political climate, like the actual climate of Northern Ireland, proved too harsh.

In 1977 another failure of a more sectarian nature occurred. Ian Paisley, who had emerged as a powerful spokesman for the loyalists, decided to return to an earlier strategy to force the British to restore self-government to Ulster. He called a general strike in May similar to the one of 1974 that had brought down the power-sharing government. Paisley had the support of the extreme loyalists and the Protestant paramilitaries, but the strike was a failure. Far fewer men stayed out of work than Paisley had expected, despite the efforts of the paramilitaries to force workers to stay home. Paisley's lack of success in this effort indicated that the Protestant workers had been angry enough in 1974 to bring down a government that included the Council of Ireland but they were not powerful enough in 1977 to force London to restore a government to the province.

Violence continued throughout the years. A wave of firebombings occurred, and two soldiers were killed when the queen visited Belfast in August of 1977. The year 1978 found London embarrassed by its treatment of internees—not for the first time. When the initial confrontations had ignited across Ulster, the British government had pressured Stormont to appoint commissions to investigate them. In 1969 two of these reported: the first in September, the Cameron Commission on the August riots; the second, the Hunt Commission on the police in Northern Ireland, in October. The reports were damaging to the Stormont regime and embarrassing to London, as the commissions called for the elimination of the B Specials and made forty-seven recommendations for changes in the RUC. The Cameron Commission reported that members of the B Specials had been part of the mob that had attacked the civil rights demonstrators at Burntollet Bridge in 1969. The RUC was described as anti-Catholic and, in the case of the Burntollet riot, charged with brutality in Derry. The reports were sensitive to the difficulties the RUC faced, such as manpower shortages and widespread violence since 1968, but the weight of the reports were clearly against the police. In 1972 the Stormont Commission reached similar conclusions concerning the RUC and its abuses of Catholics.

After internment was introduced in 1971 reports of physical and psychological abuse of the internees increased; leaving prisoners naked, hooding, i.e., putting hoods over a prisoners' heads, and beatings were alleged to be common practices at Long Kesh Prison outside Belfast. In 1971 the Compton Report investigated the interrogation of internees and found evidence of ill-treatment. In 1972 Amnesty International reported on the abuse of internees and concluded that the ill-treatment amounted to brutality. Although internment ceased in 1975 the Republic of Ireland brought the accumulated evidence before the European Human Rights Commission as both the Republic and the United Kingdom were by then members of the European Community. In 1976 London was embarrassed by the report of the European Commission that, in fact, the interned prisoners were subjected to cruelty and to brutal treatment. Prime Minister James Callahan then asked the Republic of Ireland not to take the commission's evidence to the European Court of Human Rights. Callahan argued that such an act would only exacerbate tensions as internment had been terminated and Dublin and London were cooperating on the control of cross-border terrorism. Prime Minister Lynch refused, and in 1978 the European Court ruled that the techniques used to interrogate prisoners were "inhumane and degrading treatment" and violated the European Convention on Human Rights, the first such judgment since the founding of the European Community.[3]

In May of the same year Amnesty International struck again, indicating that the treatment of prisoners was abusive and that the legal rights of suspects were regularly violated. Stung, Roy Mason, secretary for Northern Ireland, denied the allegations but appointed the Bennett Committee to investigate. That committee concluded that, in fact, prisoners were beaten, and it suggested reforms. The position of London on the whole question of the treatment of prisoners essentially was that they were not abused, but if they were, such treatment was necessary and not excessive. The vulnerability of London concerning the treatment of IRA prisoners was to surface again in 1980 and especially in 1981.

The year 1979 brought a series of brutal assassinations, not all in Northern Ireland. Killed were Richard Sykes, the British ambassador to the Netherlands; Aery Neave, a member of the British Parliament and a close associate of Margaret Thatcher; and Earl Mountbatten and three others, including his grandson. Sykes was killed in Holland; Neave, right outside of the British Parliament; and Mountbatten and the others, in Donegal Bay. At the time of Mountbatten's death an IRA ambush also killed eighteen soldiers in Northern Ireland. This trail of blood did little to further the IRA cause as public revulsion was matched by Margaret Thatcher's determination not to be bombed out of Ulster. Thatcher, who took power in 1979, had a series of meetings with Jack Lynch that led to an increased emphasis on cross-border security.

THE HUNGER STRIKES

Thatcher's greatest difficulty, however, was to come on the issue of the treatment of IRA prisoners. In 1972 William Whitelaw, secretary of state for Northern Ireland, responded to a hunger strike by IRA and loyalist prisoners by granting them a form of prisoner-of-war status that included wearing their own clothes, being able to mix freely, and doing no prison work. In 1975 the government adopted the policy of "criminalization," which held that the crimes committed by IRA and loyalist paramilitaries were ordinary crimes and the perpetrators were ordinary criminals. The policy is legally dubious as most IRA men are convicted under the Emergency Provisions Act, which justifies extraordinary measures in order to deal with terrorists and then defines terrorism as using violence for political ends. There is little doubt that the actions of the IRA men are politically motivated and that they can be subjected to arrest for questioning, detained for three to seven days, tried without a jury, and subjected to pressure to give confessions. Although these factors seem to make invoking the policy of criminalization a contradiction, they still do not necessarily justify special treatment in prison.

In 1976 the government began to phase out the special status of those IRA men who were in the H Block section (so-called because of its shape) of Maze Prison. This section contained over 900 prisoners, 600 of whom were IRA members. Four hundred and seventeen of the prisoners protested the change and began to refuse to wear prison clothes, instead covered themselves with blankets, refused privileges, and smeared their cells with excrement. The British government's response was to label their demands as a maneuver to achieve political status and thus open the possibility of amnesty. At the end of 1980 some of the prisoners went on a hunger strike in order to achieve five demands: (1) freedom to not wear prison clothes, (2) ability to freely associate or mix, (3) no compulsion to do prison work, (4) one letter, one parcel, and one visit a week, and (5) full remission on sentences (remission is one day off a sentence for each day of good behavior). After fifty-three days the strike was settled, or at least it appeared to be so. After the turn of the year, however, the prisoners felt that the government had reneged on the agreement, and Bobby Sands, a spokesman during the earlier hunger strike, began his own fast in January of 1981. Sands was followed by others who began fasting (eventually Sands and nine other men died), and this hunger strike put the British government in an embarrassing position as the demands appeared to be reasonable.

Public opinion shifted against Thatcher's policy. Three members of the Republic's Dáil went to see Sands to ask him to take the protest to the European Commission on Human Rights, which a year earlier had put pressure on the British government to meet some of the complaints of the Maze prisoners. The effect of Thatcher's uncompromising stand was to turn the complaints of the prisoners into the broader question of the whole situation in Northern Ireland. The IRA supported increased violence in the streets, and the situation reverted back to that of the early seventies. The position of London remained the same. William Whitlaw stated:

We are totally committed to continuing to maintain British troops in the province to protect the great majority of law-abiding citizens. There can be no question of ever washing our hands of the whole affair. The Army stays for as long as is needed to uphold law and order. There is no other alternative. We cannot and will not abandon Ulster to the extremists on either side. That way lies civil war.[4]

Whitelaw should have said "all-out civil war," as the record since 1969 is hardly one of peaceful relations between Protestants and Catholics. The death toll in 1981 stood at 2,100; injuries at 22,000; and the ruined families, businesses, and psyches cannot be counted.

THE FUTURE OF NORTHERN IRELAND

In books, essays, and speeches on Northern Ireland the title or the concluding section often includes the world "solution." Particular developments are cited as weak but positive indicators of any given possible solution, such as the liberal Unionists' efforts, civil rights, reform legislation, rule from London, power sharing, and the Women's Peace movement. All attempts have failed, and the province is riven as grievously as it ever has been. Hopes for a solution, movement toward a solution, or even amelioration of the conflict depend upon the explanation one favors as to the fundamental "cause" of the conflict in Ulster. John Whyte discusses three Marxist and six non-Marxist interpretations of Northern Ireland, and Arendt Lipjhart offers ten different portraits of Northern Ireland, each emphasizing one facet of the crisis such as religion, colonialism, and pseudodemocracy.[5] The conflict in Northern Ireland is certainly multidimensional, but it plays itself out in political terms. We can examine the layers of the antagonism between the communities and then the political consequences.

Ethnic Conflict

Religion plays a powerful role in the Northern Ireland conflict. The very labels used, Protestant and Catholic, ascribe an overtly religious antagonism to the conflict and submerge the religious differences within each community. Religion, however, plays the role of an integrating value system at the center of a broader network of community features that provide a distinct ethnic character for each group. Cynthia Enloe, among others, defines an ethnic group as a group of people who are culturally distinct and view themselves as being so. The group members share common beliefs and values, which to some degree set them apart.[6] The common bonds in such groups include such characteristics as religion, race, language, social mores, and national identity.

In the province of Ulster the two communities are ethnically distinct and the central, but not sole, difference is religious affiliation.[7] The difference in religion, however, is accompanied by more subtle, but real, differences in speech and interpersonal relationships. The more overt differences include those in sporting activities, social life, music, dance, and education. The last provides distinctive differences in a community's view of history, tradition, and national identity. In the historical development of the identities of the two ethnic communities, religion played a powerful role in defining the distinctiveness of the respective national or regional identities, and consequently the political center of power around which each would orbit. In the case of the Catholics it was Sinn Féin, Catholicism, Dublin, and Ireland, whereas in the case of the Protestants it was Unionism, Protestantism, London, and Britain (or its regional center, Belfast/Ulster). The lack of any great degree of inter-marriage also preserved a racial stock in each case: Scottish on the one hand, Celtic (or a Celtic blend) on the other.

None of the identified differences in the two ethnic communities nec-essarily lead to the incandescent hostility that is characteristic of Ulster as examples abound of diverse ethnic communities living together in peace socially and politically. Clearly the key ingredient is that which turns ethnic difference into ethnic hatred.

The crucial variables are conflicting political and economic interests. From the outset the concrete economic and political interests of the Ulster planters and the indigenous Catholics were almost mutually exclusive and thus par-ticularly intense. The three sets of interests that divided them were land, religion, and power. In the case of land, the conflict hinged on the expropriation of land owned by Catholics and its transferal to Scots Presbyterians. History is replete with examples in which such actions engendered severe conflict between the groups involved, even if they shared the same ethnic identity and faith. With respect to religion, the conflicting interest was not so much one of doctrine as the use of political (i.e., legal) power to eradicate one community's faith through the penal laws. The clash of political interests was over the fundamental question as to who was to rule. Picking a specific point to represent the opposition of political interests must be symbolic, to some degree, as such opposition has deep roots. Home rule, however, represented for the Ulster Protestants the blunt threat of rule by the other ethnic community, as, say, the Irish Parliament of 1782 to 1800 did not because it was based on the Protestant ascendancy. However constrained, home rule, explicitly or by implication, meant that the Catholic majority would wield power over the Protestant minority in all of Ireland, including Ulster.

The Catholic church was identified with the religious issue, of course, but also with the land issue to some degree and with the political thrust for home rule as well. To the Protestant this involvement reinforced the ethnic divide, in which religion was central, as in the clash of political interests the church cast its weight against Protestant interests. To a certain degree this opposition was ironic as the hierarchy of the Catholic church in Ireland had almost variably supported British authority (except with respect to education).

The Irish-Ireland movement at the end of the nineteenth century had the effect of evoking in the Catholics of Ulster a powerful cultural feeling that helped to define their national identity. This cultural nationalism was obviously not shared by the Protestants, but it did mean that their sense of British national identity was reinforced.

Thus ethnic distinctiveness was reinforced by political conflict, which translated the ethnic cultural differences into differences of national identity. Political contests in which power is diffused among multiple groups with crosscutting interests of moderate intensity and that take place in arenas in which political institutions have multiple access points are considered pluralist. Favorable or unfavorable outcomes are shared among the contestants, and such contests will only occasionally reinforce ethnic and cultural identity as opposed to political identity. However, when the political contest is between two groups and the favorable outcomes always favor one group, then the ethnic identity of each of the two groups will not only be reinforced, but reinforced in the context of superiority and inferiority, or oppressor and oppressed.

Thus in Northern Ireland the movement from being a part of the United Kingdom to home rule to partition created the political reality of dual minorities and the consequent impact on ethnicity. The dual minority idea is simply stated: The Catholics are a minority in Northern Ireland and have been discriminated against politically and economically. Thus they have reinforced their ethnic identity, especially the religious and national components. The Protestants are a minority in the whole of Ireland and consequently fear integration into a Catholic-dominated state in which their privileges would be eradicated. Each group points to the practices of the other. The Catholics point to fifty years of Unionist/Orange/Protestant rule in Ulster; the Protestants point to sixty years of Nationalist/Green/Catholic rule in the Republic of Ireland. It is not difficult to translate political differences into religious differences, especially for the committed on both sides. Paisley rants about the "whore of Rome," and the bishops in the Republic speak of Ireland as "a Catholic nation."

Under pressure, conflicting ethnic groups tend to reinforce their own communal values and to stereotype their vision of the "out group." Not only is the other group seen as different but as inferior, and the majority group tends to elevate the virtues of its group and denigrate the attributes of the other. In the case of the Protestants this tendency takes the form of seeing the Catholics as garrulous, lazy, dirty, and superstitious. The Catholics, on the other hand, view the Protestants as cold-blooded, ruthless, inhumane, and oppressive. In Northern Ireland the out group, or underclass, is the Catholics, and political and economic advantage blend into, and reinforce, the Protestant stereotype of superiority. In Ireland as a whole the Protestants are not an underclass, being traditionally ascendant, but they fear that they would become so in an Irish Catholic state. For the Protestants the language of ethnic solidarity tends to be the language of their central value, i.e., religion; the same is true for the Catholics in the North. The antagonism between the two communities is rooted, then, in political conflict, which is split along ethnic lines; reinforced in emotional intensity by the perceptions of minority status by both communities; and expressed in the language of the central ethnic values, religion and nationality.

For the Ulster Protestant, however, the question of nationality is more difficult. The conflict in national terms is between Irish Catholics and Ulster Protestants, but the Ulster Protestants, being Irish—i.e., residents of Ireland for nearly 400 years—do not have quite the same attitude in asserting their Britishness as the Catholics do in asserting their Irishness. The Ulster Protestant identifies with Britain in symbol and political loyalty because it is the alternative to the Irish Catholic identification. The Protestants' British nationality remains qualified, however, by the fact that the claim is really for an Ulster-in-Britain nationality. A powerful pull on the Protestants in Northern Ireland is their identification with Ulster. The Ulster Protestant may not really have a nationality at all—i.e., an Ulster nationality—but adopts the British nationality for essentially negative reasons, not to be part of Irish-Ireland. The result for the Ulster Protestant is an absolutely frantic claim to Britishness, adopted about a century ago to preserve a dominant economic and political position, which is expressed in a language of religious bigotry that repels a great number of the British. The British, in fact, do not see the Ulster Protestants as British but rather as Irish, and although Ulster is attached to the United Kingdom, it is left alone and considered to be quite distinct. Many Britons have little or no identification with the Protestants of Ulster, and that number has increased to a large degree, which leaves the Ulster Protestants in the vulnerable position of being afraid that they are not wanted by London. The ultimate expression of this fear is the ultraloyalist's shooting of a British soldier in order to remain British.

Political Solutions

The "solutions" offered for the Northern Ireland problem tend to approach the interlocking aspects of the conflict at different levels. For those people who see the problem as one of the ethnic communal conflict there is a tendency to focus on education and socialization against hostile stereotypes and to offer policies designed to reduce communal tensions. These policies include more interaction among the youth and less communal reinforcement in the schools. Religious leaders are urged to condemn the hatred and to "love thy neighbor" (this last having been tried many times to no effect). The people who stress the religious dimension focus on the need for greater toleration and in particular the dismantling of the obvious political manifestations of religious doctrine such as the Republic of Ireland's stand on the special position of the Catholic church, divorce, and contraception.

Political solutions to the Ulster crisis tend to fall into roughly three categories. In the first category Ulster stays tied to Britain in one fashion or another; in the second category Ulster becomes independent, tied neither to the Republic nor to Great Britain except perhaps by economic guarantees or something similar. A variation on the first two categories is to include the suggestion of repartition. The third category would place Ulster under the sovereignty of the Republic of Ireland. In categories one and three, suggestions for a devolved government are usually included so that Ulster would have some local control whether tied to Britain or to Ireland. Many variations on the above themes can be spun, but those three options are always at the base of the suggestions.

In each version the political difficulties are immense, and the potential for violence is high. Ulster's remaining part of the United Kingdom presents the difficulties that exist at present. The drive for majority rule on the part of the loyalists stymies the development of local rule, and the IRA quest to drive the British out of Northern Ireland ensures that the violence will continue. Whether the tactic is hunger strikes, bombing, or assassination, the extreme

Catholic wing can always cause the collapse of any dialogue at the "center" of the political spectrum in Northern Ireland. Conversely, as has been seen with power sharing and the Council of Ireland, the extreme wing of the Protestant community can sabotage any tentative links with the Republic.

An independent Ulster in many ways is the worst of all worlds. The Protestant community would be shorn of British economic and, more important, security assistance. The responsibility for security would fall to the Protestants, who would revert in all likelihood to the style of control they displayed from 1920 to 1972. A statelet of Ulster would hardly satisfy the IRA as that solution would accomplish only half of the IRA objectives, removal of the British, but not the other half, a united Ireland. The same difficulties that exist at present would prevail in an independent Ulster, i.e., the inability to form a government that would legitimately serve both communities. Thus loyalists and the IRA would clash in a bloody encounter as their ultimate political objectives would still be mutually exclusive.

Repartition is occasionally suggested in the context of the above two options so as to minimize the size of the Catholic community in Ulster. Whether in the case of remaining a part of the United Kingdom or of becoming an independent entity, repartition would hardly satisfy the IRA, which would only see a smaller geographical unit cut off from the political unity of Ireland. The anger over the original partition in 1920 would be mirrored in the present day and would place a terrible stress on the Catholics in Northern Ireland. The population distribution within Ulster is such that repartition would not mean simply redrawing the border but a large-scale movement of people. Finally, the resultant entity would be so economically frail that it would collapse without Irish or British, or dual, economic guarantees. Thus a principality would be created that would be incapable of being politically or economically self-sustaining, and the violence would probably continue.

Union with the Republic of Ireland simply shifts the pendulum of armed resistance to the Protestant paramilitaries rather than to the IRA. The transition— no matter what timing, structures, or protections were to be included—would in all likelihood be a modern replay of 1886. Absolute Protestant intransigence ("Not an inch") would raise the threat of widespread violence that could freeze Britain's political nerve at the moment of transition. Ireland also would tremble as it entertained visions of its small army fighting a guerrilla war with a million Protestants for an indeterminate length of time. The Republic must also contemplate what would actually happen were it reunited with Ulster. Although it is certainly not a theocracy, the Republic has a strong Catholic flavor. Political structures would have to be refashioned, and a "successful" guerrilla army, the IRA, would have to be assimilated.

Thus, from maintaining the status quo to establishing a united Ireland, and all solutions in between, the picture is one of continuing or escalating violence and political upheaval. Such turmoil is hardly conducive to investors, thus ensuring continuing unemployment; or to stable childhood experiences, thus perpetuating communal hatred; or to rational dialogue, thus certifying that political confrontations will never attain political consensus.

The crucial task in Northern Ireland is to delegitimize the extremes, the loyalist paramilitaries and the republican paramilitaries. The preconditions of historical conflict, ethnic tension and persistent violence, all favor the gunman. In the case of the Protestants, the leading political spokesman, Ian Paisley, is representative of the extreme wing. The spokesman for the Catholics, however, John Hume of the SDLP, is not at the extreme of his community and competes with the IRA. Both Paisley and the IRA can capitalize on the emotional surges that accompany bloodshed. If the moderates find common ground, it will invariably include some element that the extremes cannot accept. Power sharing, the Irish dimension, maintaining the link with Britain—whatever element emerged, it is a threat to the absolute positions of the extreme wings.

Trying to crush the IRA with the British army has only provoked the IRA to reorganize, professionalize, improve security, and forge international links for arms supply. A deadly standoff occurs daily, and the members of the Catholic community applaud, support, or tolerate the IRA.

The solution must begin with the British and Irish governments' declaring that at some unspecified date in the future Ulster will revert to Irish sovereignty. This statement must be accompanied by elaborate and well-publicized work on the various possible political arrangements that would bind the two sections of Ireland together. At the same time the security of Northern Ireland must be preserved so that the advantage of a violent response would be seen to be short term or nonexistent. Centrist community leaders must be strengthened by incorporating them into the process of designing the new political structures. The extremes must be left in a position in which they can only provide violence but cannot stave off the inevitable. The inevitability of the transition would confront the Protestant community with the choice of "not an inch" or pragmatic accommodation to the new status. Preservation and advancement of that community's political interests must be seen to be more valuable than a violent Armageddon. The problem of governing Northern Ireland would be, in fact, secondary to the governing of the whole of Ireland, and it is necessary to redirect some of the expenditures of political energy from the futile endeavor of creating a devolved government in Ulster to the positive creation of a new structure. Provisions would have to be made for emigration to Britain for those who chose it and for financial assistance to the government of Ireland to balance the inequities in the two regions as it absorbs the responsibility for providing social welfare.

The Republic of Ireland would have to "face the music" and do more than provide rhetorical support for the Northern Catholics. Its citizens would have to confront the implicit and explicit Catholic aspects of their government and search for a form of pluralism that could preserve the Catholic tradition of the state without imposing Catholic doctrine on people who do not profess that faith.

In a sporadic, sometimes, violent, process British authority would give way to the newly created instrument of Irish authority, and at some point the advocates of physical force would become increasingly remote from the real struggle of building a new kind of Ireland. In the indeterminate future, the ethnic affiliations of the Protestants and the Catholics would be just that, ethnic affiliations, not the stimulus to violence. However, they would probably still color the political alignment.

This solution probably has no more plausibility than the solutions noted earlier. It rests fundamentally upon two premises: The problem is basically political, and Ulster, with all its troubles, is Irish. Under this solution the remnant of British rule in Ireland would be eradicated, and everybody, it would seem, would live happily ever after. Probably not—but more might have the chance simply to live.

NOTES

1. *Northern Ireland: Constitutional Proposals* (London: Stationery Office, 1973).

2. Hume made this statement in a private conversation with the author.

3. Burns H. Weston, Richard A. Falk, and Anthony A. D'Amato, *International Law and World Order* (St. Paul, Minn.: West Publishing Co., 1980), p. 523.

4. Quoted in "Fury in Northern Ireland," *Time*, May 4, 1981, p. 13.

5. John H. Whyte, "Interpretations of the Northern Ireland Problem: An Appraisal," *Economic and Social Review* 9 (July 1978), pp. 257–282. See also Arendt Lipjhart, "The Northern Ireland Problem: Cases, Theories, and Solutions," *British Journal of Political Science* 5 (January 1975), pp. 83–106.

6. Cynthia Enloe, *Ethnic Conflict and Political Development* (Boston: Little, Brown, 1973), p. 15.

7. Examples of this distinction abound, such as the position of a Jew in Northern Ireland who will at some point in his economic, social, or political life have to decide whether he is a "Catholic Jew" or a "Protestant Jew." Catholics who become alienated from the church for one reason or another may not be very religious and may be explicitly anticlerical, but they remain in ethnic terms "Catholics."

Conclusion

IRELAND IN THE WORLD

To state that the impact of Ireland on world politics is modest is not to engage in irresponsible hyperbole. The size of the country, its peripheral geographical location, and its lack of critical resources place it among those nations that are destined to play lesser roles on the international stage. The dominant aspect of Irish foreign relations has been the country's economic and political relationship with Britain, and since 1922 the major aspect of that relationship has been Ulster. After World War II, however, new dimensions entered into Ireland's relationship with the world. They include the United Nations, the European Community, and linkages with the United States on both the Northern Ireland issue and economic investment.

The position of neutrality adopted by Ireland during World War II was continued after the war when, in April of 1949, Ireland decided not to join the North Atlantic Treaty Organization. However, the Republic did not refrain from extolling the injustices of the partition of Ireland. In a campaign that lasted for a decade, the Irish sought to hammer away on the antipartition theme in the new Council of Europe, and on any other stage they could command. In terms of the massive changes after the war the issue of partition was not as compelling as the Irish felt it should be, and eventually this propaganda effort was found to be unproductive.

In 1955 the Soviet Union dropped its ban on Ireland's entry into the United Nations. Ireland's foreign minister, Frank Aiken, believed that his country's role in the United Nations was quite important and appointed a delegation to that body that included Conor Cruise O'Brien, who was very influential in shaping the Irish position. That position was one of independence, which included supporting the nonaligned nations on many issues, anticolonial views, nuclear nonproliferation, UN peacekeeping efforts (the Irish have contributed over 16,000 soldiers for UN service in the Congo, Cyprus, the Sinai and Lebanon), and the admission of the People's Republic of China into the United Nations. By the late 1960s, however, the expansion of the United Nations, coupled with the advent of Sean Lemass as prime minister, pushed the United Nations off the Irish center stage to be replaced by the European Economic Community.

Ireland's application for membership in the European Economic Com-

149

munity had been made in July of 1961, more than a decade before membership was granted. The close economic ties between Britain and Ireland caused those two countries to move in tandem in regard to entry into the EEC, and Charles de Gaulle would not accept Britain's entry because of long-standing differences. By 1972 these differences were resolved by de Gaulle's departure from power, and on January 1, 1973, Ireland and Britain entered the EEC.

The advantages for Ireland have been numerous. They include the support offered by the European Community's Common Agricultural Policy to the Irish farmers, who have prospered considerably as a result. In addition, direct payments from the EEC have flowed into Ireland to implement social and economic development plans. Another advantage for the Republic is that it is now a part of a larger group of nations that can undertake negotiations on issues that were previously bilaterally negotiated between Britain and Ireland. The Republic is one of a group of nations, clustered with the smaller nations, to be sure, but no longer the little sister of Britain. Ireland is free to agree or disagree with Britain in the context of European policy, not under the old shadows of its colonial heritage.

Membership has had the effect of adding another "layer" of authority with respect to making policy in Ireland. Local governments and Dublin now have to take Brussels into account when considering tax policy, borrowing, farm production development plans, currency fluctuations, and a host of other issues. The Irish bureaucrats have had to learn how to deal with a large and complex European bureaucracy. Irish pressure groups confront a politically more diverse universe than in Dublin, and Irish representatives to the European Parliament interact with a more cosmopolitan assembly in Strasbourg.

With respect to Northern Ireland the European Community has served as a means for the Republic to embarrass the British government through the 1978 European Court decision on the treatment of prisoners in Northern Ireland. Less dramatic, however, has been the Martin Report, a series of proposals for EEC-supported Ulster development projects. Finally, the break with the British pound after Ireland's entry into the European Monetary System in 1979 reflects the degree to which Ireland, as a member of the EEC, has become more independent politically and economically.

Northern Ireland remains, however, an ever-present dimension of Irish–British relations, even in Europe. The direct elections to the European Parliament, instituted in 1979, produced a large victory for Ian Paisley in Ulster. The two other representatives are John Taylor, from the Official Unionist Party, and John Hume, the leader of the Social Democratic and Labour Party. Ironically enough, the three representatives have been able to cooperate in Strasbourg with respect to direct aid proposals even though on other issues Paisley has attacked both Hume and Taylor.

The rapid economic development of the Republic of Ireland and the violent crisis in Northern Ireland have created new bonds as well as new pressures and strains on Ireland's relationship with the United States. The United States has long been a haven for Irish immigrants and thus a locus of anti-British Irish sentiment. Generations of immigrants, filled with bitterness at English policies, have provided the foundation for Irish-American support of Irish causes. This support ran to millions of dollars in the nineteenth century and prompted no less a figure than de Valera to come to the United States in 1919 to seek financial aid and diplomatic recognition for the first Dáil Éireann.

As Irish-Americans were assimilated into the U.S. social structure, their images of Ireland began to soften and become somewhat romanticized. The lack of intense conflict in Ireland after 1922 meant that the 1916–1921 images of Irish nationalism were fixed in their minds (to the degree that any strong images exist at all in the second and third generations), and this romantic vision is exemplified in the St. Patrick's Day version of Ireland and Irish nationalism. Shamrocks, leprechauns, colleens, and Irish-American songs have little to do with what is going on in Ireland.

When the trouble burst upon Ulster in 1968 Irish-American attitudes were both naive and cast in an older, conservative mode. Bernadette Devlin visited the United States in 1969, and the differences between the young agitator, with her Marxist views and sympathy for U.S. blacks, and the conservative Catholic Irish, who wanted to hear echoes of the Irish fight for freedom against the Black and Tans, were painfully clear.

Eventually the support for the Provisional IRA in the United States was organized by such groups as the Irish Northern Aid Committee and promoted by papers such as the *Irish People*. The formal and informal ties between the Irish-Americans and Ireland meant that there was a steady channel of money flowing to Ulster. The money was ostensibly meant to aid the victims of the violence, but a substantial amount of it went to purchase about $1.5 million to $2.5 million worth of arms for the Provos. Other organizations attempting to influence Irish-American opinion have included the hard-line, anti-British Irish National Caucus, founded in 1974, and the Ireland Fund, which is devoted to reconciliation in Ulster and is headed by Anthony O'Reilly, president of the Heinz Corporation.

The response of the U.S. government has been formal and guarded. President Carter and President Reagan made statements in 1977 and 1981, respectively, that called for "peaceful solutions" regarding the "two traditions" in Ireland. Ford, Carter, and Reagan have all been sympathetic to the requests of the Republic and Britain that the U.S. government deport known IRA men and crack down on the transfer of guns and money to Ulster.

The most visible response in the United States to the Northern Ireland problem has come from Senators Edward Kennedy and Daniel P. Moynihan, Speaker of the House Thomas P. O'Neill, and former Governor Hugh Carey of New York. The "big four" have offered statements on Northern Ireland since 1976 and have formed the "Friends of Ireland" in the U.S. Congress. Their position is hostile to the Provisional IRA and includes a search for accommodation and reconciliation that would lead ultimately to a united Ireland. This position is consistent with that of the Republic, and it is also somewhat critical of Britain for its harsh treatment of prisoners and lack of political initiatives on Ulster. Speaker O'Neill took the position that the sale of arms to the RUC indirectly supported the oppression of the Catholic community in Ulster, so the sales were frozen.

By far the most substantial linkage between the United States and Ireland is in the area of investment. Since the initiatives of the Whitaker Plan the amounts invested from 1960 to 1980 by the top ten countries (in millions of Irish punts) are as follows:

United States	£2,119.2
United Kingdom	524.5
West Germany	428.5
Canada	336.7
Netherlands	267.0
Japan	135.8
France	129.9
Italy	102.1
Switzerland	50.9
Sweden	38.7

The magnitude of the U.S. investment, which is greater than the total of the other nine, is such that one out of every five persons employed in manufacturing in Ireland works for a U.S. firm. After Ireland entered the EEC the dam burst as U.S. investors sought access to the European market. Apple, Wang, and Analog put high-technology manufacturing plants in Ireland, as did Polaroid, Atari, Burlington, Westinghouse, Fieldcrest, General Electric, and many others. The Irish Development Authority made special efforts to attract investment from the United States, and its success is evident as 300 U.S. manufacturing and service industries have located in Ireland. This record is not unblemished as some large plants have closed, but Ireland's dependency on U.S. investment is so substantial that it is no surprise that in 1982 Prime Minister Haughey invited the members of the Economic Club of New York to "think Irish during the course of this particular week and decide to look into the many and varied opportunities Ireland has for worthwhile development projects."[1]

Ireland's rapid development has placed its future in a context that is wider than its insularity and wider than its relationship with Britain. The future of any European economy based on foreign investment and export trade is within the EEC. Ireland is irrevocably committed to Europe not only because of political choice but also because of economic necessity. The conflict in Northern Ireland, however, will ensure that a principal concern of the Republic will still be its relationship with Britain. Ireland has expanded from its historic insularity, but it appears that it will never achieve complete autonomy from its past.

FACING CHANGE

Ireland has come face to face with some of its most cherished myths and traditions since 1960, but that confrontation has not been without pain. The rapid growth of modernization that hastened the decline of the west of Ireland and opened the nation to U.S. and European secular values meant that the Republic, which was designed to preserve and nourish the Irish culture, was confronted by a decay of Gaelic, rural, nationalist Ireland. The slide of Ulster into the pit of ethnic murder and political stasis has made the traditional nationalist rhetoric on unification somewhat hollow in the face of incandescent Protestant intransigence on the one hand and the IRA's violent rejection of Dublin's position on the other.

Thus Ireland in both the short and the long run is confronted with the task of working out a new set of values that can synthesize the tradition of the past and the realities of the present. Underlying the conflicts over specific issues such as Ulster, divorce, social welfare, and the Irish language is a conflict between two different conceptions of community, organic and pluralist. The people who prefer the organic sense of community feel that the individual gains identity, security, and morality from being integrated into a social entity. Society is a moral, social, and legal whole that is cohesively bound together. Organic societies have a powerful reverence for the past; a distinctive and pervasive set of central values, such as Catholicism; and an ethnic unity that gives the society identity and strong bonds of authority, family, and culture.

The pluralist conception of society places the individual and individual preferences at the center of society. People are free to pursue diverse values, goals, beliefs, and modes of living. Neighborhood, church, and family ties are looser; geographical and social mobility are greater; and tolerance and diversity are more apparent.

In the case of the Republic of Ireland organic unity was spun out of the traditional elements of Gaelic heritage, the Irish language, and the Catholic religion. The binding of these elements to political nationalism provided the authoritative machinery to preserve that organic unity. The degree to which the organic Gaelic vision was fulfilled is displayed in the Ireland of the Free State and Republic until the early 1960s. The deficiency in that organic view of the national community is the gap between the inclusive geographical aspiration of political nationalism—i.e., eliminating partition—and the exclusive community values that had no place for 1 million people of different religious and cultural convictions.

The greater the emphasis on Ireland as Gaelic, Catholic, nationalist, green, rural, and united, the weaker the political claim on the Protestants. Conversely, the greater the emphasis on diversity and inclusiveness, the greater the dilution of the organic integrity that has served to define the Irish nation and to set it free. Irish nationalism provided the foundation for the creation of the nation. That fact alone, however, did not automatically mean that the basic needs and wants of the people would be fulfilled. The economic transformation went a long way toward fulfilling the second stage, as it were, of Irish nationhood as it provided economic opportunity and, on a modest level, the standards of life of a European nation. The third stage, yet to transpire, is the forging of a new concept of Irish political and cultural life to absorb the impact of modernization and to deal with the unsolved tangle of Irish nationhood, Ulster.

Within the Republic the tensions over censorship, religious doctrines, family law, and the consumer society reflect an organic community defending itself from the changing, superficial, and corrupting influences of the secular world. The pluralists, however, argue that diversity and tolerance need not mean the repudiation of Ireland's religious values or its political and cultural heritage. They do say that room has to be made within the heritage for religious pluralism, in order to honestly confront the Ulster situation, and for social diversity, in order to allow the individual to be free of a single set of social or religious constrictions. The plural society that should emerge from Ireland's economic transformation should be a society that reveres its past but does not live in it because Ireland has a rich future in the modern world of Europe. The Irish religious and cultural identity, the pluralists argue, will not be vibrant if it is preserved through an enforced parochial isolation. Rather, the identity and religion of the Irish should be examined and revitalized by the pressures of modernization.

The organicists clutch to tradition as they see it erode, and not only do they romanticize Gaelic, Catholic Ireland and Irish life, but they also display a degree of intolerance and authoritarianism in attempting to preserve them. The pluralists tend to delegitimize traditions and embrace somewhat too hastily a secular U.S. and European culture, which is itself under sharp attack for its triviality, narcissism, atomism, and less than profound values.

The process of economic change, especially after Ireland's entry into the EEC, and the concomitant changes in the religious, social, educational, and cultural spheres are not going to go away. If Northern Ireland did not exist, Ireland would have to cope with the friction engendered by old values being challenged by new values. Because of the Ulster problem Ireland is confronted with a dual challenge: that of reconciling the consciousness of Gaelic Ireland with the modern secular world and that of reconciling a Gaelic Republic of Ireland with the politics of the Ulster Protestant tradition. Either problem alone would be difficult enough; together they demand patience, adaptability, leadership, and courage. It may be that in the long run the differences between orange and green will be submerged in an emerging Europeanized culture in Ireland. If that situation occurs, then the problem will be one of managing the transition without violence and with tolerance for the different traditions on the island. However, if a universalization of culture does not occur, the problem of Ireland will be to forge a new form of pluralistic political and cultural identity that will preserve that which is honored and absorb that which is valuable from the new.

The people of Ireland have undergone an enormous range of experience from the grisly to the heroic: Cromwell's punishments, religious persecution, famine, rebellion, war, civil war, emigration, poverty, terrorism, regeneration, and growth. There is ample evidence that the Irish will find the strength to transcend the new challenges facing their nation.

NOTES

1. "Speeches and Statements," in *Ireland Today, Bulletin of the Department of Foreign Affairs* (April 1982).

Bibliography

Ayearst, Morley. *The Republic of Ireland.* New York: New York University Press, 1970.
  Solid treatment of Irish government and politics but too early to take advantage of the recent work done on electoral politics.

Barritt, Denis P., and Carter, Charles F. *The Northern Ireland Problem.* London: Oxford University Press, 1972.
  First published in 1962, this book contains sound research concerning social, religious, and legal discrimination in Northern Ireland.

Brody, Hugh. *Inishkillane: Change and Decline in the West of Ireland.* New York: Schocken Books, 1974.
  The lives of villagers in the west of Ireland as the young people depart and the old ways fade.

Brown, Terence. *Ireland: A Social and Cultural History, 1922–79.* Glasgow: Fontana, 1981.
  A valuable assessment of the effects of a half century of changes in Ireland and their impact on Irish identity.

Carty, R. K. *Party and the Parish Pump: Electoral Politics in Ireland.* Waterloo, Canada: Wilfred Laurier University Press, 1981.
  An excellent treatment of the Irish party system and electoral behavior; explains some of the uncommon characteristics of the Irish system.

Chubb, Basil. *The Government and Politics of Ireland.* London: Oxford University Press, 1974.
  A pathbreaking book that approaches Irish government analytically and empirically rather than historically. A second edition was published in 1982 and is as valuable as the first.

_____. *A Source Book of Irish Government.* Dublin: Institute of Public Administration, 1964.
  Indispensable documentary materials on all aspects of Irish government.

Coffey, Thomas. *Agony at Easter.* London: Penguin, 1969.
  A captivating account of the Easter Rising of 1916.

Coles, Robert. "Ulster's Children." *Atlantic* (December 1980):33–44.
  Interviews with youngsters from Northern Ireland reveal the depth to which the ethnic conflict is bred into them.

Coogan, Tim Pat. *Ireland Since the Rising.* New York: Greenwood Press, 1975.
  A brief, informative history written by a well-known journalist and editor.

155

———. *The Irish: A Personal View.* London: Phaidon Press, 1975.
This anecdotal treatment reveals the Irish personality and the peculiarities of Irish life.

Cullen, L. M. *An Economic History of Ireland Since 1600.* London: Batsford, 1972.
A thorough treatment of Irish economic history.

Dangerfield, George. *The Damnable Question.* Boston: Atlantic Monthly Press, 1976.
Particularly valuable for coverage of the years 1914–1919.

Darby, John. *Conflict in Northern Ireland.* Dublin: Gill and Macmillan, 1976.
A clear treatment of the major dimensions of the problem and the social and political institutions that reinforce polarization.

de Paor, Liam. *Divided Ulster.* London: Penguin, 1970.
An impassioned history of Ulster focusing on the discriminatory treatment of Catholics.

Farrell, Brian. *Chairman or Chief? The Role of the Taoiseach in Irish Government.* Dublin: Gill and Macmillan, 1971.
The stewardships of five prime ministers are examined for their conceptions of their role.

Farrell, Brian, ed. *The Irish Parliamentary Tradition.* Dublin: Gill and Macmillan, 1973.
An excellent collection of essays on the impact of various Irish parliaments from the time of the Gaelic kings to independence.

FitzGerald, Garrett. *Towards a New Ireland.* Dublin: Torc Books, 1973.
Insightful assessment of the relationship of North and South written by the current prime minister.

Garvin, Tom. *The Revolution of Irish Nationalist Politics.* Dublin: Gill and Macmillan, 1981.
A superb analysis of the political support for the rise of nationalism from Sinn Féin to Fianna Fáil.

Gray, Tony. *The Irish Answer.* London: Heinemann, 1966.
A somewhat outdated and uncritical evaluation of the changes in Ireland and Irish life.

Hull, Roger. *The Irish Triangle.* Princeton, N.J.: Princeton University Press, 1975.
Treats the problem of Ulster from the perspectives of Dublin, Belfast, and London and in terms of international law.

Kain, Richard M. *Dublin in the Age of William Butler Yeats and James Joyce.* Newton Abbot, Eng.: David and Charles Ltd., 1972.
Traces the cultural renaissance in Ireland that accompanied the political turmoil of the independence movement.

Kee, Robert. *The Green Flag: A History of Irish Nationalism.* London: Weidenfeld and Nicholson, 1972.
An extended study of the rise of Irish nationalism written in an engaging manner.

———. *Ireland: A History.* Boston: Little, Brown, 1982.
An excellent brief, popular history of Ireland based upon a BBC television series written and narrated by Kee.

Kennedy, Kieran A., and Dowling, Brendan R. *Economic Growth in Ireland.* Dublin: Gill and Macmillan, 1975.
Excellent analysis of the impact of the Whitaker reforms.

Laurence, R. J. *The Government of Northern Ireland*. London: Oxford University Press, 1965.
A solid explanation of the structures and processes of the now-defunct Stormont government.

Lebow, Richard Ned. *White Britain, Black Ireland*. Philadelphia: Institute for the Study of Human Issues, 1976.
Recounts the degree and nature of British prejudice with respect to the Irish and its influence on colonial policy.

Lee, J. J., ed. *Ireland, 1945–70*. Dublin: Gill and MacMillan, 1979.
An excellent collection of essays on changes in Irish groups and policies such as the media, environment, law, education, business, and labor.

Lee, Joseph. *The Modernization of Irish Society 1848–1918*. Dublin: Gill and MacMillan, 1973.
This work looks at the degree to which traditional economic, social, and political structures were swept away in the late nineteenth century.

Lipjhart, Arendt. "The Northern Ireland Problem: Cases, Theories, and Solutions." *British Journal of Political Science* 5 (January 1975):83–106.
An inventory of ten different perspectives that could serve as a foundation for explaining the Ulster crisis.

Lyons, F.S.L. *Ireland Since the Famine*. London: Collins, Fontana, 1973.
The best single history of Ireland since the famine and one of the best histories of Ireland overall.

McCaffrey, Lawrence J. *Ireland: From Colony to Nation State*. Englewood Cliffs, N.J.: Prentice-Hall, 1979.
A brief history of Ireland and the growth of nationalism.

MacGreil, Michael. *Prejudice and Tolerance in Ireland*. Dublin: College of Industrial Relations, 1977.
A revealing study of Irish prejudices and stereotypes.

Manning, Maurice. *Irish Political Parties*. Dublin: Gill and Macmillan, 1972.
The foundations and developments of the major parties are briefly and crisply presented.

Moody, T. W., and Martin, F. X., eds. *The Course of Irish History*. Cork: Mercier Press, 1967.
A well-respected collection of essays that are informative for beginner and expert alike.

Murphy, John A. *Ireland in the Twentieth Century*. Dublin: Gill and Macmillan, 1975.
A well-written, brief history.

O'Brien, Conor Cruise. *States of Ireland*. New York: Vintage Books, 1973.
Sharply written assessment of the development of the Northern Ireland problem, with O'Brien's negative interpretation of the Provisional IRA.

O'Faolain, Sean. *The Irish*. London: Penguin, 1969.
One of the most insightful books on Irish history and culture by a renowned Irish author.

O'Hanlon, Thomas J. *The Irish: Portrait of a People*. London: André Deutsch, 1976.
A journalist's critical tour of the Irish scene from urban developers to northern gunmen.

Pakenham, Frank (Earl of Longford), and O'Neill, Thomas P. *Eamon de Valera.* London: Hutchinson Publishing, Arrow Books, 1974.
> A comprehensive biography and a very favorable treatment of de Valera.

Peillon, Michel. *Contemporary Irish Society.* Dublin: Gill and Macmillan, 1982.
> A study of Irish social classes, their objectives, and their relationships with the state.

Penniman, Howard, ed. *Ireland at the Polls, 1977.* Washington, D.C.: American Enterprise Institute, 1978.
> This collection of essays by expert analysts on the 1977 election reveals a great deal about Irish politics in general.

Rose, Richard. *Governing Without Consensus.* London: Faber and Faber, 1971.
> One of the most informative and comprehensive studies of political attitudes and political dynamics in Northern Ireland.

_____. *Northern Ireland: Time of Change.* Washington, D.C.: American Enterprise Institute, 1976.
> A briefer study of the political groups and electoral competition in Ulster through 1975.

Rumpf, E., and Hepburn, A. C. *Nationalism and Socialism in Twentieth-Century Ireland.* New York: Barnes and Noble, 1977.
> A geographical analysis of the electoral support for Irish nationalism that links that support to the western farming areas.

Sacks, Paul M. *The Donegal Mafia.* New Haven, Conn.: Yale University Press, 1976.
> A detailed treatment of the Blaney political machine in Donegal that reveals the power of local political bosses.

Schmitt, David E. *The Irony of Irish Democracy.* Lexington, Mass.: D. C. Heath, 1970.
> Argues that Irish democracy is sustained by essentially undemocratic traits of authoritarianism and personalism.

Shade, William G. "Strains of Modernization: The Republic of Ireland Under Lemass and Lynch." *Eire-Ireland* 14 (Spring 1979):26–46.
> Presents some of the manifestations in Irish life of the pressures of economic growth and social change.

Whyte, John H. *Church and State in Modern Ireland.* 2d ed. Totowa, N.J.: Barnes and Noble, 1980.
> The best treatment of the whole subject and, in particular, the mother and child welfare plan.

_____. "Ireland: Politics Without Social Bases." In Richard Rose, ed., *Electoral Behavior,* pp. 619–653. New York: Free Press, 1973.
> A groundbreaking article that reveals the lack of convergence between electoral support for the parties and social class in Ireland.

_____. "Interpretations of the Northern Ireland Problem: An Appraisal." *Economic and Social Review* 9 (July 1978):257–282.
> A summary of three Marxist and six non-Marxist interpretations of the Northern Ireland problem.

Index

DATE DUE